THE GREAT FILTH

THE GREAT FILTH

THE WAR AGAINST DISEASE
IN VICTORIAN ENGLAND

STEPHEN HALLIDAY

SUTTON PUBLISHING

First published in the United Kingdom in 2007 by
Sutton Publishing, an imprint of NPI Media Group Limited
Cirencester Road · Chalford · Stroud · Gloucestershire · GL6 8PE

British Library Cataloguing in Publication Data
A catalogue record for this book is available from the British Library.

ISBN 978-0-7509-4378-9

Typeset in Sabon.
Typesetting and origination by
NPI Media Group Limited.
Printed and bound in England.

Contents

List of Illustrations

Introduction

In 1897 Queen Victoria celebrated her Diamond Jubilee, having ascended the throne in June 1837, less than a month after her eighteenth birthday. She was very proud of the fact that she was the longest reigning British monarch, having passed the record set by her grandfather George III, who reigned for almost sixty years. When she died in January 1901 she had reigned for almost sixty-four years.

Her reign was much less turbulent than that of her grandfather, which had witnessed the Seven Years War with France (1756–63) at its beginning; the Napoleonic Wars (1793–1815) at the end; and the disastrous American War of Independence (1776–83) in the middle. During Victoria's reign there was no serious likelihood that the British Isles would be invaded, despite a few scares concerning supposed threats from the French or Germans. In the colonies the Indian Mutiny was suppressed and the Zulu Wars in Africa made some headlines, but neither represented a threat to the mother country. The Boer War cast its shadow over Victoria's final years, but no one supposed that the Boers would march on London as Napoleon had intended to do.

But other battles were being fought in Victoria's towns and cities that were concerned with saving lives rather than ending them. These were battles against disease, especially against epidemic diseases, which spread swiftly in the crowded urban communities that, by the end of her reign, had become the homes of most of her subjects. This book tells the story of those battles fought against squalor, poor housing, dirty water, sewage, ignorance and, ultimately, germs. Since its focus is Victorian England, most of the men and women whose achievements are recorded in this book are British, though two of the most important, Sir Joseph Bazalgette and Sir John Simon, were of French descent. However, the critical discoveries of Frenchmen like Louis Pasteur, Germans like Justus von Liebig, Dutchmen like Anthony van Leeuwenhoek and the Italian Filippo Pacini are also recorded, because of their impact on the understanding of the causes of disease.

By the end of Victoria's reign some diseases, such as smallpox, typhus and cholera, had either virtually disappeared from the records or were in the process of doing so. Typhoid, scarlet fever and childbed (or puerperal) fever were following. Others, like whooping cough, measles, pneumonia and tuberculosis, were in decline but remained a very real threat. Another fifty years would pass before better living conditions and effective medication would provide successful remedies. The Victorians' battles were fought by doctors, nurses, midwives, social reformers, scientists and engineers. Sometimes the professions overlapped. Sir John Simon was a doctor, but most of his achievements in the field of public health were made as a public servant, first as Medical Officer to London and, later, to the Privy Council. John Snow was also a doctor who practised in Soho, but he is remembered for his careful scientific study of the Soho cholera outbreak, so he is recorded in this volume as a scientist, as is Dr William Budd, who identified the mechanism by which typhoid is transmitted. Some of those whose achievements are described in the pages that follow were ridiculed in their lifetimes and even now are less well known than they should be.

But before the doctors, nurses, midwives and scientists could do their work, other battles had to be fought by politicians, social reformers and philanthropists. At the outset of Victoria's reign the role of government was minimal. Its principal tasks were to defend the kingdom from foreign enemies and administer justice. The first of these was discharged by maintaining a powerful navy (though much smaller in peacetime, when many officers were put on half-pay, as Nelson had been) and a very small army, whose shortcomings were quickly exposed during the Crimean War. What later became the Victorian Empire largely consisted of trading posts in which government involvement was minimal. For the first twenty years of Victoria's reign even India was largely the province of private enterprise in the shape of the East India Company, and it took the Indian Mutiny of 1857 to persuade the government to assume sovereignty over the 'jewel in the crown' of empire. The judicial system was the responsibility of central government, but even this was very small (there was not even a Court of Appeal until 1907), and it was mostly run by unpaid amateurs in the form of local magistrates who were also responsible for the affairs of local government, including the Poor Law and the maintenance of roads and bridges, outside the chartered towns. Trials were conducted in the minimum time and at minimum cost, one estimate being that in the 1830s Old Bailey trials took, on average, nine minutes. After the trial, those convicted were likely to be flogged, executed or transported, thus saving the state the costs of imprisonment. It was several years into Victoria's reign before a prison building programme was instituted under the auspices of central government.

Transport was the responsibility of turnpike trusts for the main roads, canals built by entrepreneurs like the Duke of Bridgewater and, later in the reign, the railways, which in many ways exemplify the Victorian virtues: entrepreneurship, risk taking, high technology and, above all, the employment of private capital for the public good. Hospitals were dependent upon earlier philanthropists, such as John Addenbrooke at Cambridge, Thomas Guy in London and John Radcliffe in Oxford, and those who succeeded them and added to their bequests. The training of nurses at St Thomas's Hospital was made possible because Florence Nightingale used the prestige she had gained from her work in the Crimea to set up a charitable fund, amounting to £45,000, to pay for it. Education, such as it was, lay in the hands of Dame Schools offering a rudimentary education to economically inactive children; private schools, often Tudor foundations, many of which had declined into a state of torpidity by the nineteenth century; and the ancient universities of Oxford and Cambridge, which were little more than Anglican seminaries.

One of the greatest of the achievements of the Victorians, therefore, was to accept that national and local government had a responsibility for the health, education and welfare of citizens, as well as for defence against foreign invasion and domestic injustice. With this went an acceptance that the authorities would have to raise taxes both centrally and locally. As late as the 1870s William Gladstone was still hoping to be able to abolish the income tax that had first been introduced during the wars against Napoleon, but by Gladstone's time the cause was lost. A torrent of legislation regulated working practices; promoted the construction of sewers at public expense; instituted the inspection of factories, food and water supplies; built workhouses and the rudimentary hospitals they contained; laid down rules for the training of doctors and midwives; and reformed schools and universities. Big government had arrived and would not be going away. It was the most enduring legacy of Victoria's reign. It was all necessary before the reformers could begin work.

The young Queen Victoria succeeded to the throne on 20 June 1837. Four days later the *Manchester Guardian* spokesman for the city, which, above all, represented the cause of laissez-faire and small government, expressed its hopes for the new reign: 'The accession of our young queen is a circumstance full of hope and promise . . . government will be compelled to be more economical; a higher standard of civilisation will ultimately be adopted among us.'

By the time of the Queen's death, in 1901, her subjects were better educated and better fed. More of them had access to clean water, effective sewers and medical practitioners who were trained and regulated. The population's average life span had risen by almost 50 per cent. This is presumably what the *Manchester Guardian* meant by 'a higher standard of civilisation', but it had been achieved largely by the abandonment of the dream of 'more economical' government.

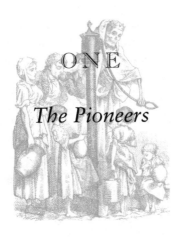

ONE

The Pioneers

The English are fools and madmen: fools because they give their children the smallpox to prevent their catching it; and madmen because they wantonly communicate a certain and dreadful distemper to their children, merely to prevent an uncertain evil.

(Voltaire, inveighing against the English practice of inoculation against smallpox)

Vaccination has been chiefly carried on by lady-doctors, wrong-headed clergymen, needy and dependent medicators and disorderly men-midwives.

(Dr Benjamin Mosley, inveterate nineteenth-century opponent of vaccination against smallpox)

VARIOLATION

In 1840, three years into Victoria's reign, the Vaccination Act was passed. Vaccination of infants with 'cowpox' to protect them against the virulent, disfiguring and often deadly smallpox was made available free of charge as a public health measure. By the same Act the earlier practice of *variolation*, which involved infecting the recipient with a mild form of the disease itself, was made illegal. This was the first significant public health measure of the reign, the first stride along a long path towards recognition that government had a role in protecting its citizens against disease as well as against foreign enemies. The Act was not particularly successful. Ignorance about medical practices made many families unwilling to risk having their infants deliberately infected with a mysterious disease, albeit one that was supposedly harmless. Further legislation was necessary before the population was protected, often against its will, and smallpox ceased to be rife. Nevertheless the 1840 Act was significant as a symbol of future intentions, and, added to a developing understanding of the causes and nature of diseases amongst doctors, scientists, nurses, midwives and politicians, it represented a notable step in the battle against epidemic disease that was one of the achievements of the reign.

EARLY PLAGUES

The *Anglo-Saxon Chronicle*, which records the years 879–1154, has left accounts of many plagues, whose occurrence is normally preceded by intimidating accounts of such phenomena as comets, earthquakes and eclipses, though the precise nature of the diseases concerned is rarely clear. This did not prevent the early writers from speculating on the causes of the disorders, often in moralising tones that survived in some quarters into the Victorian period itself. In some cases, it was thought, the simple act of looking upon a disease was sufficient to contract it. The work *Mabinogion*, which was compiled in the thirteenth century from ancient Welsh legends, recorded that in about AD 550 one Maelgwn Gwynedd 'beheld the Yellow Plague [probably jaundice] through the keyhole in the church door and forthwith he died'. St David (512–87) was thought to have escaped the plague by fleeing temporarily to Brittany.[1]

The moralising element is evident in the work of the Venerable Bede (673–735), who, in his *De Natura Rerum*, wrote that pestilence was 'produced from the air when it has become corrupted (in accordance with the deserts of men) either from excess of dryness or of heat, or from rain. Inhaled in the process of breathing, the air generates plague and death.'[2] His near contemporary Bishop Isidore of Seville (*c.* 560–636), in his great *Etymologiae*, declared that pestilence 'is produced from a corruption of the air and it makes its way by penetrating into the inward parts'.[3] Almost a thousand years later the Italian physician Girolamo Fracastoro (*c.* 1478–1553) attributed syphilis to foul air, which was no doubt a source of some relief to those who contracted it. In the absence of any knowledge of germ theory, the idea that foul air, in the form of a 'miasma', was the invariable cause of epidemics was to remain medical orthodoxy until well into the nineteenth century, when some bold spirits suggested that, in the case of cholera and typhoid, the real culprit was polluted water. In the meantime the idea that disease could be spread between people living in crowded communities prompted some authorities to take appropriate steps, albeit perhaps for reasons that were not fully understood. In 672 an outbreak of an unspecified disease among monks led Theodore, Archbishop of Canterbury, to decree at the Synod of Hertford that monks should not move between monasteries, the intention being to prevent the condition from spreading.

THE BLACK DEATH

The early writers may have had difficulty in identifying and attaching names to some of the pestilences that afflicted them, but when bubonic plague arrived in Europe it quickly acquired the name 'The Black Death' on account of its alarming symptoms: a blackening of the skin caused by haemorrhages beneath the surface and buboes, or swellings in the armpits and groin, followed by a swift and merciful death. It arrived in the port of Messina, Sicily, in October 1347 on a boat most of whose crew were already dead. Even now its precise origin is the subject of some controversy, but it is usually attributed to the bacterium *Yersinia Pestis*, transmitted by fleas that are found on black rats. It quickly spread throughout Europe, reaching England in June 1348 and eventually killing about a third of the population of Europe. Its progress had no doubt been assisted by the fact that the population was malnourished as a result of a series of poor harvests over the previous two decades, but the link between nutrition and health, which was eventually made in Victoria's reign, was not made in the fourteenth century. Like Bede, contemporary writers favoured some kind of divine visitation as an explanation. In the church of St Mary's, Ashwell, Hertfordshire, an anonymous villager carved a harrowing inscription in 1349: 'Wretched, terrible, destructive year, the remnants of the people alone remain.' The Jews, as usual, bore much of the blame and were the victims of many pogroms. The Black Death returned with less devastating consequences later in the century to a population whose previous exposure had presumably left it with some resistance. Its final onslaught on England occurred in 1665, though outbreaks occurred elsewhere in Europe until the early nineteenth century, Marseille being attacked in the 1820s, Russia at the end of the century and San Francisco, in the United States, in 1899–1900.

SMALLPOX

Epidemics of a disease that was probably smallpox were recorded in ancient Egypt and Mesopotamia (now Iraq) many thousands of years before the Christian era. The mummified remains of the pharaoh Rameses V, who died suddenly in 1157 BC, bear pustules characteristic of the disease. Europe seems to have escaped smallpox until it struck Athens in about 490 BC at the height of its prosperity. At this time such visitations were associated with the wrath of God or, in the case of Homer, gods. In the *Iliad*, book I, Homer describes a plague that falls upon the Greeks before Troy as 'arrows of Apollo', while in the Old Testament Job is afflicted by the 'arrows of the Almighty'. Perhaps it is no coincidence that the martyred St Sebastian, who is normally shown as pierced by numerous arrows, is the patron saint not only of archers but also of places afflicted by plague, where shrines to him were commonly created during the Middle Ages.

Western Europe was evidently spared the scourge of the *variola* virus that causes smallpox until some time before AD 1000, but once it had become established, shortly after that date, it spread gradually, gathering pace from about the fifteenth century. In the eighteenth century the French writer Voltaire claimed that a majority of the population would contract smallpox at some time, with about a fifth of them dying of the disease and a similar number surviving with faces marked by the pustules it left behind.[4] It was no respecter of persons. Among the more prominent English casualties was Queen Elizabeth I, who survived an attack in 1562 with a disfigured face, while Queen Mary II died of smallpox in 1694. Among foreign monarchs the Holy Roman Emperor Joseph I died of the disease in 1711, and his death was followed by those of Tsar Peter II in 1730 and Louis XV of France in 1774.

In the meantime the disease had become a weapon. The conquest of South America by the Spanish invaders in the sixteenth century was aided by the fact that the native population had no resistance to the *variola* virus, which they had never previously encountered. The first recorded outbreak occurred in the island of Hispaniola (Haiti and the Dominican Republic) in 1518, when half the native population was wiped out, but the problem became much more serious after 1520, when the disease reached the mainland through one of the soldiers of Cortés. A third of the Aztec population was killed, and when smallpox reached Peru the Inca emperor Huayna Capac was among its victims. It was also used as a threat. In 1728 the gaoler of the Fleet prison, Thomas Bambridge, demanded fees from one of his prisoners, a debtor called Robert Castell, in return for more comfortable accommodation. When Castell refused to pay the sum demanded, Bambridge, who had paid £5,000 for the office and was determined to gain a return on his investment, moved Castell to a part of the prison that was infected with smallpox. Castell died, and the matter became a *cause célèbre* when it was raised in Parliament by James Oglethorpe, who went on to found the colony of Georgia for discharged debtors.[5] In the first recorded deliberate use of biological warfare, in 1763, British troops at Fort Pitt (later Pittsburgh) deliberately distributed smallpox-infected blankets to Indians who were thought to be allies of the French enemy. Consequently, during the American War of Independence George Washington ordered that his troops be protected against the disease by a process then known as *variolation*, which had been gaining in popularity since the early years of the century.

INOCULATION

The process of *variolation*, also known as inoculation, involved the deliberate infection of one person, usually an infant, by another. This was done by rubbing matter from an infected person's smallpox pustule into a scratch on the arm of the recipient. The process was observed by Lady Mary Wortley Montagu in Constantinople while her husband was serving as British ambassador to the Ottoman Empire in 1717. Voltaire, who later wrote an account of her experiences, attributed the custom among Circassian families to a desire to obtain positions for their daughters in the harems of Turkey and Persia – opportunities that would be lost if the girls were disfigured by smallpox. The belief prevailed that, if one child were infected by another, the smallpox would be less virulent than if it were contracted later. Lady Mary had lost a brother to the disease and herself bore its scars. She persuaded the embassy surgeon, Charles Maitland, to inoculate her five-year-old, despite being warned by the chaplain that it was an un-Christian practice that would work only upon infidels. Following her return to England in 1721 she also had her four-year-old daughter inoculated, and the child became a medical curiosity who attracted the attention of the royal physician, Sir Hans Sloane. As a result, permission was obtained to test the process on six Newgate prisoners who were facing execution. The trial succeeded, the prisoners gaining their freedom as well as immunity to smallpox, and the practice received a powerful endorsement when, in 1722, the Prince of Wales's daughters were inoculated. The Foundling Hospital, created in 1741 by the sea captain Thomas Coram to care for abandoned children, inoculated its children at the age of three from the time of its foundation.[6]

The process was more readily adopted in England than in many other European countries. Reference has already been made to the deaths of continental monarchs, and the attitude towards inoculation of many foreign observers was summarised by Voltaire in his *Lettres philosophiques* when he wrote:

> It is inadvertently affirmed in the Christian countries of Europe that the English are fools and madmen: fools because they give their children the smallpox to prevent their catching it; and madmen because they wantonly communicate a certain and dreadful distemper to their children, merely to prevent an uncertain evil. The English, on the other hand, call the rest of the Europeans cowardly and unnatural. Cowardly because they are afraid of putting their children to a little pain; unnatural because they expose them to die one time or other of the smallpox.[7]

The most notable exception to the general European scepticism about inoculation was Catherine the Great of Russia. In 1768, faced

Sir Hans Sloane (1660–1753) was born in County Down, Ireland, in modest circumstances and studied medicine in England and France. In 1687 he went to Jamaica as physician to the governor and began the collection of flora and fauna for which he is remembered. He returned to England and established a very successful medical practice in Bloomsbury Place, close to the site on which the British Museum was later built. His patients included Queen Anne, George I and George II. Upon his death he bequeathed his collection of over 70,000 objects, a herbarium and library to George II in return for a payment of £20,000 to his two daughters. The money was raised through a public lottery and formed the basis of the British Museum, which was consequently founded in the year of Sloane's death and opened to the public in 1759. He was influential in promoting inoculation against smallpox and devised a drink for children made by mixing cocoa with cow's milk, based on a practice he had witnessed in Jamaica, where mothers mixed breast milk with cocoa beans. It was marketed by Cadbury's until 1885 as 'Sir Hans Sloane's Milk Chocolate'. He succeeded his friend Sir Isaac Newton as President of the Royal Society and has several London streets named after him, including Sloane Square and Hans Place.

by a severe smallpox epidemic sweeping through Russia, she contacted an English physician, Thomas Dimsdale (1712–1800), who had published a treatise, *The Present Methods of Inoculation for the Smallpox*, the previous year. Dimsdale visited Russia, inoculated Catherine and her son, the future Paul I, and was rewarded by being created a Baron of the Russian Empire.

VACCINATION

Edward Jenner (1749–1823) was a country doctor in the small town of Berkeley, Gloucestershire. The son of the local clergyman, he showed an early interest in natural history and was the first person to observe the habits of the young cuckoo in expelling other eggs from its nest. He trained as a doctor first with a local surgeon in Chipping Sodbury and later at St George's hospital, London, under the great surgeon and experimenter John Hunter, of whom he became a lifelong friend. It was on Hunter's recommendation that Jenner was employed by Sir Joseph Banks to prepare for examination specimens collected on Captain Cook's expeditions to Australia and the South Seas, so his experience and connections were considerably greater than those of most country doctors. In 1772 he returned to Berkeley and set up a medical practice. His childhood interest in natural history had familiarised him with the tale that milkmaids (who were often represented by contemporary painters as icons of beauty) retained their good looks because their work rendered them immune to the disfigurements of smallpox. He had himself been inoculated, had been very ill as a result and knew that the process could, on occasion, lead to the full effects of smallpox itself.

He observed that milkmaids frequently developed blisters on their hands, known as cowpox, which resulted from contact with the udders of cows, and he reflected upon the possibility that this minor blemish might in some way protect them from the depredations of smallpox. He was consulted by a milkmaid called Sarah Nelmes, who had developed a particularly bad case of the characteristic blisters after milking a cow called Blossom, and he extracted some pus from the blisters. This he injected into an eight-year-old boy called James Phipps, the son of his gardener, gradually increasing the amount of pus over a period of several days. He then deliberately injected the boy with smallpox on several occasions. James remained immune from smallpox. Since cowpox was a relatively harmless disease that carried with it no risk of infection from smallpox itself, it offered obvious advantages over the alternative practice of inoculation. This experiment was repeated over the years that followed, Jenner vaccinating 100 children in further tests as well as trying the procedure on himself. In those days there were no ethical or regulatory constraints upon such experiments. Jenner named the new process 'vaccination' after the Latin word *vacca* for 'cow' and published his findings in a book titled *An Enquiry into the Causes and Effects of the Variolae Vaccinae; A Disease Discovered in some of the Western Counties of England, Particularly Gloucestershire, and Known by the Name of Cow Pox.*

He submitted his findings to the Royal Society, whose president was his acquaintance Sir Joseph Banks. However, he was advised that he had not carried out enough experiments to justify such revolutionary ideas. This discouraging judgement was influenced by the fact that cowpox was confined to a few areas, so that doctors who wanted to experiment with the new process were dependent upon Jenner to supply them with pus at a time when such a substance was difficult to transport over any but the shortest distance. This clergyman's son also encountered resistance from churchmen, who thought it was profane to inject into human beings material from a diseased animal. James Gillray was one of the cartoonists who lampooned the practice by showing people growing cows' heads. One of the fiercest critics of vaccination was a doctor called Benjamin Mosley (1742–1819), who described the arguments in favour of vaccination as 'the ravings of Bedlam'[8] and claimed that cow hair would grow on the scabs that formed after vaccination – scabs that in the early days could be unsightly. He later added that 'vaccination has been chiefly carried on by lady-doctors, wrong-headed clergymen, needy and dependent medicators and disorderly men-midwives'.[9]

Despite such strictures, the prospect of escaping the dreaded disease was so attractive that criticism melted away. By the time that Mosley wrote, the great majority of medical practitioners were practising vaccination. Jenner developed ways of preserving cowpox microbes by drying them on to threads of glass and began to supply the material to doctors in Britain and abroad, calling himself 'vaccine clerk to the world'. The process of vaccination was adopted more rapidly in other nations, often using material supplied by Jenner himself. Bavaria was the first nation to make vaccination compulsory, in 1807, while Denmark, Sweden, Prussia, Hungary, Romania and Serbia all imposed the practice before Britain did. In recognition of the value of his work, the British government awarded him the substantial sum of £10,000 in 1802 and a further £20,000 in 1807. He received tributes and presents from Napoleon, a man not normally noted for being well disposed towards the English, and from a delegation of North American Indian chiefs. His statue stands in Kensington Gardens. The 1840 Vaccination Act made the practice of inoculation with the disease itself illegal, free vaccination with cowpox being offered in its place, and in 1853 vaccination was made compulsory for all infants within four months of birth, a fine of £1 being imposed on parents who failed to comply. There were, however, no effective powers of enforcement, and the fine, once paid, put an end to the matter, which meant that reasonably wealthy families could flout the law, though poorer families, for whom £1 could amount to a week's wages, were under greater pressure to comply.

The measure was fiercely resisted in some quarters by those who formed the *Anti-Vaccination League* and contended that it amounted to an unwarranted interference with the liberty of the subject. The 1867 Vaccination Act was more effective, again prohibiting the old practice of inoculation and imposing repeated fines for those who neglected to have their infants vaccinated. As late as 1871 the newspaper the *Graphic* praised one Anne Supple for refusing to 'be a party to the poisoning of her baby' when she was prosecuted for failing to have the child vaccinated during an epidemic that, over three years, claimed 44,000 lives. Local authorities like the London County Council gave further impetus to the vaccination movement by requiring a vaccination certificate from all citizens applying for public housing. Yet as late as 1898 the distinguished scientist Alfred Russell Wallace (1823–1913), who had shared with Charles Darwin the discovery of the mechanics of evolution, wrote a pamphlet entitled 'Vaccination: A Delusion'.

SMALLPOX HOSPITALS

Outbreaks of smallpox continued to occur while the process of vaccination spread gradually through the population. In the meantime the disease was contained through the creation of isolation hospitals, to which sufferers would be sent in the hope that the uninfected population would thereby be protected. In the eighteenth century smallpox hospitals were set up by charities at places like Windmill Street, off Tottenham Court Road and Battle Bridge, on the present site of King's Cross station, but as the population expanded these became too small. In 1867 the

Metropolitan Asylums Board was established to care for London's sick poor, and the board set about creating three hospitals funded by the ratepayers. They were constructed at Stockwell to the south and at Homerton and Hampstead to the north. The Hampstead site had a particularly interesting history. The site chosen lay just south of Hampstead Heath itself, which, by 1867, was becoming a fashionable residential area. The prospect of having as neighbours a multitude of highly infectious patients was very unattractive to the wealthy residents, whose opposition to the scheme was led by Sir Rowland Hill, inventor of the Penny Post, who lived nearby.

The site was nevertheless purchased in 1868, and was opened in 1870, using temporary buildings, to accommodate the victims of an outbreak of relapsing fever, transmitted by ticks, which had arisen in the East End of London. This condition, also known as 'sweating sickness', was characterised by a high temperature, nausea and severe headaches and about 30 per cent of sufferers died. It is now treated effectively by antibiotics but remains common in Ethiopia and the Sudan. The Hampstead hospital was, in effect, Britain's first fully state-run hospital and could claim to be the first stirrings of the National Health Service that emerged eighty years later. By the end of 1870 the hospital was filled with smallpox victims who had been taken from workhouses and whose growing numbers caused further alarm to the local residents. In November 1871 *The Times* carried a report of a delegation to the Local Government Board in Whitehall led by the Hampstead MP Lord George Hamilton.[10] The residents protested that the site was unsuited to such a use; that cases of smallpox had arisen among the local population that were attributed to the hospital; that holidaymakers frequenting the local pubs (including the celebrated Bull and Bush) were particularly vulnerable to infection and would carry the disease back to their own communities; that 'property in Hampstead had deteriorated to the extent of £100,000 since the hospital had been there'; and that local traders had been adversely affected by the constant passage of ambulances and hearses. The residents even offered to pay the cost of having the hospital relocated elsewhere.

As a result of the petition a Parliamentary Select Committee examined the matter. It established that patients had communicated with local residents over the hospital walls and that ambulance men and relatives of the infected often stopped for refreshment at The George (which still stands on Haverstock Hill), thus providing opportunities for the local populace to become infected through contact. However, MPs concluded that these incidents did not amount to a reason for moving the hospital. The dispute rumbled on for several years, Rowland Hill's part in the campaign being taken over by his son until the Metropolitan Asylums Board bought him off, literally, by purchasing his house and incorporating it in the hospital. After 1882 smallpox patients were accommodated on three ageing ships, *Atlas*, *Endymion* and *Castalia*, which were moored in the Thames near Dartford. The Hampstead hospital continued to be used to isolate and treat patients with infectious conditions like scarlet fever and was later used for polio victims. In 1948, with the creation of the National Health Service, the Hampstead hospital became part of the Royal Free Hospitals group, and in 1973 the Royal Free Hospital itself was moved from its site in Grays Inn Road to the Hampstead site, where it remains.

THE DEATH OF SMALLPOX

Smallpox was a long time dying. The mortality rate associated with the disease fell throughout the nineteenth century, the last major epidemic occurring in the late 1830s, when 2.3 persons per 1,000 contracted the disease: as many as 12,000 deaths per annum. Sir John Simon complained that vaccination rates fell away after epidemics and drew attention to 'an appreciable amount of utterly incompetent vaccination',[11] which explains why, even in the last decade of the century, 30 per cent of smallpox deaths occurred among people who believed that they had been vaccinated. Nevertheless, by the 1870s the mortality amounted to less than one person in 2,000.[12] In 1872 the Public Health Act established sanitary authorities in ports that could quarantine ships believed to contain passengers who were carrying infectious diseases, but as late as 1901–3 2,000 cases occurred in Liverpool as a result of unnotified cases arriving in the port. London's final epidemic occurred in 1902. In October 1977 the last case of smallpox was recorded in an unvaccinated hospital cook in Somalia. In 1980 the World Health Organisation declared that smallpox had finally been eliminated from the population. Samples of the *variola* virus are kept in secure conditions in laboratories in Russia and the United States. The possibility of destroying them has been discussed, but they have been retained in case a new strain of disease emerges for whose cure an understanding of the workings of *variola* would be beneficial.

Other diseases were to prove more difficult to understand or manage.

TWO

A Nation of City-Dwellers

The stranger, during his visit, feels his breathing constrained, as though he were in a diving bell; and experiences afterwards a sensible and immediate relief as he emerges again into the comparatively open street.

(John Simon, London's Medical Officer, describing a visit to a slum)

Of all the achievements of the Victorian era history will find none worthier of record than the efforts made to ameliorate the lives of the poor, to curb the ravages of disease and to secure for all pure air, food and water, all of which are connoted by the term 'sanitation'.

(The journal *Public Health* on the occasion of Victoria's jubilee, 1897)

THE MOVE TO THE CITIES

In 1801, at the time of the first census, Great Britain was primarily a nation of country dwellers. Of a national population of 10,686,000, about 30 per cent lived in towns and cities. London accounted for 959,000 of these. By 1851 the figure had risen to 54 per cent, and in 1901, at the end of Victoria's long reign, 78 per cent of the population were town or city-dwellers. In the course of one century the average Briton had moved from being a countryman to a townsman.[1] Moreover, in the same period the total population of Great Britain had almost quadrupled, so the move to the towns was further augmented by this unprecedented growth in numbers. London itself had experienced a sixfold increase in population by the time of Victoria's death in 1901 and was by far the greatest metropolis the world had ever seen, but other cities, though smaller, had seen an even greater increase in population and in the consequent pressure on their resources. The figures in the following table speak for themselves.[2]

Population of	Census years		
	1801	*1851*	*1901*
Liverpool	82,000	376,000	704,000
Birmingham	71,000	233,000	522,000
Manchester	75,000	303,000	645,000
Glasgow	77,000	345,000	762,000
Sheffield	46,000	135,000	409,000

This movement of population did not proceed at a steady pace throughout the century. The great port cities of Glasgow and Liverpool were overwhelmed by waves of Irish immigrants during the potato famine of the 1840s. There was a further surge from the 1870s when the government's free trade policies led to the importation of cheap food from America and the Empire, causing a serious depression in Britain's farming sector and what one writer has described as a stampede to the towns by unemployed agricultural workers.[3] The communities receiving this human tide were in no condition to accommodate the new arrivals who had come to work in Blake's 'dark, satanic mills'. Before the passing of the Municipal Corporations Act in 1835 most of the affairs of local government were conducted by magistrates, and the role of government of any kind in matters of sanitation, water supply or public health was barely recognised. In the disapproving words of G.M.Trevelyan, the first serious writer of English social history, the process of urbanisation was characterised by 'a rampant individualism, inspired by no idea beyond quick money returns . . . Town planning, sanitation and amenity were things undreamt of by the vulgarian makers of the new world.'[4] This is not to suggest that dwelling conditions in the countryside were ideal. William Cobbett, scourge of London, 'The great Wen', and of town-dwellers, described the village of Cricklade in Wiltshire as 'that villainous hole' and added that its agricultural labourers 'seem miserably poor. Their dwellings are little better than pig beds and their looks indicate that their food is not nearly equal to that of a pig.'[5] This is no rural idyll, but at least in the countryside fresh food was near at hand and the population could dispose of its relatively small quantities of human waste by depositing it on the surrounding fields of grateful farmers. The absence of fields and farmers from the great urban communities was to have fatal consequences for many of the century's townsmen when the great cholera epidemics struck.

DEATH IN THE CITY

The urbanisation of the population was not accompanied by a corresponding improvement in the facilities for the new residents. It has been estimated that for about forty years after 1780 crude death rates fell and life expectancy increased,[6] but the statistician William Farr, who campaigned for better public health measures,[7] observed that this encouraging trend was reversed from about 1816. Nevertheless, at the outset of his career as Compiler of Abstracts (Chief Statistician) to the Registrar-General, he struck an optimistic note, writing in his second annual report: 'There is reason to believe that the aggregation of mankind in towns is not inevitably disastrous.'[8]

The unwelcome upturn in mortality rates that Farr had observed coincided with a series of poor harvests, the release of many soldiers and sailors at the end of the Napoleonic Wars on to a market short of jobs, and the gathering pace of the movement to the towns and cities.[9] Death rates were 22.4 per 1,000 population in 1838 as William Farr began his work as chief statistician to the Registrar of Births, Marriages and Deaths, and they remained above 20 until the 1880s, falling to 15 in the first decade of the twentieth century.[10] Children were particularly vulnerable. An examination of Farr's annual reports and those of his successors reveals the depressing fact that more than 15 per cent of children failed to reach their first birthday throughout the nineteenth century, and Farr's attitude to this problem was at times fatalistic.

Writing of the depressing levels of infant mortality, he commented that infants were 'feeble; they are unfinished; the molecules and fibres of brain, muscle, bone are loosely strung together . . . It is not surprising that a certain number of infants should die.'[11] Farr had worked as a surgeon's assistant and qualified as an apothecary early in his career, though he never practised in either capacity, and one can only assume that these highly unscientific judgements were based on his own observations. The 'certain number' began to fall only in 1902, as new regulations governing the training of midwives began to take effect.[12]

The difference in death rates between rural and urban areas was remarked upon by many commentators, beginning with the *Lancet*, which in 1843 published the following information on the average ages at death of different social groups in rural Rutland and rapidly expanding Liverpool.[13]

Area	Ages at death (years)		
	Gentry	Farmers and tradesmen	Labourers and artisans
Rutland	52	41	38
Liverpool	35	22	15

William Farr seized upon the information he compiled to draw attention to the high incidence of premature death in towns and cities and published league tables of mortality with the intention of shaming municipal authorities into measures to improve public health. Preston in Lancashire was one of the most dangerous towns in the kingdom for infants, since more than 20 per cent of them failed to reach their first birthday. London was safer at just under 16 per cent, but Farr went further and showed that, within the metropolitan area, a child's chance of dying was much greater if he was born in the East End than in Hampstead, while life expectancy for those fortunate enough to survive childhood was almost forty years in the wealthy parish of St George's, Hanover Square, compared with thirty-four in the East End parish of Whitechapel.[14] One of the most dangerous things that could happen to a sick city-dweller was to be sent to hospital. Upon her return from the Crimean War, Florence Nightingale reflected upon her experiences there and the effects of good hygiene upon the survival rate of the casualties for whom she had cared. In her book *Notes on Hospitals* she commented:

> It may seem a strange principle to enunciate as the very first requirement in a hospital that it should do the sick no harm. It is quite necessary nevertheless to lay down such a principle, because the actual mortality in hospitals, especially those of large crowded cities, is very much higher than any calculation founded on the mortality of the same class of patient treated out of hospital would lead us to expect.[15]

She was also acutely aware of the shortcomings of the system of Medical Officers of Health. She described the position as 'a busy man with a private practice covering a very large area, who earns a pittance for doing a most important public duty',[16] and in her 1894 work 'Health Teaching in Towns and Villages'[17] proposed to supplement him with 'a fully trained nurse for every district and a health missioner'. The 'health missioners' would be women of good character and education who would undergo a course of fifteen lectures by the Medical Officer and would visit people in their homes and give instruction on hygiene and sanitation to *prevent* illnesses from arising. In her own words: 'Not Bacteriology but looking into the drains is the thing needed.'[18] The first 'missioners' (later called health visitors) were trained in Buckinghamshire, where Florence Nightingale lived, and they began work in the 1890s.

In 1891 one of Farr's successors compared the fates of 100,000 children born in the rural counties of Hertfordshire, Dorset and Wiltshire with a similar number born in the textile towns of Blackburn, Preston and Leicester. More than 90 per cent of the country-born children reached their first birthday, while only 78 per cent of the children born in towns did so.[19] The *Lancet* further drew attention to the ghoulish fact that some parents were well prepared to benefit from the vulnerability of their infants. It cited one father who, in 1861, received the considerable sum of £34 3s by subscribing to numerous infant burial clubs.[20]

So towns and cities were dangerous places to live, but what could be done about them?

THE HEALTH OF CITIES

In 1848, in an attempt to improve the health of the population, and especially those living in towns and cities, the government created the General Board of Health. It was a product of Edwin Chadwick's *Report into the Sanitary Conditions of the Labouring Population of Great Britain*,[21] which has been described by a subsequent writer as 'a masterpiece of protest literature'.[22] The publicity it received and the widespread concern that it generated drove the Whig government of Lord John Russell, for the first time in British history, to set up an organisation that was concerned with the health of the population as a whole. The Public Health Act, 1848, which set up the board, conferred powers upon local boards of health (who were often in practice the local town council) to construct sewers, water supply networks and public baths; to control offensive trades like glue making and rendering; and to clear cellars that were being used as dwellings. In practice, the reluctance of local authorities to spend money meant that these powers were rarely used. In the ten years of the General Board of Health's existence, 1848–58, only 103 communities even set up local health boards. The ten years that followed the demise of the General Board under the abrasive Edwin Chadwick and its replacement by the Privy Council Medical Department saw the creation of a further 568 local boards, an achievement that probably owed much to the diplomatic skills of Sir John Simon at the Privy Council in persuading some of the more complacent communities into unaccustomed activity.[23] However, the mere existence of a local board was no guarantee that it would actually do very much.

The Inspectors and Medical Officers who were responsible for identifying and eliminating the worst sanitary practices were usually poorly paid, and the esteem in which they were held may be illustrated by the verdict of a vestry clerk who, as late as 1884, upon being questioned by a Royal Commission about the qualifications required by an Inspector of Nuisances, replied: 'If a man was endowed with common sense I think it would be about as good a training as he could have.'[24] Medical Officers were not much better off. Only in 1872 was it made compulsory for local authorities to employ a Medical Officer, and it was a further three years before it was specified that they had to be medically qualified. The value placed upon their services may be judged by the fact that, in that latter year, 1875, Lincoln's Medical Officer was paid £15 per annum, while the wealthy district of Hampstead valued its Medical Officer's services at only £50. By comparison, a town clerk could expect to be paid £2,000. Even these meagre payments were resented in some quarters. In 1872, following a campaign mounted by Nottingham, the Local Government Board offered to pay half of the salaries of Medical Officers and Inspectors, but even so only eight out of forty-four municipalities with populations exceeding 35,000 took up the offer. Obstruction came from more surprising quarters as well. In 1842 the normally progressive Chartist periodical the *Northern Star* opposed an Act promoted by Leeds to improve its sanitation on the grounds of expense, while as late as 1887 the Treasury declined to grant £100 towards the cost of research into the effects of water quality on infection rates.[25] There were exceptions. Dr W.H. Duncan of Liverpool and John Simon of London were highly valued by their communities,[26] while Robert Rawlinson, later President of the Institution of Civil Engineers, was an Inspector for the General Board of Health, but they stand out from the mass of poorly paid, undervalued local officials who struggled with urban disease.

Sometimes they also had to struggle with their employers. Sanitary inspectors, besides being underpaid, were also subject to the political influence of councillors, who were often themselves slum landlords. As late as 1899 the *Lancet* drew attention to the insecurity felt by many Medical Officers of Health:

> It is not an uncommon thing for a Medical Officer, while endeavouring to have some insanitary property put in a proper state of repair, to find that a quantity of it is owned by a member of the sanitary authority – i.e. by one of his masters, by one of the men who have absolute power to discharge him neck and crop.[27]

Such situations prompted the campaigning evangelical clergyman Charles Kingsley to argue that middle-class women of philanthropic disposition should carry out such inspections, a suggestion that prompted the creation of the 'Ladies Sanitary Association' in

1857.[28] Kingsley, who was a clergyman more than he was a writer (he was the author of *The Water Babies*), argued that 'the moral state of a city depends on the physical state of the city; on the food, water, air and lodgings of the inhabitants' and was a powerful advocate of sanitary reform. The Sanitary Act of 1866, following the last great cholera epidemic, enabled the Home Secretary to intervene where he felt that local authorities had not acted with sufficient energy, but his actions were frequently constrained by the limits on expenditure imposed by the Treasury. Little real progress was made until the Local Government Act of 1871, which enabled the Local Government Board to sanction loans for local public works. In its first year the board sanctioned loans of little more than £267,000, but by the time of Victoria's Jubilee in 1897 the figure was almost £6,000,000.

THE GOVERNANCE OF TOWNS AND CITIES

Following the passage of the Municipal Corporations Act of 1835, a recognisable structure existed for the management of urban communities, but many battles had still to be fought before the administrative structure was reflected in activities that would benefit the health of the population. The Act itself had done away with the self-perpetuating oligarchies that were the descendants of medieval charters, and it gave to male ratepayers the responsibility for electing councillors, who, in turn, received the right to carry out improvements such as drainage and street cleaning. Many of the new industrial towns, which had no form of municipal government at all, could apply for incorporation. However, evidence that firmer measures would be required before the newly elected councils could be galvanised into productive activity is to be found in a survey carried out by the Health of Towns Association. This was established in 1844, its founding document declaring that its aim was 'to substitute health for disease, cleanliness for filth, order for disorder, economy for waste, prevention for palliation, justice for charity, enlightened self-interest for ignorant selfishness, and to bring to the poorest and meanest air, water and light'.

The greatest achievement of the association was the passing of the Public Health Act of 1848, which required local Boards of Health to be set up in communities where the death rate exceeded 23 per 1,000 inhabitants or where 10 per cent of ratepayers requested it. In the same year, 1848, thirteen years after the Municipal Corporations Act had been passed, the association sent a questionnaire to towns asking: 'Have the authorities of the town given any indication of their knowledge of the kind and degree of influence which the condition of suburban districts exercises over the health of the town?' The reply from Canterbury was, at least, honest:

A few of the town council are quite aware of the influence which defective drainage has upon the public health but a large number will not acknowledge it and the greater number are so much opposed to public expenditure for any purpose that there is no hope of effectual means being resorted to by them for the public good.[29]

A question to Oxford asking what plans the city had for obtaining a clean and economical supply of water drew the equally candid reply of 'never, and not likely to do so until compelled by Parliamentary interposition'.[30] It was such attitudes that had led Edwin Chadwick to despair of local democracy and to declare that 'the affairs of the parish are best governed in the absence of its representatives', and, on another occasion, that 'the worst company would be better than the best corporate municipality'.[31]

The prospects of the kind of 'Parliamentary interposition' to which Oxford had referred were much diminished by a combination of reluctance on the part of ratepayers to pay for municipal improvements and a widely held and doctrinaire belief that government activity of almost any kind was a tyrannical interference with the liberties of Englishmen. One of the most ardent advocates of this viewpoint was a barrister of Lincoln's Inn called J.Toulmin Smith, who wrote a series of pamphlets whose inflammatory character was matched only by their length and tedium. In 1849, in a 384-page document entitled 'Government by Commissions Illegal and Pernicious', he invoked Magna Carta, Sir Edward Coke and the Common Law in attacking the centralising tendencies of government-appointed commissions, singling out for special criticism the Metropolitan Commission of Sewers, which, for one year, had been struggling ineffectively to improve the sewerage of London. He attacked the Commission as 'one of the best illustrations of the vices of the system' for its 'folly and waste and inadequacy'.[32] He founded a journal called the *Eclectic Review* to publicise the activities of his 'Anti-Centralisation Union', which suggested that engineers who were trying to improve sewerage and water supplies were simply lining their own pockets at the public expense. He did not lack either confidence or bravado, since in 1852 he gave voice to these beliefs at a meeting of the Institution of Civil Engineers, informing his audience that the role assigned to sewers should be left to nature.[33]

THE GOVERNANCE OF LONDON

If communities like Canterbury and Oxford showed a degree of complacency in their attitudes to municipal government and public health, then the situation in London itself could be described as one of frustration generated by anarchy. As Victoria ascended the throne, the sanitary affairs of her capital were still governed by a Bill of Sewers that had been passed in 1531, during the reign of Henry VIII. It established eight commissions to govern their respective areas:

- The City
- Greenwich
- Holborn and Finsbury
- Poplar and Blackwall
- St Katherine's
- Surrey and Kent
- Tower Hamlets
- Westminster

Each commission was able to adopt its own practices in the design, shape and size of sewers, but they all agreed that the task of the sewers was to carry away rainwater, the connection of house drains to the system being specifically forbidden. House waste was accommodated in cesspools, collected at intervals by nightsoilmen and sold to farmers as manure. No commission was required to coordinate its plans with any other, so that large 'upstream' sewers in Holborn could be connected to 'downstream' sewers in the city, which could be both smaller and of a different shape. In such circumstances floods were inevitable and a frequent occurrence during heavy rainfall, but the situation was made more hazardous by the fact that house waste, including sewage, was often surreptitiously added to their contents.

In addition to the eight sewers commissions, London was governed by a confusing multitude of local authorities. The Square Mile of the City itself had its City Corporation and Lord Mayor, dating from the twelfth century, with authority that has been jealously guarded into the twenty-first century. Outside the boundaries of the City itself about two million people were governed by the vestries of more than ninety parishes, precincts and liberties, ranging in size from the Liberty of the Old Artillery Ground, Bishopsgate, with 1,500 inhabitants, to the prosperous parish of St George's, Hanover Square, with 60,000. Some of these bodies were 'open' and elected by ratepayers, while others were 'close' or 'select', the members being nominated by 'principal inhabitants' whose ancestors had been nominated for the purpose when the body was created in earlier centuries. One of the largest and most chaotic, St Pancras, had been changed from an 'open' to a 'close' vestry in 1819 by a local Act of Parliament. One hundred and twenty-two vestrymen were thus created, holding office by virtue of the value of the property they held in the parish. Overlaying such vestries was an apparatus of about 300 different boards for paving, lighting and other amenities, which had been established by over 250 Acts of Parliament. These Acts created some 10,000 commissioners for the purpose. The confusion engendered by this web of responsibilities was revealed when the rector of Christchurch, Regent's Park, asked the General Board of Health what he could do to improve sanitation in his parish. He was told:

> In the parish of St Pancras, where you reside, there are no less than sixteen separate paving boards, acting under twenty-nine Acts of Parliament, all of which would require to be consulted before an opinion could be pronounced as to what might be practicable to do for the effectual cleansing of your parish as a whole.[34]

In 1848, in an attempt to deal with the sanitary problems caused by London's chaotic local government, the government replaced the eight sewers commissions of Henry VIII with one Metropolitan Sewers Commission, the members nominated by the government. The government feared that an *elected* body in the capital might prove too powerful and present a challenge to the national government itself. Over the next seven years one commission succeeded another, as each wrestled ineffectively with the problems of London's drainage, lacking both the money and the authority to take the decisive actions that were required, while calling down upon themselves the wrath of Toulmin Smith and others who viewed them as excessively powerful. As commissions quarrelled among themselves, offended the government of the day or declared themselves impotent to discharge the tasks entrusted to them, one commission replaced another, until six altogether had retired from the field.

Finally the government conceded, with some reluctance, that the problems of the capital would be solved only by an elected body, which might thereby command the confidence of the metropolitan ratepayers who would have to pay for its activities. The necessary measure, the Metropolis Local Management Bill, was introduced to Parliament by Sir Benjamin Hall. As it made its way through Parliament, *The Times* commented: 'There is no such place as London at all . . . it is rent into an infinity of divisions, districts and areas . . . Within the Metropolitan limits the local administration is carried on by no fewer than three hundred different bodies, deriving powers from about two hundred and fifty local Acts.'[35]

While accepting the principle of an elected body to govern the metropolis, the government was anxious to accommodate the existing interests of the vestrymen who had administered the capital for centuries. Henceforward, however, all vestries would be 'open', elected by all ratepayers with property of a certain value. The vestries would, in turn, elect members of a central Metropolitan Board of Works, forty-six in number. The principle of *direct election* of the central body by ratepayers would have to wait for the advent of the London County Council in 1889. Local vestries would be responsible for such local amenities as street sewers, while the Metropolitan Board would be responsible for the main drainage of the metropolis as well as major streets, bridges and other measures affecting the capital as a whole. Medical Officers would be employed by vestries rather than by the Metropolitan Board, and the *Lancet*, always alert to developments that affected the health of the populace, writing of the vestry Medical Officers, declared rather grandly that 'the honour of the profession will be largely in their keeping'.[36] The Metropolitan Board would have the power to levy rates to pay for its works, but ratepayers who felt that their payments outstripped the benefits they gained from the board's works could appeal to the Court of Quarter Sessions: a formula certain to result in much delay and litigation. Moreover, the government, mindful of the challenge to its authority that could be represented by a body acting for the metropolis as a whole, retained the right to approve any expenditure upon public works of over £50,000 and also required the board to submit its plans for the main drainage for the approval of the Commissioners of Works and Public Buildings, headed by a government minister. Clause 136 of the Metropolis Local Management Act was unambiguous:

> Before the Metropolitan Board of Works commence any sewers and works . . . the plan of the intended sewers and works . . . shall be submitted by such Board to the Commissioners of Her Majesty's Works and Public Buildings; and no such plan shall be carried into effect until the same has been approved by such Commissioners.

Having created this body of vestries, which would be firmly rooted in local interests and which further protected the rights of individual ratepayers by giving them the right of appeal to the courts, Parliament was still unwilling to confer upon that body the right to design its own sewers: a symbol of the uneasy relationship that existed between the national government and local authorities. The anxieties that Parliamentarians felt over entrusting too much authority to a municipal body were expressed by Mr R.D. Mangles, MP for Guildford. Referring to the question of the authority of the Metropolitan Board of Works over London's affairs in a debate, he argued that 'the question was really one of an imperial character and ought to have been so treated by the legislature'.[37] The effects of the government's 'veto' and its eventual withdrawal in the face of the 'Great Stink' are discussed below.[38]

So in the middle of the century the government of Victorian London still lacked the powers it required to deal with the capital's sanitation problems, while other local authorities were reluctant to use such powers as they had because of a doctrinaire reluctance to do very much and an even greater reluctance to spend money. This affected the health of their residents at many levels.

HOUSING

One of these was housing. In 1844 Friedrich Engels, collaborator and supporter of Karl Marx, wrote in his work *Conditions of the Working Class in England* about housing conditions in Manchester, then approaching the height of its prosperity as the cotton capital of the world:

> Such is the Old Town of Manchester, and on rereading my description I am forced to admit that, instead of being exaggerated, it is far from black enough to convey a true impression of the filth, ruin and uninhabitableness, the defiance of all considerations of cleanliness, ventilation and health which characterise the construction of this single district, containing at least twenty to thirty thousand inhabitants. And such a district exists in the heart of the second city of England, the first manufacturing city of the world.[39]

Other public figures shared his concern, and some tried to influence the course of events. In 1842 Dr Thomas Arnold, the celebrated headmaster of Rugby School, wrote to his friend the writer Thomas Carlyle proposing the formation of a society, the object of which would be to collect information as to the condition of the poor throughout the kingdom. Nothing came of this proposal, possibly because it coincided with the publication of Edwin Chadwick's *Report into the Sanitary Conditions of the Labouring Population of Great Britain*, published the same year.[40] Other writers followed Chadwick's example. In 1851 Henry Mayhew (1812–87), lawyer, playwright, journalist and co-founder of *Punch*, published *London*

Labour and the London Poor, an account of the squalid living conditions endured by many city-dwellers. One of his most moving descriptions is of an eighteen-year-old girl, recently delivered of a child who had died at birth, sharing a room 9 feet square with her mother and another woman, the roof leaking, so that, in the mother's words, 'we never want rain water, for we can catch plenty just over the chimney-place'.[41] Later Mayhew described the 'mud-larks', of both sexes and all ages, who earned a living scrabbling in the mud- and sewage-laden shores of the Thames in search of pieces of wood, coal, copper nails and anything else that was usable or saleable. The worst part of London for working-class housing was Bethnal Green, where endemic poverty was exacerbated by the dependence of the population upon employment in the London docks, which was available intermittently at the whim of the dock managers. In 1844 the *Northern Star* published an account by a local clergyman, the Revd G. Alston. Referring to the efforts of Charles Blomfield, Bishop of London, to arouse public interest in the conditions in which the poor lived, he wrote: 'I believe that till the Bishop of London called the attention of the public to the state of Bethnal Green, about as little was known at the West end of the town of this most destitute parish as the wilds of Australia or the islands of the South Seas.'[42]

At least these unfortunate people had a roof over their heads, albeit a leaking one. They were more fortunate than the prostitutes described by Engels as living in Green Park 'in full view of Queen Victoria's windows',[43] whose unfortunate circumstances were described in *The Times* in 1843. A long and indignant article, unusual in its lavish use of capital letters, concluded by reminding the readers that 'within the most courtly precincts of the richest city on GOD'S earth there may be found night after night, winter after winter women young in years, old in sin and suffering, outcasts from society ROTTING FROM FAMINE, FILTH AND DISEASE'.[44]

Nearly forty years later, in 1889, Charles Booth produced his 'poverty map' of London in which he used a colour-coded map of London to illustrate the levels of deprivation suffered by inhabitants of streets in each area. The long gap between Mayhew's protest and Booth's map is a reminder of the limited progress that had been made in the meantime in improving the living conditions of the urban working class, as improvements in housing struggled to keep pace with the ever-rising urban population. It was not for lack of trying. A series of legislative measures from the 1840s onwards had encouraged local authorities to take an interest in the housing conditions of their citizens. Thus the Towns Improvements Clauses Act of 1847 allowed councils to demolish insanitary dwellings, and in 1851 Lord Shaftesbury's Labouring Classes Lodging Houses Act conferred upon local authorities the powers to build houses themselves and to borrow money for the purpose, the loans being secured against the rates. However, there was an almost universal reluctance to use the legislation in the ways that the reformers intended. Reference will be made elsewhere to the measures taken by Dr Duncan in Liverpool to clear that city's insanitary courts and cellars and the difficulties he faced even when backed by a supportive town council.[45] However, local authorities were slow to exercise the powers given to them by the Act. An obsessive desire to keep down the rates ensured that they rarely had the money needed either to purchase and demolish the insanitary dwellings of rapacious landlords or to build their own. The Nuisances Removal and Diseases Prevention Act of 1855 was more effective, since some enterprising Medical Officers of Health used the fear of diseases like cholera to cajole their councils into closing down tenements that the Medical Officer declared dangerous.[46]

Some idea of the degree of squalor that had to exist before the local authority would take action may be gained by reading some of the Medical Officers' accounts. John Simon, in his first report as Medical Officer to London, commented in 1849 on visits to the slums: 'The stranger, during his visit, feels his breathing constrained, as though he were in a diving bell; and experiences afterwards a sensible and immediate relief as he emerges again into the comparatively open street.' Simon went on to declare many such dwellings 'permanently unfit for habitation'.[47] Andrew Mearns, author of *The Bitter Cry of Outcast London*, described the experience of a sanitary inspector who visited a cellar containing a father, mother, three children and four pigs. In another room was a man with smallpox, while in a third was the body of a dead child.[48] Local authorities were themselves aware of the effects of overcrowding on the health of their populations, and the London County Council (LCC), which took office in 1889, was among the most active in identifying the problem. Soon after taking office, the LCC commissioned a study of the relationship between overcrowding and mortality, and the results were presented in the 1892 report of the council's Medical Officer of Health. The council defined 'overcrowding' as people living more than two to a room, and the report compared the death rates of different boroughs according to this criterion:

Percentage of people living more than two to a room	*Death rate per 000 residents*
15	17.5
16–20	19.5
21–25	20.2
26–30	21.7
31–35	23.9
>35	25.0

The relationship between overcrowding and mortality was clear, but not everyone was convinced that government intervention in housing, or any form of public welfare, was benign. This was the age of Toulmin Smith and laissez-faire, when the instincts of most public figures told them to do as little as possible and that at minimal cost to the public purse. It was a time when *The Economist* could declare: 'Suffering and evil are nature's admonitions; they cannot be got rid of; and the impatient attempts of benevolence to banish them from the world by legislation, before benevolence has learned their object and their end, have always been more productive of evil than good.'[49]

Thus, when the Marquess of Salisbury, future Prime Minister, proposed in 1883 the establishment of a Royal Commission on Working Class Housing, declaring that 'laissez-faire is an admirable principle but it must be applied on both sides', the Liberty and Property Defence League, founded the previous year, was ready with its counter-arguments, as it was for the proposals of Dr Druitt, President of the Society of Medical Officers of Health. In 1870 Dr

Druitt called for decent housing to be provided by public authorities, while Dr Buchanan, who visited some of London's worst tenements in the St Giles area, close to the present site of Tottenham Court Road underground station, suggested rather more tentatively that local authorities might just consider the matter: 'I feel it my duty to raise the question, at whatever risk of being thought wild and Utopian.'[50] These sentiments were not those that had long been held by the Liberty and Property Defence League, whose chairman, Lord Wemyss, ridiculed the idea of state provision of housing in uncompromising terms: 'he could conceive of nothing which would be more prejudicial than that . . . if they built houses, would they not furnish them? Would they put fire in the grate or food in the cupboard?'[51]

Another half century was to pass before such revolutionary ideas as public housing would be acceptable, but in the meantime some further steps were taken. Acts of 1868 and 1875 (the 'Torrens Act' and 'Cross Act' respectively, named after the MPs who promoted them) encouraged slum clearance measures by local authorities, but once again their provisions were weakened by the generous compensation they promised to slum landlords. W.T. Stead in the *Pall Mall Gazette* fulminated against the injustice of paying compensation to slum landlords,[52] but the sacred nature of property rights was such that the *Law Times* declared that the Cross Act was 'altogether divergent from the *laissez-faire* doctrine which for so long a period was held to be the guiding principle of English politics'.[53]

A further problem concerned the difficulties authorities faced in rehousing those who had been evicted from demolished properties. The Housing Act of 1900 enabled local authorities to buy land beyond their boundaries to house slum dwellers, and this led, in time, to the creation of the huge council estates at places like Becontree in Essex by the London County Council. A further Act of 1903 enabled the Local Government Board to force local authorities to undertake slum clearance measures. Moreover, the housing situation was helped by the fact that, in the last three decades of Victoria's reign, standards of living rose rapidly, though unevenly. An analysis of rents, prices and wages in this period gives some surprising results, based on an index of 100 in 1870.[54]

William Thomas Stead (1849–1912) was born in Embleton, Northumberland, the son of a Congregationalist minister and, after a rudimentary education at home, began to contribute articles to the Darlington newspaper the *Northern Echo*. In 1871, aged only twenty-two, he became its editor and used its pages to campaign for social reform, including votes for women and Irish Home Rule. In 1880 he moved to London, where Gladstone's protégé John Morley employed him as a journalist on the *Pall Mall Gazette*, handing over to Stead the editor's chair when Morley entered the House of Commons. Stead introduced to that rather staid publication such techniques as banner headlines, illustrations and human-interest stories, so that it quickly became a very influential periodical. In the first year of his editorship, 1883, Stead ran a series of stories on child prostitution. In 1885 Stead purchased, for £5, Eliza Armstrong, the thirteen-year-old daughter of a chimney sweep, to show how easy it was to procure young girls for prostitution and published the story under the title 'The Maiden Tribute of Modern Babylon'. An embarrassed government had him prosecuted at the Old Bailey for kidnapping a minor and he spent three months in prison. Nevertheless the government amended the law by raising the age of consent to sixteen. Stead also campaigned against the arms trade and for the rights of trade unions. He was nominated for the Nobel Prize for peace but was drowned when he travelled to a speaking engagement on *The Titanic* in 1912, making no attempt to enter the overcrowded lifeboats.

Year	House rents	Prices	Wages
1870	100	100	100
1898	123	71	165

The sharp increases in wages that characterised these years was more than adequate to cover the more modest increase in rents, with favourable consequences for the living conditions of many town and city-dwellers. Moreover, the decline in the price of food that accompanied the arrival of grains and meat from the New World and the Empire had a beneficial effect upon nutritional standards, as will be discussed later.

Despite the many problems that local authorities faced in improving the quality of housing, some progress was made even before the 1900 Housing Act. Thus Sir Joseph Bazalgette, who contributed so much to the health of the capital,[55] demolished some of London's foulest tenements, in the St Giles district, in order to build Charing Cross Road, rehousing altogether some 40,000 Londoners through this and other street improvement schemes. Paradoxically, such measures sometimes displaced problems rather than solved them. The Royal Commission on Working Class Housing was established in 1883, with a formidable membership that included the Prince of Wales, Cardinal Manning, the authors of the Cross and Torrens Acts and Lord Salisbury. The commissioners commented that, because of the urgent desire of working-class people to live close to their places of work, the demolition of slums in one place led to worse overcrowding nearby. Notting Hill was cited as an example of an area that had been degraded in this way.[56] The most radical proposal came from a partially dissenting member of the Commission who argued that 'the only effectual remedy is for local authorities to be empowered to purchase both land and dwellings in those parishes, towns and cities which can be described as populous and as liable, under ordinary conditions, to be overcrowded'. Parliament was still not yet ready to embrace the concept of public housing.[57]

More progress was made in Birmingham, where, by 1875, under its dynamic mayor Joseph Chamberlain, many slum dwellings had been cleared and factories and new residential districts located to the suburbs. In London, Charles Booth, author of the colour-coded 'poverty map', and the Cambridge economist Alfred Marshall, who served on a Royal Commission on the aged poor in 1893, advocated the removal of slum dwellers from London to suburbs, a proposal influenced by the Cheap Trains Act of 1883, which promoted early morning and evening travel at cheap fares. These enabled working people to travel to work from the suburban communities that were springing up along the railway lines into the great cities, especially

London. However, the real development of suburban London, of Metroland and of the 'Garden Cities' such as Welwyn and Letchworth, would have to wait for the new century and the new reign. Nevertheless, in 1900 a popular novelist wrote of London that 'narrow streets have yielded to broad, handsome thoroughfares; whole areas that were once little better than slums have been cleared and vast hotels and splendid shops stand where, only a few years back, the thieves and ruffians of London herded'.[58]

The author was no doubt more familiar with Bazalgette's broad thoroughfares such as Charing Cross Road, Northumberland Avenue and the Victoria Embankment than he was with the burrows of the East End, but he was, perhaps, right to detect the first stirrings of the municipal conscience in the provision of decent housing.

PHILANTHROPISTS: THE AMERICAN, THE LADIES AND THE LORD

While Victorian local authorities took the first hesitant steps in the provision of public housing, the demand was further met to a modest degree by philanthropists, prominent among whom were George Peabody, Angela Burdett-Coutts, Octavia Hill and Montagu Corry, first Baron Rowton. George Peabody (1795–1869) was born in Massachusetts but moved to London in the 1830s, where, with Junius Morgan, he founded a bank that was the ancestor of the later J.P. Morgan. In 1851 he was responsible for ensuring that American products featured in the Great Exhibition of that year when he put up his own money to meet the costs of exhibiting, which the American Congress had refused to bear. In 1862 he used his great wealth to found the Peabody Trust with a donation of two and a half million dollars, an unimaginably large sum for the time, the aim of the trust being to provide decent, subsidised housing for working-class people. The Peabody Trust insisted that all its residents be vaccinated, thus giving impetus to the controversial campaign to eradicate smallpox.[59] The Fabian Writer Beatrice Potter (later Beatrice Webb, 1858–1943), when writing in 1887 about the poor living conditions endured by casual workers in the London docks, commented that those with permanent positions in the docks chose to live at a distance in places like Hackney and Forest Gate, unless they could find a 'Peabody', model dwellings that offered a refuge from the surrounding squalor. In the twenty-first century the Peabody Trust owns or manages nearly 20,000 properties across 30 London boroughs, housing about 50,000 people. It is often in the news, not always to its advantage. In 2005 the Trust was praised for the quality of its new residences in Boxley Street, Canning Town, and criticised for attempting to sell flats in Vauxhall that it could not afford to refurbish to the standards required for contemporary living. Upon his death in 1869, Peabody, with the consent of the Queen, was temporarily interred in Westminster Abbey, before his remains were taken to America by the Royal Navy, where he was buried in the town of his birth, Danvers, Massachusetts, which changed its name to Peabody in his honour.

Angela Burdett-Coutts (1814–1906) used her great wealth to promote many philanthropic causes, notably the welfare of the poor. She was the daughter of the radical politician Sir Frances Burdett (1770–1844), who was himself gaoled for three months for denouncing the Peterloo massacre of 1819. He married Sophia Coutts, scion of the wealthy banking family, and it was through this connection that, in 1837, aged twenty-three, Angela became the wealthiest woman in England with a fortune of £1.8 million, a condition of the will being that she would forfeit 60 per cent of her inheritance if she married a foreigner. Numerous marriage proposals followed her inheritance (one of them supposedly from the future Napoleon III of France), but they were all rejected. The word 'eccentric' hardly does justice to one who, as a young woman, herself proposed (unsuccessfully) to the aged Duke of Wellington and who married, at the age of sixty-six, her secretary, William Bartlett, aged twenty-nine, who changed his name to Burdett-Coutts upon marriage in the reverse of the normal procedure. Since the young man had been born in America, she thereby yielded up most of her inheritance, but since she gave away some £4 million to charitable causes, this loss did not prove to be an insuperable deterrent. Queen Victoria described the marriage as 'positively distressing and ridiculous'. Angela used her St James's Square home to entertain such figures as William Gladstone, Michael Faraday,

Charles Babbage and Charles Dickens, who dedicated his novel *Martin Chuzzlewit* to her memory and encouraged her to found many 'ragged' schools for poor children.

The good causes she supported are almost too numerous to mention. She paid for the construction of many churches in London and elsewhere and endowed bishoprics in South Africa, Australia and Canada. She was a major early supporter of the RSPCA and gave money to Dr Livingstone in his missionary journeys in Africa and to Stanley in his search for Livingstone. She also supported causes in Nigeria and Sarawak.

However, her main contributions to the welfare of the poor comprised the establishment of a hostel for homeless women, Urania Cottage in Shepherd's Bush, which she planned with Charles Dickens, and the construction of model tenements at Nova Scotia Gardens, Bethnal Green, in place of the foul tenements that had existed before in this most notorious corner of London, known as 'The Jago'. She also paid for the creation of drinking fountains providing wholesome water, an inestimable benefit for those who could not afford a piped supply, the most prominent example being still visible in Victoria Park, Hackney. When she died, 30,000 people filed past the coffin of the woman who was called 'the Queen of the poor', and the future Edward VII described her as, 'after my mother, the most remarkable women in the kingdom'.

Her near contemporary Octavia Hill (1838–1912) was born in Wisbech, Cambridgeshire, the eighth daughter of a wealthy corn merchant and banker. She was the granddaughter of Dr Thomas Southwood Smith, who promoted a moralistic view of medical theory.[60] Through her mother, Southwood Smith's daughter, she became acquainted with some of the leading figures of the Christian Socialist movement and also with the art critic and social commentator John Ruskin. In 1856 she began to work at the Working Men's College in Great Ormond Street and later started a school, together with some of her sisters, in Nottingham Place, Marylebone, where she became acquainted with the squalid housing conditions of many of her neighbours. In 1864 she succeeded in interesting the wealthy Ruskin in plans for improving the dwellings of the poor and, with his assistance, was able to buy three houses, which she upgraded for her tenants. Ruskin suggested that she put the project on a commercial basis, offering to pay a 5 per cent dividend to investors, a decision that led to a substantial increase in the funds available to her. By the time of her death she was managing some 6,000 dwellings, many of them on behalf of the Ecclesiastical Commissioners. She was also active in securing the preservation of open spaces for the recreation of working people, safeguarding Parliament Hill Fields from development and taking an active part in the creation of the National Trust.

A fellow campaigner for better housing, Montagu William Lowry-Corry (1838–1903), had a lifetime that almost exactly matched the reign of Victoria. He was a grandson of the Earl of Shaftesbury, from whom he perhaps inherited his philanthropic genes, and spent most of his working life as private secretary to Benjamin Disraeli when the statesman was both in and out of office. In 1880, when the Conservatives fell from power, Corry was created Baron Rowton, and in 1890 he donated £30,000 to set up a trust to build and run decent common lodging houses for working men. The first Rowton House opened at Bondway, Vauxhall, in 1892, and in its first year over 140,000 beds were let at sixpence a night, offering such luxuries as clean sheets, washrooms and hot water, the last a luxury normally only to be found in the public wash houses that more enlightened local authorities had been establishing since Liverpool built the first municipal wash house in 1841.

Five other Rowton houses followed, of which the best known was Tower House in Fieldgate Street, Whitechapel, which housed some notable residents. Jack London (1876–1916) described Tower House as 'the Monster Doss House' in *The People of the Abyss* (1903) and recorded that it was 'full of life that was degrading and unwholesome',[61] but other equally censorious commentators were kinder. Thirty years later, in *Down and Out in Paris and London*, George Orwell (1903–50) wrote of Tower House:

> The best lodging houses are the Rowton houses where the charge is a shilling, for which you get a cubicle to yourself and the use of excellent bathrooms. You can also pay half a crown for a special, which is practically hotel accommodation. The Rowton houses are splendid buildings and the only objection to them is the strict discipline with rules against cooking, card playing etc.[62]

Tower House's most notorious resident left no record of his impressions, though the fact that he spent a fortnight there in 1907 suggests that he appreciated the standard of accommodation it offered. This was Iosif Vissarionovich Dzhugashvili, better known as Joseph Stalin, who rented a sixpence a night cubicle while attending the fifth congress of the Russian Social Democratic and Labour Party in Whitechapel. The building has since been converted into luxury flats, and the only Rowton House still used for its original purpose is Arlington House in Camden, known as 'Dracula's Castle' or, for its largely Irish population, 'The Mickey'.

NUTRITION

The early years of Victoria's reign included the 'hungry forties', a period especially remembered for the Irish potato famine, which has tended to overshadow the poor harvests, low wages and high levels of unemployment in Britain itself that led to riots and, of course, the Chartists' agitation. Yet it was during the hungry forties that was enacted the legislation that was to have a dramatically beneficial effect upon the price of food. The repeal of the Corn Laws in 1846 removed the protectionist measures that had kept out cheaper foreign grains since the time of the Napoleonic Wars, to the benefit of the great landowners. Their repeal split the Conservative Party of Robert Peel but opened the ways to cheaper sources of supply, which, combined with a steady improvement in wages later in the century, were very beneficial to the nutrition of working people.[63] At about this time Dr R.B. Howard, surgeon to the Royal Infirmary and Workhouse, Manchester, conducted and published *An Enquiry into the Morbid Effects of Deficiency of Food*. He drew attention to the fact that those suffering from malnutrition were much more vulnerable to disease than were well-nourished members of the population.[64] Further enquiries by others confirmed these findings. Dr Howarth, Medical Officer of Health for Derby, observed that deaths among bottle-fed infants were three times those of breast-fed infants, a difference that could be attributed to the fact that as much as one quarter of the milk supplied by dairies to towns and cities was seriously adulterated.[65] Similar observations were made by Medical Officers in Liverpool and Poplar, East London, where Irish and Jewish residents had continued to breast feed according to the practice of their countries of origin with beneficial results for their babies. This led to an early 'breast is best' campaign, which has been echoed in a further campaign with the same slogan conducted by midwives in the twenty-first century. Now as then, evidence suggests that breast milk is more nutritious and safer than other kinds (including proprietary products), coming as it does when required and ready sterilised. From the 1890s the pasteurisation of milk gathered pace, making it safe for children and adults to drink, and in 1899 an attempt to improve the quality of milk for children was made by the establishment of municipal infant milk depots, which were supplied only by farms that had been inspected. Liverpool was the first town to create one. In the meantime, however, mothers could take comfort from the fact that sick and peevish infants could be tranquillised with one of ten proprietary brands of opium that were freely available until the Pharmacy Act of 1868 restricted its sale to qualified pharmacists.

In 1867 one third of the children examined at Great Ormond Street Hospital suffered from rickets, while in 1884 *every* child examined at a Glasgow hospital suffered from this condition associated with poor nutrition. It was not only infants who suffered from malnutrition. An inquiry carried out on behalf of Sir John Simon as Medical Officer to the Privy Council ascertained that 30 per cent of the labourers questioned had eaten no meat but bacon, their diet being largely dependent upon bread and potatoes. A study by the philanthropist Joseph Rowntree (1834–1925) in York among thirteen-year-old boys demonstrated that middle-class children were on average 3½ inches taller and 11¼ pounds heavier than those of the labouring classes. His son Benjamin Seebohm Rowntree (1871–1954) calculated that, to support a minimum level of 'physical efficiency', a working-class family in York needed an income of 21s 8d a week, whereas 6.8 per cent of York's labouring population had incomes below this level. The Rowntrees raised the wages in their chocolate factories, arguing that a healthy, well-fed workforce would also be a reliable and efficient one. The American writer Jack London (1876–1916) commented on the short stature of the English compared with Americans and Scandinavians. Having encountered an Englishman taller than himself, Jack London jokingly commented that the man would be a candidate for the Lifeguards, only to learn that the man was, indeed, a member of that regiment.[66] Charles Booth's remedy for poverty among the elderly was in many ways more radical. He argued for a pension of 5s a week to be paid to men and women over sixty-five to keep them out of the workhouses, but this measure had to wait for the new century, the Liberal government and Lloyd George's Old Age Pension Act of 1908.

The quality of the food available as well as the quantity was an issue. Red lead was commonly used in cheeses like Gloucester to enhance their colour and was added to mustard for the same reasons. Chalk was added to milk to make it whiter and to flour in order to make it more bulky and thereby enhance the grocer's profits. The law of the times was so inadequate that it is doubtful whether some of these practices were illegal until the passage of the Adulteration of Food, Drink and Drugs Act in 1872. The Act permitted public analysts to be appointed by local authorities, the ancestors of our environmental health and trading standards departments.

Despite the mounting evidence that diet had a direct impact on the health of the population, it was left to market forces to go some way towards remedying the problems. From the late 1870s the cost of staple foods fell by as much as 30 per cent, as the government's free-trade policies allowed the importation of cheap food from America, Europe, Australia and New Zealand. This had a severe impact upon Britain's hard-pressed farmers but benefited the urban population, as consumption of bread fell while that of sugar, milk and meat rose. Even so, Charles Booth's survey estimated that labouring men spent as much as a quarter of their wages on alcoholic drink.[67] It is interesting to reflect that, earlier in the century, it was estimated that the inmates of the notorious and disease-ridden Millbank Penitentiary (1821–90) were receiving the equivalent of 3,500 calories per day in their diet. It became known for that reason as 'the fattening house', and the level was reduced to 2,600 calories per day. In 1900 it was estimated that the daily intake of labouring classes was a little over 2,000 calories at a time when they were required to undertake hard, physical work. The present recommended levels for a workforce that is less physically active are

3,580 for a man and 2,930 for a woman.[68] The consequences of this poor diet were observed among recruits for the army of the Boer War, when many volunteers were considered physically incapable of soldiering, but it was not until the advent of the First World War, with its need for mass recruitment, that the full implications of poor diet were appreciated, and almost half a century had to pass before such measures as free school milk and free school meals for needy families were accepted as a responsibility of government.

'NOXIOUS VAPOURS'

In his Ode 'Composed upon Westminster Bridge, September 3rd, 1802' Wordsworth referred to the city as

> All bright and glittering in the smokeless air.
> Never did sun more beautifully steep
> In his first splendour valley, rock or hill.

Within a few years of Wordsworth's celebration of the quality of London's air its citizens were being assailed by foul smells. A later chapter will deal with the contribution to this noxious compound of London's sewage,[69] but the pages that follow will discuss the role of smoke in damaging the health of Londoners and other city-dwellers. By 1819 Wordsworth's fellow poet Shelley could write in the opening lines of 'Peter Bell the Third' that

> Hell is a city much like London –
> A populous and a smoky city.

It was in the middle of the nineteenth century that London began to be called 'The Smoke' and to be plagued by the mixture of smoke and fog ('smog') that envelops the adventures of Sherlock Holmes and the novels of Charles Dickens. Foreigners were astonished at this phenomenon. The French writer Hippolyte Taine (1828–93), in his *Notes sur l'Angleterre* (1872), wrote that 'no words can describe the fog in winter. There are days when, holding a man by the hand, one cannot see his face', and referred his readers to the works of Dickens to gain some insight into the nature of London fog.[70] In one week in February 1880 London recorded more deaths than at any comparable period outside the great cholera epidemics, and the deaths were attributed to fog. The Black Country also acquired its unhealthy name and reputation at this time for the huge volumes of black smoke that came billowing from its furnaces. To these unhealthy brews were added the specialist toxic vapours of soap makers, alkali works, tripe boilers, tanners, glue makers and a multitude of similar establishments that sprang up in towns and cities in support of Britain's industrial economy. In 1889 Oscar Wilde's poem 'Symphony in Yellow' referred to London's fog-laden atmosphere:

> And like a yellow silken scarf
> The thick fog hangs along the quay.

Nor were the hazards only in the air. In the 1870s London had 1,500 slaughter houses with over 300,000 cattle being brought to London annually for slaughter and 1,500,000 sheep to market. To these must be added the many horses used to draw carriages and, later, omnibuses, and it is not surprising that the streets of London and other cities are estimated to have accommodated ten million tons of animal droppings by the end of the century.

Throughout Victoria's reign Horseguards Parade was permanently covered in a thick layer of soot, and *Punch* commented in 1851 on the measures being taken to clean up the capital in preparation for the Great Exhibition of that year. In an article headlined 'London with a Clean Front on' it proclaimed: 'Our good city of London is determined to deck itself out for the coming exhibition in its very best. Every street is either whitewashing its face or rubbing up its dingy complexion with a fine layer of London cement.'[71] Some early attempts to abate the nuisance had unintended consequences. The Metropolis Smoke Nuisance Abatement Act of 1853 led to a number of industries relocating to the outskirts of the capital, so that the residents of previously rural locations like Blackheath discovered that they now needed to keep their windows closed throughout the year. Birmingham and other cities adopted similar measures whose effectiveness was vitiated by the fact that the maximum fines amounted to £2 a day.

Sir John Simon, in evidence to the Royal Commission on Noxious Vapours in 1878, described the extent of the problem: 'It is not a question of a few manufactories, but of industries all over the country, which in relation to man are causing pollution of the air in degrees sufficient to make them a common law nuisance.'[72] Not everyone agreed with him. When the Earl of Derby, a former Prime Minister, complained about smells from the St Helens Alkali works invading his estate, the local paper commented: 'Noxious as are the vapours, St Helens cannot be said to be unhealthy. The large amount of high-priced labour which these works provide would cause the inhabitants to rise as one man if the legislature tries to change it.'[73]

The Royal Commission was given a very similar message. Alkali works, cotton mills and potteries all produced huge volumes of noxious vapours, but they also produced cleansing agents, cheap washable clothing and sewer pipes respectively. One witness told the commissioners: 'You cannot have manufactures carried on without suffering these disabilities; half or two thirds of your incomes is derived directly or indirectly from manufacturing industry and you must take the rough with the smooth.'[74]

The commissioners were also told that factory inspections would amount to a violation of English liberty. There were other less principled objections to the suppression of noxious trades, not the least of which was reluctance on the part of local authorities to lose payers of high industrial rates from the poor districts in which such industries were frequently located. Nor was there a proven link between lung disease and pollution of the air, many believing that exposure to smoke, in particular, was actually beneficial to the lungs. In 1843 the protesting inhabitants of Woolwich were informed that the rank fumes of gunpowder issuing daily from the arsenal were a powerful disinfectant, and this view was further illustrated in the experience of the Metropolitan Railway, the world's first underground line, which opened in 1863 between Paddington and Farringdon. The trains were hauled by steam engines, which were supposedly designed to minimise the release of steam and smoke into the underground tunnels, but their effectiveness may be judged by the experience of one passenger, as he reported it in a letter to *The Times* in 1879:

The condition of the atmosphere was so poisonous that, though a mining engineer, I was almost suffocated and was obliged to be assisted from the train at an intermediate station. On reaching the open air I requested to be taken to a chemist close at hand . . . Without a moment's hesitation he said 'Oh, I see Metropolitan Railway', and at once poured out a wine glass full of what I conclude he designated *Metropolitan Mixture*. I was induced to ask him whether he often had such cases, to which he rejoined 'Why, bless you sir, we often have twenty cases a day'.[75]

Reports like this one led the Board of Trade to set up a Committee on Ventilation of Tunnels on the Metropolitan Railway, which was informed by the Metropolitan Railway's general manager, Colonel John Bell, that the asphyxiating fumes were actually beneficial, especially for people with lung diseases. He attributed his own recovery from tonsillitis to frequent exposure to the 'acid gas' in the tunnels and assured the committee that Great Portland Street station was 'actually used as a sanatorium for men who had been afflicted with asthma and bronchial complaints'.[76]

Noxious vapours were also recorded in Manchester by Friedrich Engels, who described in detail one of the Manchester 'Courts', an enclosed area of housing similar to those criticised in Liverpool by Dr W.H. Duncan.[77] Engels wrote:

At the bottom flows, or rather stagnates, the Irk, a narrow, coal-black and foul-smelling stream, full of debris and refuse . . . In dry weather a long string of the most disgusting, blackish-green slime pools are left, standing on this bank, from the depths of which bubbles of miasmatic gas constantly arise and give forth a stench unendurable even on the bridge forty or fifty feet above the surface of the stream.[78]

KEEPING CLEAN

At a time when few dwellings, especially those of the labouring classes, had ready access to hot water, the problems associated with keeping the human body or the clothes it wore clean could be insuperable. Edwin Chadwick, in his *Report into the Sanitary*

Conditions of the Labouring Population of Great Britain, had recorded that in some places distilled urine was the only cleansing agent commonly used. Following the example of Liverpool, which had established the first public wash house in 1841, there followed the foundation of the Association for the Establishment of Baths and Wash Houses for the Labouring Poor. This charitable organisation raised money to build a bathhouse in St Pancras, which opened in 1846, and in its first two years attracted 280,000 bathers and 90,000 who used its laundry facilities. This no doubt disappointed the doomsayers who had argued that the poor *liked* being dirty; that their clothes would fall apart if washed; and that the baths would become places of debauchery.[79] Other public bath- and wash houses soon followed, many built by local authorities, who typically charged one penny for a cold bath, twopence for a warm one and a penny an hour for the use of the laundering facilities. The most notable surviving wash-house building may be seen in Old Castle Street, Whitechapel, where the Victorian façade has been preserved on a building that now houses the magnificent Women's Library of London Metropolitan University. Poplar Borough Council, close to Whitechapel, handed out free disinfectants to its residents on Saturday mornings, with the threat that houses that did not put the disinfectant to good use would be fumigated.[80] In 1897 the Cleansing of Persons Act, usually referred to in its passage through Parliament as the 'Verminous Persons Bill', promoted the establishment of more public wash houses and authorised local authorities to clean and disinfect persons afflicted by vermin. The effects of these measures in reducing the incidence of the classic 'filth disease', typhus, can be seen in the table on p. 58.

Eventually, technological solutions were found to the problems of polluted air. The electrification of the underground railway network in the early twentieth century removed the smoke from the tunnels. Robert Smith (1817–84), a chemist who was appointed chief inspector of works under the Alkali Act of 1874, showed manufacturers how to turn harmful waste into profitable by-products. In the 1890s incinerators were built in Shoreditch and Oldham to burn some of the animal droppings on Britain's streets and generate electricity, though as late as 1904 the Grand Junction Canal was conveying almost 50,000 tons of manure from

Paddington basin to be applied to the Hertfordshire countryside.[81] The 1875 Public Health Act had specified that furnaces should consume their own smoke 'as far as may be practicable, having regard to the manufacture or trade' – hardly a resounding call to action. However, the development of new furnaces that not only consumed their own smoke but also saved fuel, like the patented 'Bodmer' furnace adopted by the Truman brewery in Spitalfields, gave a financial motive as well as an ethical one. Yet another half century had to pass after Victoria's death before decisive measures were taken to clean up the air we breathe. The Great Smog of 1952, a combination of fog, smoke and vehicle exhaust fumes, killed 12,000 people in London alone. It prompted the Clean Air Act of 1956, which restricted the use of certain polluting fuels and banned black smoke.

THE ACHIEVEMENT

So what had been achieved by all this activity, entered into by local authorities at first very tentatively but later in the century with more enthusiasm? In 1897, on the occasion of Victoria's Diamond Jubilee, a special edition of *Public Health* had no doubts at all: 'Of all the achievements of the Victorian era history will find none worthier of record than the efforts made to ameliorate the lives of the poor, to curb the ravages of disease and to secure for all pure air, food and water, all of which are connoted by the term "sanitation".'[82]

We may have our doubts about this degree of self-congratulation, but some steps had been taken. Urban communities, including most notably the capital itself, had some form of coherent government with a reasonable degree of authority to build and clean houses, construct sewers, appoint Medical Officers of Health and control noxious trades. In most quarters there was no longer a fatalistic attitude towards the inevitability of death in cities, and some serious attempts had been made to establish the relationship between overcrowding, poor nutrition and poor health. By the end of the century mortality rates had fallen significantly, so that during Victoria's reign mortality rates fell from 22 per 1,000 population to 15, and average life expectancy had risen from the late thirties to the early fifties. This record was seriously blemished by the fact that infant mortality did not begin to fall until 1902, the year after Victoria's death, when trained and registered midwives became more readily available. However, as we have seen, much remained to be done. The construction of serious numbers of council houses did not gather pace for another twenty years, and the regulation of air quality had to wait for another half century of developments both in technology and in political will. In the meantime much of the urban population ate inadequate food, breathed foul air and lived in insanitary conditions. Three generations would pass before the word 'slum' would cease to be commonplace in describing large areas of urban Britain.

THREE

Science, Scientists and Disease

I can only say this, that I have been very careful to write nothing but what was ye product of careful observation.
(Thomas Sydenham, explaining how he categorised diseases and their symptoms)

. . . many very little living animalcules, very prettily a-moving. The biggest sort had a very strong and swift motion and shot though the spittle as a pike does through the water.
(Anthony van Leeuwenhoek's observations, through a microscope, of bacteria from his teeth)

NEW SCOURGES

The movement of population into towns and cities, which was such a marked feature of the Victorian age and whose progress was described in the preceding chapter, increased greatly the opportunities for infectious diseases to spread. Working families who had been accustomed to living in isolated communities found themselves in much closer proximity to their neighbours, often in slum tenements that lacked basic amenities such as clean water and lavatories. Fortunately, epidemics of bubonic plague had disappeared from Great Britain in the seventeenth century, though its reappearance in Russia in the last decades of the nineteenth century caused some anxiety. It is impossible to estimate what would have been the effect of an outbreak in overcrowded communities of a highly infectious disease like smallpox, since, by the time Victoria ascended the throne, a remedy for that condition had already been discovered. There were still many battles to be fought before vaccination was accepted and applied on a broad scale, but there was, at least, an understanding among the medical profession and much of the population of how to combat the disease.[1]

Unfortunately, other diseases were ready to take the places of these ancient scourges, some of them well designed to prey upon the residents of crowded towns and cities or upon patients in hospitals, where the importance of good hygiene was understood little if at all. Moreover, success in conquering them depended not only upon recognition of their true causes, often slowly achieved, but also upon the different rates at which disease prevention measures advanced throughout the century in disciplines as varied as engineering, public health measures and, last of all, the practice of medicine itself. Furthermore, attempts to combat them were bedevilled by fierce disagreements about their character and causes among well-intentioned and often very distinguished public servants.

Early writers were of little use. Hippocrates (*c.* 460–*c.* 380 BC), whose texts were in reality the product of many writers spread over six centuries, rejected the ideas that illnesses were caused by the wrath of the gods and accurately described the symptoms of pneumonia, but his contribution to an understanding of the causes of specific diseases revolved around his idea of 'humours': blood, yellow bile, phlegm and black bile. Disorders in any one of these would account for different types of illness, a belief that was to bedevil an understanding of disease during the centuries that followed. Galen (AD 131–201), who had practised medicine in Turkey and in Rome, taught that pestilence was caused by such phenomena as eclipses, comets, earthquakes and tidal waves. This did not help much, and the fact that Galen was a believer in one God helped to ensure that his views took a firm hold on medical theory in the Christian communities of Western Europe throughout and beyond the Middle Ages. Andreas Vesalius (1514–64), an anatomist and physician who was born in Brussels, wrote *De humani corporis fabrica*, which remained the definitive anatomical text on the human body for three centuries, but it did not have much to say about what caused it to go wrong. The Renaissance physician Girolamo Fracastoro (*c.* 1478–1553) suggested in his work *De contagione* that contagion could be spread by living organisms, which he called 'seminaria', and could be passed from person to person by 'water, air or any other means'. Although this was on the right lines, Fracostoro's analysis was too vague to be of much practical use to physicians.

Fracastoro's near contemporary Paracelsus (1493–1541) developed some interesting and controversial ideas on the causes and treatment of disease, but his capacity for antagonising colleagues was such that his theories were less influential than they deserved. He was born in Switzerland, his father being a physician from Swabia in modern Germany and his mother Swiss. His real name was Theophrastus Bombastus von Hohenheim, and the nature of his personality may be inferred from the fact that the word 'bombastic' was derived from his middle name. He adopted the name 'Paracelsus' late in life to indicate that he was beyond (that is superior to) the Roman writer Aurelius Celsus, whose collection of Roman medical knowledge in his work *De re medicina* had been rediscovered in 1428 and was treated with some reverence by Paracelsus' contemporaries. Paracelsus was brought up in Austria and was awarded his bachelor's degree by the University of Vienna, possibly gaining his doctor's qualification in Ferrara. He spent much of his life travelling, visiting Ireland, Moscow, Egypt, Palestine and Turkey.[2]

His distinct contribution to medicine was the belief that physicians should make a detailed examination of patients rather than relying only upon examining their urine, as was the common practice. He appears to have had a low opinion of virtually all his colleagues, claiming that 'all they do is gaze at piss', and, on occasion, publicly burning their books. He caused further offence when, in 1527, he announced to the inhabitants of Basle, where he was briefly a professor of medicine, that he was going to reveal to them the greatest secret of medicine and proceeded to produce a bowl of fresh human excrement. As his audience departed from the scene, he chided them: 'if you will not hear the mysteries of putrefactive fermentation you are unworthy of the name of physicians.'[3] The concepts of fermentation and putrefaction were to be paramount in many of the theories of disease causation of the Victorian age. Along with his belief in the importance of examining patients went a degree of scepticism about the value of some of the remedies then in use, such as the practice of pouring boiling oil on wounds, a process that could kill a patient through shock. Like most of his medical contemporaries, he practised alchemy, but unlike others he did not believe that its ultimate goal was to produce gold. He believed, rather, that its true purpose was to devise remedies for disease, views that he expounded in his book of medical alchemy *Archidoxa* ('arch-wisdom'), which established his reputation as a pioneer in advocating the use of chemicals to treat certain illnesses. Paracelsus later found renewed fame through an occasional appearance in the *Harry Potter* stories!

DISTINGUISHING DISEASES

Some early attempts to distinguish between diseases and to classify them according to their symptoms and treatment were made by pioneers like 'the English Hippocrates' Thomas Sydenham (1624–89). Some mystery surrounds Sydenham's early history, since, after attending Oxford University and becoming a Bachelor of Medicine, he was a soldier in the Parliamentary army during the Civil War, and, after the Restoration of Charles II, he was understandably reticent about his activities during that sensitive period. He was very well connected, studying under Christopher Wren before the latter moved from natural philosophy (science) to architecture, and was also friendly with Robert Boyle and John Locke. He appears to have studied on the Continent, and by 1655 he was practising in London, where he compiled his great work 'Method of Curing Fevers by Original Observations', which attempted to identify specific illnesses by bedside observations rather than by contemplating the works of ancient writers. He himself wrote: 'I can only say this, that I have been very careful to write nothing but what was ye product of careful observation.'[4] He was particularly interested in epidemics, having observed the last visitation of the Black Death in 1665 and a number of smallpox epidemics, and he developed the theory of an 'epidemic constitution' – environmental conditions related to air, seasons, climate and similar factors – which could prompt outbreaks of disease. He argued that fevers were nature's way of expelling harmful influences from the body and concluded from this belief that the physician should work with the grain of an illness rather than against it. This led him to adopt a number of common-sense remedies for his patients such as fresh air, warm clothing and clean water to drink, which, at a time when knowledge of medicine was rudimentary, at least did no harm to patients, unlike the practice of bleeding, which Sydenham used in moderation.

In the following century the *First Lines on the Practice of Physic* (1781) by William Cullen (1710–99) became Europe's standard text on medical practice. He used the presence of high pulse rates, headache, fever, chills and similar symptoms to distinguish between different diseases but left unanswered the questions of what caused them to arise and, more importantly, what caused them to spread rapidly through communities. His contemporary William Withering (1741–99), a graduate of the University of Edinburgh, was chief physician to the Birmingham General Hospital and a member of that city's celebrated Lunar Society, whose members also included Joseph Priestley, James Watt and Erasmus Darwin. Withering's particular interest was botany, which led him to discover that *digitalis*, a product of the common foxglove, could strengthen contractions of the heart in cardiac patients. He thereby made early use of drug therapy in treating disease, even though the cause of the condition remained unclear, and, in the process, earned a rebuke from Erasmus Darwin for poaching patients from his son, Robert Darwin (father of Charles), by offering 'solemn quackery of large serious promises of a cure'.[5] An early opportunity to achieve a greater understanding of the causes of disease was lost by political events in France. From 1770 to 1790, in an exercise of unprecedented scale, the Société Royale de Médicine conducted a study of the relationship between weather, food, hygiene and disease, using thousands of questionnaires completed by doctors throughout France. The information was not analysed because of the turmoil that followed the French Revolution.[6]

Some writers took a harsh economic view of mortality. The French writer René Villermé (1782–1863) studied relative mortality rates in affluent and impoverished arrondissements of Paris. He concluded, in his influential work *État physique et moral des ouvriers* (1840), that disease was caused by malnutrition, which was caused by poverty, which was in turn caused by the iron laws of economics against which there was no remedy. At about the same time in Germany the physician Johann Peter Frank (1745–1821) took a similarly 'economic' view of public health in his nine-volume work *Medicinischen Polizei*, where he traced links between communal health, a large population and material prosperity. Such arguments were highly acceptable in the English body politic, whose economic policies were governed by the doctrine of laissez-faire.

COUNTING THE DEATHS

From 1838 the statistician William Farr (1807–83) recorded the numbers of deaths occurring annually, together with their causes. Farr's contribution to the development of effective public health measures is discussed in greater detail later,[7] but it is instructive at this point to examine his records and those of his successors in order to identify those diseases that were gradually conquered by the Victorians and those that had to wait for later centuries and more advanced medical knowledge. The table that follows shows the number of deaths occurring from nine diseases that were prevalent as Victoria ascended the throne and whose passage through her reign illustrates the advances in some disciplines and the limitations of others. Cholera is discussed separately, because its mortality came, not in a steady stream, but in four sudden visitations, like Old Testament plagues, which caused more fear in all sections of society than did the greater death toll in the more relentless but less spectacular diseases. William Farr developed a 'nosology' or classification of diseases to help him with the compilation and presentation of statistics, but, as his medical colleagues developed a greater understanding of the nature and causes of disease, so his categories changed. Thus the disease we know as 'tuberculosis' was earlier described as 'consumption' or 'phthisis', while deaths arising from infections acquired during childbirth were variously described as 'childbed fever', 'puerperal fever' and 'metria'. Typhus and typhoid were not distinguished from each other until 1869, while typhoid was sometimes referred to as 'enteric fever'. Some of Farr's categories, moreover, are intriguing. Thus, in his first report, covering the last six months of 1837, his category 'violent deaths' includes such bizarre activities as 'eating cucumbers' and 'drinking boiling water'. Dropsy, gout and intemperance account for a few hundred deaths annually, while 'teething' among infants accounts for several thousand. 'Hooping cough' did not acquire its initial 'W' until the 1850s.

The deaths attributable to the diseases were as follows in England and Wales in the period 1840–1910.[8]

Disease				Years				
	1840	1850	1860	1870	1880	1890	1900	1910
Smallpox	10,876	4,753	2,882	2,857	651	16	85	19
Typhus				3,520	611	151	29	5
Typhoid	19,040	15,435	14,084	9,185	7,160	5,146	5,591	1,889
Scarlet fever	21,377	14,756	10,578	34,628	18,703	6,974	3,844	2,370
Whooping cough	6,352	8,285	8,956	12,528	14,103	13,756	11,467	8,797
Measles	9,566	7,332	9,805	7,986	13,690	12,614	12,710	8,302
Pneumonia	19,083	21,138	26,586	25,147	27,099	40,373	44,300	39,760
Tuberculosis	63,870	50,202	55,345	57,973	51,711	48,366	42,987	36,334
Childbed fever	3,204	3,478	3,409	4,027	3,492	4,255	4,455	2,806

A number of patterns emerge from this table. Smallpox and typhus had practically disappeared from the records by the end of Victoria's reign. Scarlet fever and typhoid were shortly to join them, though not before the latter had claimed the life of the Prince Consort and nearly killed the Prince of Wales. Whooping cough, measles, pneumonia and tuberculosis remained major scourges. However, the situation was improving faster than the figures suggest, since the modest decline in deaths in three of these during the last three decades of the century (pneumonia being the exception) must be seen in the context of a rapidly rising population. Thus the deaths per 1,000 citizens were declining faster than the bare figures show. The decline in deaths from childbirth, which did not occur until the first decade of the new century, was caused by specific legislative measures governing the training of midwives.[9]

THEORIES OF DISEASE

At the beginning of Victoria's reign there was virtually no understanding of how any of these diseases was caused, with the single exception of smallpox. The degree of bewilderment and ignorance that affected the populations of European countries in the face of epidemic disease may be illustrated by the anxious comment and speculation that accompanied the approach of the first great cholera epidemic, which reached Great Britain via the port of Sunderland in 1831. The precise origins of the disease remain a mystery, but it is now known that cholera is usually spread by water that is contaminated by the faeces of someone infected with the disease, though it can also be spread by flies that have been hatched in diseased faeces or have fed on it. In the absence of this knowledge, the epidemics that afflicted Britain between 1831 and 1866 were the subject of conjecture informed by despair.

In November 1831, early in the first outbreak to strike Britain, the *Lancet* reported from Vienna that a community of Jews from Wiesnitz in Austria had escaped cholera by rubbing their bodies with a linament containing wine, vinegar, camphor powder, mustard, pepper, garlic and ground beetles.[10] One imagines that such a treatment would have kept other people at a safe distance but would have done nothing to fend off the cholera germs, which they were likely to consume in polluted water. In September 1849, at the height of the second epidemic, *The Times* published a series of articles, stretching over three days, in which the possible causes of the disease, and its remedies, were discussed.[11] The writer listed the then current theories, starting with 'the Telluric theory which supposes the poison of cholera to be an emanation from the earth'. He went on to describe the 'Electric theory', which attributed disease to atmospheric electricity, and the 'Ozonic theory', which laid the blame on a shortage of ozone. He briefly considered the idea that the epidemic was caused by emanations from sewers and graveyards' but decided that 'for such an hypothesis we can find no solid foundation'. More space was devoted to the 'Zymotic theory', which was particularly associated with the distinguished professor of organic chemistry at the University of Giessen, Justus von Liebig (1803–73). Liebig believed that some compounds were inherently unstable and that, under the influence of temperature, electricity or friction, they could be prompted into a condition akin to fermentation, as with yeast. He further believed that the putrefaction of bodies that had suffered from disease could produce ammonia, which could be 'the means by which the contagious matter received a gaseous form',[12] thereby creating a 'miasma' in the atmosphere that would spread the infection through breathing. Liebig believed that blood was particularly susceptible to this process, and most particularly the blood of children, because, he believed, their blood contained 'wastes' from growth processes.

'THE ISAAC NEWTON OF AGRICULTURAL SCIENCE'

Liebig was himself the son of a dealer in painters' supplies and other chemicals. He was born at Darmstadt in Germany in 1803 and quickly became intrigued by the substances that he found in his father's stores and workshop. His formal education was curtailed when his experiments were the cause of an explosion at the gymnasium he attended, a result later repeated in the family home. His parents therefore apprenticed him to an apothecary, in the hope that his activities would be more constructively employed, and he attracted the attention of the Grand Duke of Hesse, who paid for him to study in Paris as a pupil of the distinguished French chemist Joseph Gay-Lussac. He became an assistant professor at the University of Giessen, which was later named after him, and he has a strong claim to be one of the founders of the modern science of chemistry. He demonstrated that plants feed on carbon dioxide from the air and on nitrogen, potassium, phosphates and other minerals in the soil. He invented an early form of baby food, and in 1865 founded the Liebig Meat Extract company, ancestor of the Oxo cube. His many British admirers included Michael Faraday and Dr William Budd, whose seminal contribution to the science of disease will be discussed below. Liebig was described by one English admirer as 'the Isaac Newton of agricultural science',[13] and wrote the first definitive work on the subject, which was translated into English as 'Chemistry in its Application to Agriculture and Physiology' (commonly referred to as Liebig's *Agricultural Chemistry*). The *Lancet* described Liebig as 'a man of the century'.

He believed that putrefaction was a cause of illness, but that, if the source of the putrefaction was returned to fields as manure, it would decompose and feed plants. He believed that disease in living bodies was analogous to the process by which decomposition nutrified the soil. Decomposition was thus a danger in streets and water supplies but beneficial when it occurred in the soil. Thus it was 'both the source of disease and the key to continued agricultural production'.[14] There is, of course, a great deal of truth in these beliefs: manure is as beneficial in soil as it is harmful in drinking water.

However, Liebig's influence in Great Britain was such that his mistaken ideas were as influential as his enlightened ones. His contribution to the science of agriculture cannot be denied, but his conviction that unstable compounds and putrefaction were the principal means by which diseases were spread was influential in establishing the 'miasmatic' theory of disease propagation as an orthodoxy that long persisted, to the detriment of public health and in the face of a mounting body of evidence. When Liebig made the far-reaching (and unsustainable) claim that 'it is a universal observation that the origin of epidemic diseases is often to be traced to the putrefaction of large quantities of animal and vegetable matter',[15] many hesitated to disagree with such a renowned authority. If Liebig had been correct, then it would presumably have been fatal to stand near a large compost heap. In 1849 the *Lancet* summarised Liebig's ideas as understood by the General Board of Health: 'a single infected person, and much more a large body of infected persons, localising themselves in the midst of a population predisposed to disease and actually under an epidemic influence, may act on that population systematically, that is, as the leaven which sets in action the fermenting mass.'[16]

Liebig was especially critical of the wasteful and harmful consequences of the adoption of the water closet, which became an increasingly popular feature of middle-class homes from the early nineteenth century, with widespread consequences for the sanitation of London and other large cities.[17] In one of his *Familiar Letters on Chemistry* he referred to these devices, then virtually unknown beyond Britain's shores, and their effects: 'contrivances arising from the manners and customs of the English people, and peculiar to them, render it difficult, perhaps impossible, to collect the enormous quantity of phosphates which are daily, as solid and liquid elements, carried into the rivers.'[18]

He was an early advocate of sustainable agricultural practices, believing that the quantities of phosphates and other chemicals used as fertilisers was finite and that, by flushing away potential manure, the English who so admired his work were sacrificing the future of the planet to their own sanitary whims. In 1862 the influential periodical *The Builder* quoted extensively from the English translation of Liebig's influential *Agricultural Chemistry*. Liebig observed that, from the 1840s, large quantities of guano (bird droppings) were imported to England from South America and used as agricultural fertiliser to produce food that eventually found its way into the increasingly fashionable water closets:

> The introduction of water-closets into most parts of England results in the loss annually of the materials capable of producing food for three and a half million people; the greater part of the enormous quantity of manure imported into England being regularly conveyed to the sea by the rivers . . . like a vampire it hangs upon the breast of Europe, sucking its life blood.[19]

Liebig's advocacy of the recycling of human waste attracted support from some unusual quarters. Charles Kingsley, Anglican clergyman, Cambridge history professor, author of *The Water Babies* and prominent pamphleteer, adopted Liebig's 'fermentation' theory wholeheartedly and in his curiously titled essay 'Yeast: A Problem', published in 1850, drew attention to the *moral* consequences of wasting potential manure by pouring it into the Thames. In 'A Mad World, my Masters' he argued that immorality resulted from filthy living conditions and asserted that clergy should for that reason become sanitary reformers, while in 'The Agricultural Crisis' he supported Liebig's proposals for recycling.

CONTAMINATED SOIL

These ideas spawned some ambitious, but ultimately fruitless schemes for turning sewage into a commercial product, but Liebig's

Guano is one of the least celebrated aspects of the commercial and agricultural revolutions that began in Britain in the eighteenth century and gathered pace in Victoria's reign. Guano consists of the solidified droppings of seabirds and bats and is particularly rich in nitrogen, phosphorus, ammonia and other chemicals that are of great value in agriculture. Its potential was realised in the nineteenth century, when guano to a depth of several metres was discovered on Pacific islands off the coast of Peru, whose dry climate helped to ensure that the valuable nitrates were not washed out by rainfall. Its value was such that it was the cause of a war between Bolivia and Chile, when Bolivia, backed by Peru, attempted to impose a tax on Chileans who were harvesting the guano. In 1856 the United States Congress passed the Guano Islands Act, which encouraged US citizens to take possession of any islands with guano deposits that were not already under the jurisdiction of another state. In 1842 the first shipload was imported to Great Britain by George and William Gibbs. It was an instant success with farmers, being richer and more easily managed than human excrement extracted from cesspools, and led to the collapse of the 'nightsoil' trade, with immediate consequences for the sewerage of cities.[20] Guano was the foundation of the Gibbs family's enormous fortune, which, from 1863, was devoted to the building of Tyntesfield, a magnificent Victorian Gothic country house 7 miles from Bristol, now in the possession of the National Trust. Many attempts were made to create a substitute for guano from human waste, 417 patents for such processes being filed between 1856 and 1876 by such companies as the Native Guano Company. None proved to be economically sound.

incidental influence on theories of disease propagation was more damaging, since his reputation as a first-class scientist gave currency and authority to the 'miasmatic' theories of other scientists. One of the most influential was his countryman and near contemporary

Max von Pettenkofer (1818–1901). He was one of eight children born to the wife of a small farmer but was brought up and educated by his uncle, who was apothecary to the court of the king of Bavaria. He studied medicine in Munich and successfully applied to join Liebig's laboratory at the University of Giessen, attracted by the growing reputation of the older man. He started the research into meat extracts that Liebig later turned into a commercial product and left Giessen to become a professor of chemistry at Munich, where he was soon confronted by the cholera and typhoid epidemics of the 1850s. He further developed Liebig's theories that epidemics were caused by 'fermentation' in putrefying, diseased bodies by arguing that the harmful ferment was not transmitted to others unless the earth in which the bodies were buried was itself contaminated by diseased faeces and itself fermented. This was the 'Telluric' theory described by *The Times* in 1849.[21] The combination of putrefying, diseased corpses and faecally contaminated soil worked together to produce 'a specific Cholera-Miasma which is then spread along with other exhalations into the houses'.[22] The 'exhalations' would, of course, be characterised by a very unpleasant smell, so the theory fitted very well the experiences of the residents of epidemic-ridden communities, where the smells of raw sewage and decaying bodies were all too familiar. The theory was embraced by many English authorities including Lyon Playfair (1818–98), Professor of Chemistry, pupil of Liebig and later a government minister, who informed a Royal Commission that the practice of administering opiates to infants by mothers in an attempt to calm them was made necessary because the children were made irritable by foul air: 'On the removal of these causes the general inducement to the continuance of the system would cease, for the irritability and difficulty of management of children would diminish with their increased health.'[23]

The idea that epidemic disease could be caused by filth was taken up by Charles Murchison (1830–79), physician to the London Fever Hospital and to St Thomas's Hospital. In his book *Continued Fevers of Great Britain*, published in 1862, he argued that typhoid could arise spontaneously from filth, and he adopted the term 'pythogenic' to describe fever generated by rottenness, which created a miasma. Nevertheless, in 1873 he traced an epidemic of typhoid to a polluted milk supply, thereby pointing in the direction of the true cause. In other quarters the 'pythogenic' theory took more eccentric forms. In 1842 Sir Francis Head, a former colonial governor, supported the theory by arguing that some of the new settlements in the Americas had been rendered dangerous by the ploughing of virgin soil, thereby exposing decaying vegetable matter and the 'miasms' that arose from it.[24]

Pettenkofer's proposed remedy for the cholera and typhoid epidemics was to improve burial practices and urban sanitation, which had the required effects of removing the results of putrefaction and sewage contamination from both the atmosphere

Sir Francis Bond Head (1793–1875) was descended from a Portuguese Jew called Ferdinando Mendez who came to England in 1662 as physician to Catherine of Braganza, wife of Charles II. The family name was changed to Head in the following century. Head became a lieutenant in the British army in 1811 and fought at Waterloo. In 1824 he was appointed manager of the River Plate Mining Association and was dispatched to Argentina at the head of a force of Cornish and German miners. After a 1,000-mile march they learned that the mining concession had also been sold by the local authorities to a rival consortium, who had arrived first. Further marches of 1,200 miles in search of other suitable seams proved equally fruitless. In 1835 Head was appointed governor-general of Upper Canada, where he quelled a revolt by pro-American sympathisers, setting their boat on fire and dispatching it over Niagara Falls. As a reward for his services he was made a baronet in 1836 and returned to England, taking a circuitous route to avoid a rumoured assassination attempt by his earlier victims. He devoted the rest of his life to writing pamphlets with alarming titles like 'The Defenceless State of Great Britain', prompted by the supposed threat from the emperor of France, Napoleon III, who in fact lived out his last days in exile in England.

and the water supply. He thus did the right things for the wrong reasons. So confident was Pettenkofer that cholera germs alone were harmless that in 1892, during a virulent epidemic in Hamburg, he publicly swallowed water that was known to contain cholera bacteria. In this enterprise he was joined by one of his most devoted followers called Emmerich. They both suffered diarrhoea and excreted samples of the *Vibrio cholerae* for several days but suffered no worse effects, probably because they had developed immunity from an earlier, mild infection.[25] The concept of immunity was understood at the time in relation to diseases like smallpox, but no such connection was made with Pettenkofer's dramatic gesture, thereby briefly setting back the cause of medical science.

DISEASED CELLS

Further progress towards an understanding of the causes of epidemic disease was made by another German and contemporary of Pettenkofer, Rudolph Virchow (1821–1902). He was born in Pomerania and qualified as a doctor in Berlin in 1843 but devoted his life to research rather than to the practice of medicine. He became politically active as a result of his appointment to a commission set up to investigate an epidemic of typhus in Silesia, where the principal victims were an oppressed Polish minority under Prussian rule. He formed the view that the cause of the outbreak lay in the filthy and impoverished state of the population and prescribed 'democracy, education, freedom and prosperity' as a cure. This did not endear him to the Prussian government any more than did his participation, as a Liberal, in the abortive and short-lived 1848 uprising in Berlin. Nevertheless, he enjoyed a successful political career as a member of the Berlin City Council, where he was a strong advocate of improved sewerage and water supplies and set up the city's first statistical service, collecting data on the relationship between social conditions and death rates. He was later elected to the German Reichstag (1880–93), where he was such a doughty opponent of Bismarck's aggressive military policies that at one point the Iron Chancellor challenged him to a duel (which was never fought). His reputation throughout the world was unsurpassed. In 1892 he was awarded the Copley Medal, the highest award made by the Royal Society (Captain James Cook and Charles Darwin were earlier winners), and his eightieth birthday in 1901 was celebrated by a torchlight procession in Berlin and similar celebrations as far afield as Japan and Russia.

Virchow's main contribution to medical science was as the virtual founder of the concept of cellular pathology. He rejected the idea, inherited largely unaltered from ancient writers, that disease was an infection of the whole body, in favour of the theory that it arose from alterations in certain cells, different cells being associated with specific diseases. His celebrated work *Cellular Pathology as Based upon Physiological and Pathological Histology* argued that the cell was the ultimate irreducible form of every living element and from it emanated all the activities of life both in health and sickness. He further argued that such disturbances could arise from, or be exacerbated by, social conditions of the kind he had found in Silesia. However, in some respects he was reactionary. He did not accept Pasteur's germ theory of disease causation and was, no doubt as a result, unable also to accept that infections could be transmitted between patients on the hands of doctors, as argued by Ignaz Semmelweis.[26] In his later years he began to follow an entirely new career when he visited and assisted Heinrich Schliemann in the excavation of Troy from 1879.

MICROSCOPES

Clues about the true causes of disease, germs, were lying neglected in the work of a Dutchman born two centuries earlier, Anthony van Leeuwenhoek (1632–1723). He was born in Delft, the son of a basket maker, and worked variously as a draper, surveyor and civil servant. He helped to wind up the estate of his contemporary the painter Jan Vermeer, who died bankrupt and was probably a childhood friend of Anthony. He appears to have been influenced by the book *Micrographia*, published in 1665 by the scientist Robert Hooke (1635–1703), whose magnified illustrations of plant and animal life forms inspired Anthony to grind lenses, make microscopes and use them to make observations. His highly developed skills enabled him to make microscopes that magnified over 200 times, far greater than any previous instrument, and in the

1670s he began a correspondence with London's Royal Society that lasted half a century in which he described and illustrated the objects he had seen through his microscopes. Many of his letters were translated from Dutch into Latin or English and printed in the *Philosophical Transactions of the Royal Society*. These led to his election as a Fellow of the Royal Society in 1680, thus joining a company that included Robert Hooke himself as well as Christopher Wren, Robert Boyle and Isaac Newton. In September 1683 he reported the results of his examination of the plaque from his own teeth, where he observed 'many very little living animalcules, very prettily a-moving. The biggest sort had a very strong and swift motion and shot though the spittle as a pike does through the water.' Leeuwenhoek's 'animalcules' were the first recorded observation of bacteria, but their significance was not fully appreciated by the Royal Society's Fellows, and as late as 1806 a well-known Baltimore surgeon called John Crawford lost his reputation and his practice for maintaining that disease was spread by microscopic organisms, which he called by Leeuwenhoek's name 'animalculae'.

Over the years that followed Leeuwenhoek's discoveries, microscopy languished as a branch of medicine. It was used mostly by geologists for examining rock formations and by those who followed Robert Hooke in their desire to examine insects and plants. These were the purposes for which the Microscopical Society of London was formed in 1840, and it was not until 1869 that the General Medical Council recommended that doctors be trained in the use of the instrument. However, in the meantime a group of pioneers in Bristol had set up a group that met at the home of Dr William Budd on 9 July 1849 with the intention of using microscopes for medical research. They called themselves by the almost unpronounceable name of 'The Microscopical Sub-Committee of the Medico-Chirchurgical Society' and would eventually lead William Budd himself to a series of ground-breaking discoveries on the nature of typhoid and cholera.

WILLIAM BUDD AND TYPHOID FEVER

William Budd (1811–80) was born in North Tawton, Devon, the son of a doctor. Some have identified William's own son, George, also a doctor, as the model for Dr Watson of the *Sherlock Holmes* stories. William studied in London, Edinburgh and Paris and spoke French, German and Italian fluently, gifts that enabled him to become acquainted with the ideas of continental authorities like Justus von Liebig, whom he met in 1842. He probably caught typhoid while in Paris and, having recovered, believed that he contracted a mild version of the illness in London early in his career.[27] He became physician to the Bristol Royal Infirmary and a director of the Bristol Waterworks Company, an office that reflected his belief that a supply of clean water was at the time one of the most effective means of combating disease. Typhoid was unusual in that, unlike many diseases, it was not primarily associated with poor living conditions. Queen Victoria probably suffered from it as a young woman, Albert the Prince Consort probably died from it in 1861 and the Prince of Wales, later Edward VII, almost died from it ten years later before making a full recovery. Typhoid was long confused with typhus, the two conditions first being distinguished by Dr William Jenner (1815–98), physician to Queen Victoria. In 1849–51, Jenner, who was not related to the more famous namesake who developed the process of vaccination, published a series of papers arguing that two separate diseases existed and that he, Dr Jenner, had suffered attacks of each of them! Typhus, carried by fleas, was a disease associated with filthy, crowded conditions, a fact that accounted for its popular name *gaol fever*. Deaths from the two diseases were recorded separately from 1869. Deaths from typhus itself fell rapidly from 1870, as the effects of the Public Baths and Washhouses Act of 1846 began to take effect. This Act encouraged local authorities to build such facilities in urban areas, and, after a slow start, the effects of cleaner clothes and cleaner people were reflected in the decline of typhus. Further impetus was given by slum clearance measures, so that, by the turn of the century, 'gaol fever' was no longer a severe threat to the lives of urban communities. The effects of these measures have been described in the previous chapter. The evidence is clear from the table on p. 58.

Budd was never convinced that typhoid was propagated mostly by foul air, or *malaria* as it was sometimes called. In his definitive work of 1873, *Typhoid Fever: Its Nature, Mode of Spreading and Prevention*, he challenged the orthodox view in uncompromising terms: 'It is stated by doctors Arnott, Kaye and Southwood-Smith that the malaria arising from putrefying animal and vegetable matters produced typhoid fever . . . I cannot subscribe to their opinion that this cause is adequate, of itself, to produce a contagious fever.'[28]

His first investigation of the disease occurred in the autumn of 1847 at Richmond Terrace, Clifton, where he noted an outbreak in thirteen houses drawing water from a well, which he suspected of being tainted with sewage. His next encounter with a local epidemic was at Cowbridge, Somerset, where eight fatalities occurred among visitors who were attending a ball, the only common factor between them being water from a well close to the drains of the inn where they had stayed and which, two days earlier, had accommodated a man recovering from typhoid. However, it was the third local epidemic that convinced him that sewage-tainted water was the cause. A fellow doctor, Henry Grace, father of the famous cricketer Dr W.G. Grace, drew his attention to an outbreak in some farm cottages on the outskirts of Bristol.[29] The disease had originated with the father of a family who had been working in the sewers in nearby Bristol. The house in which the family lived had drains that emptied into a nearby stream, from which water was drawn. Those who shared the father's cottage escaped infection, as did those living upstream of the dwelling. However, several residents living downstream from the source of the infection themselves caught the disease.

This and other evidence led him to conclude that 'the living body of the infected man is the soil in which the specific cause of the fever breeds and multiplies' and that 'this poison may communicate the fever to other persons in two principal ways – either by contaminating the drinking water or by infecting the air'.[30] It is interesting to reflect that, despite the evidence he had adduced that sewers and polluted water were the cause of the outbreaks he had studied, he was unwilling to absolve foul air from all blame. Was he hedging his bets or did he believe that, by thus nodding in the direction of the orthodox miasmatic explanation of disease propagation, he would make his 'waterborne' theory more acceptable? In his later examination of cholera epidemics he was to show less hesitation. Writing in the *Lancet* nine years later he was a little more confident, asserting that 'the sewers may be looked upon, in fact, as a direct continuation of the diseased intestine'.[31]

Despite his early reservations, his message was understood by his colleagues, who, from the 1860s, began a programme of sealing wells that were suspected of being polluted by sewage. These measures, together with the steadily improving sewerage of major cities such as London and Liverpool, ensured that typhoid deaths fell steadily from 1840. However, the decline in deaths hit a plateau in the last decades of the century, as may be seen from the table on p. 58. Further falls in mortality had to await improvements in the constant supply of water to households in the new century and the emergence of effective treatment for the disease. This occurred in 1898 with the development of a vaccine against typhoid by the English immunologist Sir Almroth Wright in 1898. An antibiotic treatment for typhoid followed fifty years later, in 1948.

'TYPHOID MARY'

A later century was able to distinguish between different types of carrier of the disease. Acute carriers pass the typhoid bacilli in excrement for a short time during and after the onset of the illness. Chronic carriers can pass on the infection in this way for years, while the most dangerous of all, because they are often unrecognised, are those who pass the bacilli in excrement without ever showing symptoms of the disease themselves. Of these the most notorious is 'Typhoid Mary' Mallon (1869–1938), an Irish immigrant to the United States. In 1907 Mary had worked as a cook for the family of a banker called Warren, who had rented a summer home on Long Island and suffered a severe outbreak of typhoid. The owner of the home was anxious to identify the true cause of the outbreak because of a well-founded fear that no one else would wish to rent the property in the future. He therefore hired a civil engineer called George Soper, who was experienced in such matters. Soper investigated Mary Mallon's employment history and discovered that typhoid had followed her from job to job. The New York City public health inspector isolated Mary for three years at a hospital on North Brother Island in the East River. In 1910 she was released on condition that she did not work in the preparation of food, but the

Sir Almroth Wright (1861–1947) was born in Yorkshire and died in Buckinghamshire, a year after his retirement at the age of eighty-five. He was the son of an Irish clergyman and a Swedish mother and was educated at Trinity College Dublin. His memory and energy were such that he studied both modern languages and medicine at the same time, graduating with high honours in both, and he claimed to have memorised more than a quarter of a million lines of poetry. He worked variously as a clerk in the Admiralty, as a demonstrator in the pathology department of Cambridge University and in a similar post at the new University of Sydney, Australia. Upon returning to England in 1891, he was appointed Professor of Pathology at the army medical school, Netley, Hants., where he undertook a series of experiments on the use of vaccines to combat disease. One such experiment in which he used himself as the guinea pig almost proved fatal. His experiments with an inoculation against typhoid were more successful, but the unpleasant side-effects of the treatment caused the authorities to hesitate before administering it. As a result, troops serving in the Boer War were not inoculated, resulting in the deaths of over 9,000 troops, while almost a quarter of the troops were incapacitated by the disease. In 1902 he was appointed pathologist and bacteriologist at St Mary's Hospital Medical School, Paddington, where he was soon joined by a number of other distinguished scientists, one of whom was Alexander Fleming. Wright was knighted in 1906.

job she was found, working in a laundry, did not pay well, and in 1915 she returned to cooking under the false name of Mrs Brown, infecting twenty-five people while working in a New York maternity hospital. She was arrested and sent back to North Brother Island, where she remained until her death in 1938, becoming something of a celebrity and the subject of frequent interviews by journalists. Mary appears never to have accepted that she was the cause of typhoid deaths and resisted her arrests violently. She ended her days as a helper at the hospital on North Brother Island, which was used as a quarantine centre for those affected by infectious diseases. She eventually died of pneumonia, but an autopsy found live typhoid bacteria in her gall bladder. She probably infected about forty people, of whom three died.

CHOLERA

Reference has been made earlier in this chapter to the alarm caused as cholera approached Great Britain in its relentless progress across Europe from its birthplace in Asia.[32] In reality, the steady stream of deaths from pneumonia and tuberculosis much exceeded those caused by cholera, but the greater terror engendered by cholera arose from its plague-like character – a sudden, unexplained epidemic that carried off thousands of citizens in a most unpleasant, undignified way and over a relatively short period and was the most terrifying visitation since the seventeenth-century plagues. The deaths attributable to cholera in the nineteenth century are shown in the following table.[33]

Dates	London	Great Britain
1831–2	6,536	32,000
1848–9	14,137	62,000
1853–4	10,738	20,000
1866	5,596	14,000

Moreover, while the other diseases were normally associated with insanitary living conditions, cholera was indiscriminate. The misfortunes of the royal family in its exposure to typhoid have already been noted, but the disease was normally more common among the poor. Cholera made no concessions to rank. The first three epidemics struck Mayfair as well as Whitechapel; Kensington as well as Bermondsey. Only the final epidemic, which struck Whitechapel with unprecedented intensity in 1866, was confined to the poorer inhabitants, and that had more to do with engineering than with household cleanliness.[34] The final characteristic of cholera that made it particularly feared lay in the course that it followed. The first casualty of the disease was twelve-year-old Isabella Hazard of Sunderland, where the disease first came ashore in autumn 1831. On 16 October, having attended church, this healthy child was suddenly overcome by stomach pains, vomiting, unquenchable thirst, spasms and diarrhoea of unimaginable ferocity, which drained the body of liquid and left her skin a dark blue colour. Nutrients were expelled from her body in what contemporaries later described as 'rice water evacuations', until the blood thickened to a point where it could no longer function effectively. She died the following day, the first of almost 130,000 victims. A person who was healthy at breakfast could be dead by tea time, and some victims were so sick that they often seemed dead before death came. In these respects, the rapidity with which the epidemic spread, the relentlessness of its attacks on rich and poor alike and the undignified end that awaited its victims, cholera most resembled the dreaded bubonic plague of earlier centuries.

For these reasons it attracted similarly superstitious reactions. Some Anglican clergymen believed that cholera was a punishment for sin and in particular for proposals to enfranchise Britain's prosperous and patriotic Jewish community. Nonconformist clergy were agreed that sin was the cause, but lay the problem at the door of the demon drink. There was an understandable reluctance to have any contact with the corpses of the victims of cholera, accompanied by anxiety on the part of the authorities to bury them as soon as possible. At Seven Dials, in the heart of the notorious St Giles district of London,[35] even the police refused to have anything to do with a cholera corpse. Eventually a group of watermen agreed to bury the corpse for the generous sum of 5s each – a good day's wage for each of them. Faced with the 1831–2 epidemic, a temporarily constructed Board of Health recommended, as preventative measures, the consumption of generous quantities of roast beef (for those who could afford it); of potatoes and stale bread for those who could not (it being vaguely understood that the mould on stale bread had some curative properties); and the avoidance of excessive quantities of fruit and vegetables.[36] Other remedies included brandy, laudanum, ammonia, sulphuric acid and the application of boiling water and hot bricks to parts of the victim's body. One can only hope that, in such cases, death came quickly.[37]

By the late 1840s a number of respected authorities were approaching, hesitantly, an understanding of the ways in which cholera was transmitted. In July 1849 the Microscopical Sub-Committee of the Bristol Medical-Chirchurgical Society, already referred to above, met at the home of William Budd and reported that it had found 'singular bodies' in the evacuations of cholera victims. Its findings were passed on to the Royal College of Physicians, though later experiments by that body failed to find similar organisms in samples of drinking water drawn from areas in which cholera was prevalent. There is no way of knowing whether this failure was due to poor microscopes, unlucky choices of water samples or poor observation influenced by a reluctance to admit that water, rather than air, could transmit the dreaded disease. At this point William Budd himself, while observing that patients using a particular hospital privy were vulnerable to cholera, held to the belief that the speed with which the disease spread suggested that air, rather than water, was the culprit: 'The poison accumulates on so vast a scale that, exhaling into the air, it broods like a great miasm over large districts, and in a manner to admit of its being carried by currents of air to indefinite distances with its deadly powers intact.'[38]

He nevertheless reported to *The Times* in 1849 that cholera was 'a living organism of distinct species' with 'funghoid' characteristics which *could* be conveyed in water[39] as well as in air or food. Nine days later a long article in *The Times* rejected Budd's theory on the grounds that in India and Europe cholera had travelled upstream along rivers like the Ganges and Danube, overlooking the fact that the geography of sewers and cesspools did not necessarily follow that of the rivers.[40]

Nine years later Budd departed further from the idea that the true cause lay with polluted air. The onset, character and ultimately beneficial consequences of the 'Great Stink' of 1858 are described later,[41] so suffice it to say at this point that the long, hot dry summer of that year, which converted the Thames into a stinking open sewer, provided a first-class test of the miasmatic theory. Budd drew attention to the fact that, despite the appalling smell hanging over London, the mortality rate was low. He wrote of the Great Stink: 'The hot weather passed away; the returns of sickness and mortality were made up and, strange to relate, the result showed not only a death rate of below the average but, *as the leading peculiarity of the season*, a remarkable diminution in the prevalence of fever, diarrhoea and the other forms of disease commonly ascribed to putrid emanations' (emphasis in original), adding that the miasmatic theory 'will take its place in that limbo of discarded fallacies to which other superstitions have long been consigned'.[42]

The statistician William Farr confirmed Budd's claims. The deaths per 100 persons living were recorded as follows:

Place	Average 1849–58	1858
England	2.246	2.303
London	2.425	2.356

Against the national trend, London had actually been healthier in the year of the Great Stink than in the decade that preceded it. By 1865 Budd was prepared to argue that 'Asiatic cholera is propagated exclusively by the characteristic discharges from the intestinal canal of persons affected with it', and his remedy against the epidemic that was approaching across the Continent and would soon ravage Whitechapel was to 'throw chloride of lime into privies every night and morning'.[43]

Despite this evidence, the official report of the Board of Health managed to accommodate the phenomenon of polluted water within the miasmatic theory by allowing the water to act as the *predisposing cause*, while continuing to place the immediate cause of the spread of the epidemic firmly in the air:

> It is difficult to arrive at any other conclusion than that streams polluted by the refuse of large masses of people so deteriorate the air as to operate in the time of a destructive epidemic, when all depressing agents have increased force, injuriously on the human frame, and thereby predispose it to the attacks of disease.[44]

JOHN SNOW ON CHOLERA

In the meantime, the most significant contribution to an understanding of the true causes of cholera epidemics was being made elsewhere by Dr John Snow, whose study of cholera was a model of the scientific, investigative approach to medical research and clearly identified water as the medium by which the disease was transmitted. John Snow (1813–58) was born in York, the son of a labourer, and owed his medical career to the generosity of a relative who paid the hundred-guinea fee for him to be apprenticed to a surgeon in Newcastle.[45] While studying in that city he became both a teetotaller and a vegetarian, characteristics not normally associated with student life. He was later described by his friend, the distinguished surgeon Sir Benjamin Ward Richardson, in affectionate but stark terms: 'He took no wine nor strong drink, he lived on anchorite's fare, clothed plainly, kept no company, and found every amusement in his science books, his experiments and simple exercise.'[46] An early practitioner of anaesthesia, he was one of the first to use chloroform for this purpose, administering it to Queen Victoria for the birth of Prince Leopold in 1853. His early contact with cholera occurred during the first epidemic of 1831–2, when, while still a student, he attended an outbreak at Killingworth, a colliery town near Newcastle more often remembered as the home, at the time, of the railway engineers George and Robert Stephenson. He earned his living as a doctor, but his careful scientific observations, which led him to discover the true cause of cholera, earn him a place in a chapter about science and scientists. In 1843 he opened a practice at 54 Frith Street, Soho, and in 1849, during the second great cholera epidemic, his observations led him to publish a paper called 'On the Communication of Cholera' in which he suggested that water polluted by sewage might be the medium by which cholera was transmitted. He further argued that the practice of flushing water closets into the river made the 1849 epidemic worse.[47] He developed his thesis in a series of articles in the *Medical Times and Gazette*, writing: 'If the general use of water-closets is to continue and to increase, it will be desirable to have two supplies of water in large towns, one for the water-closets and another, of soft spring or well water from a distance, to be used by meter like the gas.'[48]

Snow's Frith Street surgery was close to the offices, in Greek Street, of a young engineer called Joseph Bazalgette, whose great engineering works would, within twenty years, protect London's water supply from sewage infected with cholera and other fatal diseases. Sadly, there is no record that the two pioneers ever met. During the 1854 epidemic Snow observed that a high incidence of cholera was occurring among persons drawing water from a well in Broad Street, Soho (now Broadwick Street), not far from his Frith Street surgery. Further investigation showed that a sewer passed close to the well (a sewer that later investigations showed to be leaking). Snow persuaded the Parish Council to remove the pump handle, and the epidemic abated. The site of the pump is now marked by a granite kerbstone outside a public house named after the teetotal doctor – the John Snow. Some authorities were prepared to acknowledge that polluted water might have some role in the propagation of cholera when it worked with other factors, but none was prepared to accept that water was the principal medium by which disease was spread, despite the evidence of Snow's observations and the lucidity of his arguments:

> Rivers always receive the refuse of those living on the banks and they nearly always supply, at the same time, drinking water of the community so situated . . . the water serves as a medium to propagate the disease amongst those living at each spot and thus prevents it from dying out through not reaching fresh victims.[49]

This is a remarkably accurate description of the way in which cholera is transmitted, but few were convinced by his hypothesis, so, in 1857, the year before his early death from a stroke, Snow published a study of mortality rates in two South London parishes. He compared the mortality from cholera in Christ Church, Lambeth, with that of St Saviour, Southwark. The Lambeth water was supplied mostly by the Lambeth company and the water of Southwark by the Southwark and Vauxhall company. In the 1848–9 cholera epidemic the mortality in Lambeth had been the higher of the two parishes. In the 1853–4 outbreak the position was dramatically reversed, the Southwark mortality being almost six times that of Lambeth.

In the intervening five years James Simpson, engineer to the Lambeth company that now supplied the healthier parish, had moved its water intake to Seething Wells, Thames Ditton, above Teddington Lock, as required by the 1852 Metropolis Water Act.

There it was untainted by sewage borne upstream by the tideway. The Southwark company continued to draw its intake from the tidal Thames near Vauxhall. This marked difference in the incidence of disease could not be explained by 'miasma', since the customers of the two companies were breathing the same air. Snow never identified the organism that actually caused cholera, and the sanitary establishment remained unconvinced.

Snow recommended that the water companies use filters and that water be boiled during cholera outbreaks, and the General Board of Health at this time did examine a number of different filtration systems. They engaged in debate on the relative merits of different techniques, materials, thicknesses of filter beds and related matters, but the debate was uninformed by any clear theories of disease propagation or of the effectiveness of physical, chemical and biological processes involved in filtration. The dilemma of the investigators is reflected in their comments on the capital's well water: 'The waters from the shallow wells of London, perfectly bright as they are, frequently present, under examination, evidence of impurities derived from innumerable cesspools and sewers with which the metropolis is riddled and traversed: but those impurities may not be detected by the senses.'[50]

WATER

It is always dangerous to apply the wisdom of hindsight to the errors of earlier times, but, given the evidence collected by John Snow and his lucid arguments, why were his contemporaries so reluctant to accept his conclusion that cholera was spread through polluted water? Two explanations suggest themselves. British cities in the mid-nineteenth century were very smelly places, the stench arising from a mixture of sewage, horse droppings, offal and smoke. The Great Stink of 1858 is examined later, but it is appropriate at this point to observe that the stench arising from the sewage-ridden Thames was such that the Palace of Westminster almost had to be abandoned by Lords and Commons alike. On the other hand, unless one was equipped with a powerful microscope, it would be impossible to see cholera or any other germs in a glass of water. Twenty years later Sir Edward Frankland (1825–99) would develop chemical and biological tests of water purity. In the meantime, many dismissed Snow's theories as conjecture. In the circumstances it was reasonable to assume that disease entered the body via the nose rather than by the mouth. The second explanation concerns interest groups. Water companies were large and powerful organisations, among the biggest commercial concerns of their time. They had a strong interest in deflecting criticism to other quarters and were very skilled at doing so. The statistician William Farr, whose work is described in Chapter 5, encountered the resolute opposition of the East London Water Company when he investigated Britain's last cholera epidemic in 1866 and commented bitterly on the skill with which the company had concealed its own shortcomings until he finally penetrated its defences.[51] In his own words:

As the air of London is not supplied like water to its inhabitants by companies the air has had the worst of it. For air no scientific witnesses have been retained, no learned counsel has pleaded; so the atmosphere has been freely charged with the propagation of plagues of all kinds; while Father Thames and the water gods of London have been loudly proclaimed innocent.[52]

In such circumstances, and in the absence of any clearly defined germ theory of disease propagation, it must have been very tempting to conclude that epidemics were spread exclusively by foul-smelling air rather than by water that looked clean unless examined under a powerful microscope. Moreover, this appeared to offer a convenient explanation for the very rapid spread of the disease. A report on the 1854 epidemic commented:

The suddenness of the outbreak, its immediate climax, the short duration, all point to some atmospheric or other widely diffused agent still to be discounted and forbid the assumption in this instance of any communication of the disease from person to person, either by infection or by contamination with the excretions of the sick.[53]

Many authorities had recognised the link between filth and disease without understanding the role of water, rather than air, in promoting epidemics. However, in the absence of a germ theory of disease, Snow failed to persuade many during his lifetime. Almost ten years after his death, his diagnosis came to be accepted by some influential public figures, but others remained sceptical well into the twentieth century. One of them was the redoubtable Florence Nightingale, who in 1910 went to her grave believing that disease was caused by a bad smell, not by a polluted water supply. In the meantime, however, engineers were turning their attention to the smells.[54]

VIBRIO CHOLERAE

It fell to others to establish the theoretical explanation for cholera by identifying the bacillus that caused it. A neglected pioneer in this respect is the Italian Filippo Pacini (1812–83). He was the son of a cobbler and gained his doctorate at the University of Pisa in 1840, after initially intending to become a priest.[55] He died in poverty after devoting his modest income to caring for his two sisters and to his scientific work, prominent among which was the development and use of more powerful microscopes than had hitherto been available. In 1854 he identified the cholera bacillus in the blood and faeces of the victims of an epidemic in Florence, the same year that John Snow was conducting his analysis of the Soho epidemic, as described above. Neither man was aware of the work of the other, and the discovery of the cholera bacillus was not credited to Pacini until 1965. He recognised that death from cholera was caused by the loss of water from the body, thereby preventing blood from flowing and functioning normally, and he recommended the use of intravenous saline drips to maintain the patient while the cholera was emitted from the body. Although the disease was the main item on the agenda of seven successive international sanitary conferences between 1851 and 1892, the work of neither Snow nor Pacini was considered. Pacini's work was little known outside his immediate circle, so the discovery of the *vibrio cholerae* is usually attributed to the German scientist Robert Koch (1843–1910). Koch, like Filippo Pacini and John Snow, was from a family of modest means and overcame many obstacles to gain a place at university, where he studied mathematics, natural sciences and, eventually, medicine. He developed techniques, still in use, for cultivating, staining and isolating germs, which he first devoted to the identification of the organism that causes anthrax in animals (1876) and tuberculosis (1882). His reputation underwent a setback when in 1890 he announced that he had found a cure for tuberculosis. Within days 1,500 doctors had descended upon Berlin, where he worked at the Imperial Health Office, only to learn that Koch had been mistaken.

In 1883, by which time cholera epidemics had been absent from Great Britain for seventeen years, Koch travelled to Egypt to study an outbreak in that country. Like Pacini, of whose work in Florence Koch and his colleagues were unaware, he found an unfamiliar bacillus in the bodies of cholera victims, but he could not be sure whether the bacillus was a cause or a consequence of the disease. When the epidemic subsided in Egypt, Koch travelled to India, where cholera was still prevalent, and, using the techniques he had developed in Berlin, he succeeded in isolating and cultivating the bacillus, which he found in polluted ponds and streams. In January 1884 he announced his discovery, observing that the cholera bacillus, which he called *vibrio cholerae*, was 'a little bent, like a comma' (thus giving it its alternative name the *comma bacillus*) and that it was transmitted in polluted water, thus making an important addition to Pacini's discovery. He thereby dealt a fatal blow to all but the most resolute advocates of the 'miasmatic' theory and confirmed the theory that had first been advanced so cogently by Dr John Snow thirty-five years earlier. Koch returned to Berlin a hero and was rewarded by being given draconian powers by Kaiser Wilhelm II to deal with a severe cholera epidemic that descended upon Hamburg in 1892. In 1905 his achievements were internationally recognised when he became one of the early recipients of the Nobel Prize for Medicine.

The work of engineers in bringing about a sharp decline in the incidence of typhoid and other waterborne diseases after 1840 and in eliminating cholera from Britain will be discussed later.[56]

LOUIS PASTEUR AND GERM THEORY

In the meantime, the idea that diseases, especially epidemics, could be transmitted by living organisms specific to each disease rather than by a general 'miasma' was coming to be accepted through the work of a small number of pioneers. The failure of the eminent Fellows of the Royal Society to appreciate the significance of the 'animalcules' reported to them by Anthony van Leeuwenhoek has already been noted above.[57] Two centuries passed before it fell to Louis Pasteur (1822–95) to deliver the final blow to the 'spontaneous fermentation' theories of Liebig, Pettenkofer and their many followers by the development of germ theory. Pasteur was descended on his father's side from a long line of tanners, though his father served with distinction in Napoleon's Peninsular Army before taking up the family trade. Louis's mother was a farmer's daughter. Louis himself was born in Dôle in the Jura region of eastern France and, after a slow start, received his baccalaureat from the Collège Royal de Besançon, though his performance in physics was described as 'passable' and in chemistry 'mediocre'.[58]

Despite these perceived weaknesses, he gained his doctorate in physics and chemistry at the École Normale Supérieure in Paris in 1847 and went on to become a professor in Lille, then at the heart of the French textile and brewing industries. He became involved in studying problems in the production of alcohol, in fatal illnesses among silkworms and in the production of wine, these studies occupying him for eleven years. As a result of these and similar studies, he identified microscopic living creatures (bacteria) that promoted fermentation, some in the presence of oxygen (aerobic) and some in its absence (anaerobic). This was the foundation of his 'germ theory' of disease causation. He further discovered that, by heating wine for a few moments to a temperature of 60°, he could destroy harmful microbes that damaged the wine. This process, which came to be called 'pasteurisation', was later applied to milk.

Pasteur's germ theory was very quickly accepted in England. Joseph Lister learned of it in 1865 and made the connection with his own theory that hospital infections could be caused by a 'pollen-like dust', leading him to experiment with carbolic acid sprays in his operating theatres.[59] Following the death of Pasteur in 1895, Lister was among those who paid fulsome tributes to the Frenchman in the pages of the *Lancet*, where he referred to 'the brilliant and far-reaching discoveries of Pasteur which have revolutionised both medicine ands surgery', and even Rudolph Virchow, who long opposed Pasteur's theories, delivered a eulogy that the *Lancet* also recorded.[60]

In a paper read before the French Academy of Sciences in April 1878, Pasteur asserted:

> As the result of my first communications it appeared that the ferments, so called, are living beings, that the germs of microscopic organisms abound in the surface of all objects, in the air and in water; that the theory of spontaneous generation is chimerical; that wines, beer, vinegar, the blood, urine and all the fluids of the body undergo none of their usual changes in pure air.[61]

Pasteur shares with Robert Koch the distinction of having founded the science of bacteriology by virtue of their almost simultaneous discovery of the anthrax bacillus in 1876. In 1880, in a paper entitled 'Concerning the Extension of Germ Theory to the Causes of some Common Illnesses', he identified other microbes that were particularly associated with certain diseases. One of these was the cause of puerperal (childbed) fever, deaths from which exceeded 4,000 a year in the last decade of Victoria's reign as a result of transmission from mother to mother on the infected hands of doctors and untrained midwives. The struggles by a group of determined women who overcame this scourge are described in Chapter 6. Pasteur's role in the early development of bacteriology was to demonstrate that diseases were caused by specific germs, not by smells, thereby, in the words of a later writer, doing 'more than anyone to promote the biological theory of fermentation and to discredit the theory of spontaneous generation'.[62] Koch's contribution was to develop experimental processes that linked individual germs to their own diseases, beginning with cholera and tuberculosis. Many years would pass before remedies against some of these were to be found, but once the work of Pasteur and Koch had entered the mainstream of scientific thought the scientists at least knew what they were looking for.

SCOURGES THAT REMAINED

By the end of the century smallpox had been largely eliminated by vaccination and typhus by better hygiene. Puerperal fever, as described in Chapter 6, was being overcome by better hygiene practices in childbirth, while engineers, by providing clean water and effective sewage treatment, had virtually eliminated cholera from the lives of Britons and were well on the way to disposing of typhoid. The work of Pasteur and Koch had taught doctors and scientists to look for specific agents as the causes of tuberculosis, pneumonia, measles, scarlet fever and whooping cough.

Pneumonia existed in the time of Hippocrates, who, as observed at the start of this chapter, identified and described it and placed its causes in the traditional framework of the four humours, and in particular the phlegm. He was particularly interested in the sputum (through which the disease can be spread) and the difficulty some sufferers experienced in expelling it, writing: 'It is exceedingly bad when there seems a great quantity of matter in the throat and yet nothing to spit off. It is indeed in all cases dangerous when nothing is expectorated.'[63]

Galen distinguished between pneumonia characterised by black spittle, which he attributed to a condition affecting the black bile 'humour', and that which produced red spittle, which was due to a disorder of the blood. The latter was to be treated by the practice of bloodletting. This remedy was also proposed by Thomas Sydenham, a practice he normally avoided but that he justified by explaining that 'the blood of such people afflicted with pneumonia has become laden with phlegmatic humours collected during the winter and when put into motion by the approaching spring a persistent cough arises. This forces the humours to the lungs.'[64]

The process of bleeding survived as a treatment until well into the nineteenth century throughout Europe, a fact that reflects the helplessness of the medical profession in the face of the disease and helps to explain why it was one of the most persistent killers until well into the twentieth century. It had to wait until the latter half of the twentieth century before effective antibiotic treatments were available to combat it.

Tuberculosis or TB, also called 'The White Plague' to invite a comparison with the Black Death, is probably as old as the domestication of animals by humans. Some outbreaks have been identified with confidence in England during the medieval period, and it was becoming relatively common in Britain from the seventeenth century, one of its better-known victims being John

Bunyan (1622–88). Tuberculosis is normally transmitted between humans by droplets, typically as a result of sneezing, coughing or spitting, though it can be caught from milk infected with the bovine form of the disease. It is typically associated with poor nutrition, crowded dwellings and damp, unhealthy living conditions. It initially affects the lungs, but can spread to bones and joints, causing the sufferer to experience difficulty breathing and making movement painful. In the nineteenth century it was a source of great fear, which was reflected in great art, being a central feature both of Puccini's *La Bohème* and Verdi's *La Traviata*.

The decline in the incidence of the disease in the last decades of the nineteenth century (see the table on p. 58) owed something to the improvement in living conditions but probably owed more to a recognition that infected milk was a prime cause of the disease. In Manchester in the 1890s a survey revealed that almost one fifth of that city's milk supply was affected by TB,[65] and this led to a public health campaign designed to improve hygiene in dairies and to encourage citizens to boil milk. These measures, combined with the introduction of pasteurisation, brought about a gradual reduction in the incidence of the disease, though Sir John Simon's attempts to have the disease made notifiable in the Infectious Diseases Notification Act of 1889 was unsuccessful, and TB did not achieve this status until 1912. The first hospital designed specifically for TB was opened in 1842 (it later became the Brompton Hospital), but the sanatorium movement did not gather pace until the end of the century, leading to the isolation of sufferers in hospitals where the treatment consisted mostly of breathing cold, clean air. Seaside towns like Margate, conveniently placed for sufferers from the workhouses of London, accommodated dozens of such establishments in the later decades of the nineteenth century.

Robert Koch's discovery of the tubercle bacillus in 1882 (for which he was later awarded the Nobel Prize) had told the scientists what to look for, but no treatment for the condition was developed until 1943, when Streptomycin was developed by Albert Schatz, a research student at Rutgers University, New Jersey. From that time TB began a rapid decline in the developed world, but the drug had one major drawback: it had to be administered, as a course, by intramuscular injection, which encouraged many sufferers, once they began to feel better, to discontinue the treatment. New strains of TB thus mutated, and this, combined with the continued prevalence of poor living conditions in many parts even of the developed world, have ensured that there are more sufferers in the twenty-first century than there were in the 1950s. It is a depressing thought that, at the World Economic Forum in Davos, Switzerland, of the world's leading economic powers in January 2006, tuberculosis was identified as one of the principal causes of sickness and mortality. Almost nine million people a year suffer from the disease, of whom two million die.

The modest fall in deaths from the traditional childhood diseases that is evident from the figures in the table on p. 58 also owed something to better living conditions as the century ended. A rise in the cases of measles and whooping cough occurred from the 1780s and has been related to an increase in the price of grain[66] as well as to the crowding-together in poor dwellings of those moving from the country to the towns. Poor nutrition and a deficiency of vitamin A are common features of these illnesses, and doctors at the time commented that, while well-nourished children often caught these diseases, they rarely died of them. Scarlet fever arrived in the middle of the nineteenth century, and deaths attributable to it rose rapidly until about 1875, a period that, again, coincided with a rise in the price of grain. From the latter date the number of deaths fell rapidly, and it has been suggested that the suddenness of the fall may owe something to the fact that a degree of resistance had arisen in the resident population. Again, whooping cough and scarlet fever had to wait for the development of antibiotics in the latter half of the twentieth century before these ceased to be a source of anxiety for parents. In the case of measles and whooping cough, there was a further wait for the immunisation programmes that have occasionally caused anxieties of their own. The Victorians had no remedies for these conditions beyond decent homes, clean water, clean clothing and adequate food. The processes by which the causes of many of the diseases identified in this chapter came to be eliminated by sanitary reformers, engineers, midwives, scientists and doctors will be discussed in the chapters that follow.

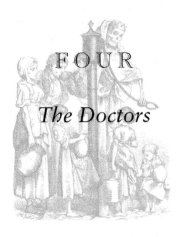

FOUR

The Doctors

*A well of sewage four feet deep, filled with this stinking fluid,
was found in one cellar under the bed where the family slept.*
(Dr W.H. Duncan, Liverpool's Medical Officer, describing
housing conditions in the city in 1843)

*Animals will scarcely thrive in an atmosphere of their own
decomposing excrement; yet such, strictly and literally
speaking, is the air which a very large proportion of the
inhabitants of the City are condemned to breathe.*
(John Simon describing living conditions in London
in the 1850s)

THE CAUSES OF DISEASE

The medical profession was scarcely better equipped to deal with
the plagues of the nineteenth century than it had been to deal with
the Black Death. In the absence of any clear understanding of the
causes of disease, doctors, like politicians and public servants, could
do little more than wring their hands in despair and offer their own
plausible (but usually mistaken) explanations for the misfortunes of
their fellow citizens. Indeed in some quarters the profession was
barely reputable. In the seventeenth century the great French
dramatist Molière, who had himself suffered at the hands of
expensive quacks, had wrought his revenge by lampooning the
profession as greedy, ignorant and complacent. Practices like
bleeding patients, in the belief that harmful influences were thereby

removed from the body, had been practised since medieval times and survived well into the nineteenth century, with results that were far from beneficial. As late as 1836 a Medical Officer from Edinburgh reported that he had cured a case of fever in a child by bleeding.[1] Fortunately few poor people could afford the doctors who inflicted these harmful treatments and resorted instead to traditional folk remedies, some of which were probably effective. Covering the patient with a red cloth to draw out the heat for a patient with a fever from influenza at least kept him warm and did no harm. Covering a bad cut with wet, mouldy bread could bring anti-bacterial fungus into contact with harmful microbes long before Alexander Fleming saw penicillin in his petri dish. Cloves of raw garlic were recommended for a variety of conditions, and such beliefs may owe something to anti-bacterial properties in that maligned vegetable.

In official circles outbreaks of diseases like cholera, typhoid, typhus (also known as *gaol fever* and often confused with typhoid) and other scourges were variously attributed to loose living, foul air, over-indulgence in alcohol and, in one case, the consumption of excessive quantities of plums. The word 'epidemic', which entered the language in the seventeenth century to mean a prevalent condition, came to be applied to such outbreaks when they inflicted significantly more than the normal levels of mortality. As the century progressed, insanitary living conditions, combined with inadequate arrangements for the disposal of sewage and the pollution of water supplies came to be accepted, slowly and rather reluctantly, as true causes of epidemics, but even then medical practitioners had few remedies to hand. Nourishing food, clean water and rest in clean linen were often the most effective remedies, but these were beyond the means of the poor. Laudanum, a product of opium, was an effective painkiller but liable to produce addiction, as the writers Thomas de Quincey and Samuel Taylor Coleridge found to their cost. The more benign aspirin was not available until 1899, as the century ended. Surgery was, of course, available when absolutely necessary but carried its own horrors in the days before anaesthetics and its own risks after anaesthesia came into use. The great merit of surgery without such sedation as ether and chloroform had to offer was that it was performed rapidly. When anaesthetics were applied and surgery was performed more slowly and carefully, the exposure of open wounds to infection actually increased the number of deaths until Joseph Lister persuaded his sceptical colleagues to adopt antiseptic measures that made surgery safer.

Joseph, Lord Lister (1827–1912), son of a distinguished scientist who had improved the design of the microscope, was educated at a Quaker School and remained deeply religious throughout his life. He studied at University College London and in 1856 he became an assistant surgeon at Edinburgh Royal Infirmary. Three years later, aged only thirty-two, he became Regius Professor of Surgery at Glasgow University, and in 1861 he was appointed surgeon at Glasgow Royal Infirmary. By this time anaesthetics were in common use for surgical operations, and the slower pace at which surgery was consequently carried out led to the deaths of almost half the patients as the result of wound infection, known as *hospital disease*. The construction of new, cleaner buildings at Glasgow did not reduce the death rate, and Lister hypothesised that infection might be caused by a 'pollen-like dust'. When, in 1865, Pasteur suggested that living organisms in the atmosphere could cause decay, Lister made the connection with his own theory and began to clean wounds with a solution of carbolic acid. Lister's theatre sister suffered from the effects of carbolic acid on her hands and thus introduced the use of rubber gloves in the operating theatre. In 1867 Lister informed the British Medical Association that his wards at Glasgow had been rendered free of infection. His ideas were more readily accepted in Germany than England, where 'miasmatic' beliefs held that there could be no infection unless there was a foul smell. However, the facts spoke for themselves, and honours followed his success. He was created Baron Lister in 1897, was appointed one of the twelve original members of the Order of Merit in 1902 and became President of the Royal Society in 1895.

THE QUACKS

In the meantime the field was open to quack doctors who offered a variety of mostly ineffective and occasionally harmful treatments in a profession that was subject to only the lightest regulation. The London College of Physicians had been licensed in 1518, the Barber-Surgeons Company in 1540, and the Society of Apothecaries in 1617, each of them authorised by the Crown to admit applicants to practise medicine in London. Outside the capital this task was discharged by bishops upon the advice of medical practitioners. Many such practitioners favoured a diagnostic method known as 'urine gazing', which held that inspection of a patient's discharges enabled a wide range of afflictions to be identified. The energies of these licensing authorities in the early years appear to have been mostly devoted to protecting their interests from one another, and any effective role they might have exercised in regulating the profession was in any case vitiated by the fact that they had no control at all over patent medicines. Only in 1858, with the passing of the Medical Act of that year, was the General Medical Council established, with authority over a single register of qualified medical practitioners, and it took a further Act of 1886 to establish common examination procedures for surgeons and physicians.

The first royal patent, for the manufacture of stained glass, was granted in 1449, but in the seventeenth century, under the impecunious Stuart monarchs, the granting of patents was exploited by the Crown as a means of raising revenue. Applications for patents for medicines did not have to show that they were effective, only that they were new. From this time, therefore, many remedies of doubtful value received royal patents, some of them peddled by reputable practitioners, some of them exploiting their royal connections to the uttermost degree by decorating their premises and labels with the royal crest.[2] Thus, while 'Hooper's Female Pills' are deservedly forgotten along with their inventor, the inventor of 'Dr Radcliffe's Famous Purging Elixir' is still remembered in Oxford's John Radcliffe (1650–1714) Hospital and Radcliffe Infirmary, the latter founded with a legacy partly derived from the elixir. Likewise, Thomas Beecham (1820–1907) successfully made the transition from quackery to respectability with Beecham's pills, cornerstone of a mighty corporation that eventually emerged as GlaxoSmithKline.

Such remedies were usually offered for chronic or cosmetic afflictions rather than for acute conditions like cholera or typhoid. The death of the sufferer from an acute illness undermined confidence in the remedy as well as losing a customer, whereas a long-term condition like scurvy, ague, dropsy, gout or disfigurements arising from smallpox not only guaranteed a long-running source of income but also benefited from the incidental improvements in these conditions as a result of remissions that were in fact due to better diet, living conditions or the natural course of the disease. Remedies for infertility and sexual inadequacy were also widely marketed for similar reasons. Only in the nineteenth century was a serious challenge mounted to the purveyors of patent medicines. It was led by Thomas Wakley (1795–1862), founder and first editor of the *Lancet*, which he founded in 1823 and used as a vehicle to attack such quacks as James Morison, whose wealth and status were such that he rode in a carriage decorated with a coronet and attended by footmen. The *Lancet* headline 'Murder by Morison's Pills' in 1836 summed up Wakley's views on 'Morison's Vegetable Universal Pills', which were recommended for consumption at up to thirty a day and claimed to cure virtually all known illnesses, including cholera. The promotion of such remedies was, of course, assisted by the development in the eighteenth century of newspapers and magazines, which, from an early stage, were happy to welcome advertisements for patent medicines in their pages.

THE EMERGENCE OF A PROFESSION

Despite these limitations, a few doctors were responsible for advancing understanding of the true causes of epidemics and for suggesting means by which they could be prevented. Many of the most prominent advocates of the varying explanations for disease propagation were of Scottish origin, while others, including Lister himself, studied in Scotland. This is no coincidence. Medical education was firmly established in Scottish universities long before it reached that stage elsewhere in Europe. The University of

Thomas Wakley (1795–1862) was the son of a Devon squire whose main interest lay in breeding racehorses. Thomas, the youngest of eleven children, was apprenticed to an apothecary in Taunton and later qualified as a surgeon at Guy's Hospital, London. While practising as a doctor in London, Wakley became friendly with the radical journalist and later MP William Cobbett (1763–1835), who persuaded Wakley to publish the *Lancet* with a view to reforming the medical profession. Publication began in October 1823, and the journal was relentless in its campaigns against the autocratic and self-serving colleges of surgeons, physicians and apothecaries. He also campaigned against the Corn Laws, which inflated the price of bread for the poor; against slavery; against the stamp duty on newspapers; and for Parliamentary reform. All these causes eventually triumphed. In 1835 he was elected to Parliament and spoke so effectively against the conviction of the Tolpuddle Martyrs that, when they were eventually reprieved, Wakley held the place of honour in the celebration of their pardons in 1838. He was also instrumental in securing the passage of the Medical Act of 1858, which set up the General Medical Council.

Aberdeen had a chair of medicine before 1550, and by the second half of the eighteenth century Scottish universities were producing ten times as many graduates in medicine as were Oxford and Cambridge. In the first half of the nineteenth century the gap widened further, with Scotland producing 7,989 graduates, while Oxford and Cambridge could manage only 273 between them. Edinburgh University was the first to appoint a professor of medical jurisprudence (forensic medicine), a discipline whose methods of careful observation and enquiry were to become critical in the understanding of the causes of epidemics in the densely populated urban communities that sprang up in the nineteenth century. Nor was it by chance that many of the most innovative doctors practised in Liverpool, Britain's most rapidly growing community and the scene of some its most intractable social problems. As the century progressed, a number of themes emerged that were to define the medical profession's approach to the problems of urban disease: fresh air, clean water, adequate diet, clean dwellings and an experimental, investigative approach to medical problems. Some of the most distinguished theorists and practitioners in one field were fierce critics of the views of others, but by the end of the century it was accepted by most that each element had its part to play in the conquest of urban disease. Each of the doctors featured in this chapter made a contribution to the science of medicine under at least one of these headings.

DR JAMES CURRIE

One of the first doctors to develop significant theories about the spread of disease in urban populations was the Scottish polymath James Currie (1756–1805), friend and biographer of Robert Burns. He was also a pioneer in his concern with each of the themes to which reference has been made: air, water, diet, cleanliness and the experimental method. The work he did and the theories he advanced were harbingers of those developed by his Victorian successors. Currie was born on 31 May 1756 in the parish of Kirkpatrick-Fleming, Dumfries, a few miles from Gretna Green. His father was the local minister. His early education was at the grammar school in nearby Dumfries, but in 1771, aged fifteen, he set sail for America, where, instead of making his fortune as planned, he was an unwilling participant in the early stages of the American Revolution. On 14 September 1774 he wrote to his aunt 'you will by this time have heard of the destruction of the East India Company's tea by the people of Boston', an early reference to one of the most celebrated incidents in the process that led to war.[3] The following year he made a prescient comment on the looming conflict: 'I am clearly of the opinion that though the colonies may be distressed, they can never be conquered: and that if matters should ever get to that height, it would probably end in the ruin of the mother country.'[4] There followed a harrowing return to England during which he was shipwrecked, seized by rebels and narrowly avoided being drafted into the revolutionary army.[5]

Having landed safely in Deptford in May 1777, he entered Edinburgh University to study medicine, later transferring to Glasgow, where he completed his degree in 1780. He set up in practice in Liverpool in the same year, being appointed physician to the Liverpool Dispensary in 1781 and to the Liverpool Infirmary in 1786. He soon made enemies by arguing for a general vaccination of the population against smallpox (a process then regarded with suspicion) and by campaigning against the slave trade, to which the rapidly growing port owed much of its prosperity. One of his correspondents was William Wilberforce himself, to whom Currie wrote a fifteen-page letter (Currie's letters were rarely short) urging the great abolitionist to try to gain the confidence of some of the more liberal Liverpool merchants.[6]

LIVERPOOL'S HOUSING

Following his appointment in Liverpool, Currie quoted[7] with some scepticism a contemporary guide to the town written by William Moss, surgeon to the Liverpool lying-in charity (maternity hospital), which claimed: 'Such is the generally healthy state of the town that infectious fevers are *never known* to prevail and it is very rare to hear of a person dying of a fever of any sort.'[8] Any illusions he had about the health of the rapidly growing community were soon dispelled. Little more than a village in 1700 with a population of 4,240,[9] the community grew rapidly after 1717 when it built the first wet dock in England. By 1797 the population of Liverpool was estimated as 63,000,[10] and by 1811 its 104,000 inhabitants made it second in population only to London among British cities, a position Liverpool held until overtaken by Glasgow in the 1860s.[11] This human tide was not accompanied by any improvements in sanitation, a particular scourge being 'gaol fever' or typhus, a condition associated with filthy, crowded, airless conditions. As early as 1784, in his 'Medical Survey of Liverpool', William Moss had written that human remains were disinterred and 'dragged forth to a public view and disclosed to the prying eye of a wanton curiosity'.[12] The first population census, of 1801, commented that 'a large proportion of the population were living in cellars and typhus fever and other diseases carry off many each year in the lower, crowded parts of the town'.[13] In 1797 Currie estimated that, in the previous seventeen years, 213,305 patients had been treated at the dispensary, of whom 48,367 had typhus.[14] Currie also campaigned for the establishment of a lunatic asylum separate from the workhouse, and the Liverpool Asylum was completed in 1790.[15] Currie was particularly alarmed at the proportion of the population living in cellars (he estimated 7,000 in 1797) and a larger number (about 9,000) living in enclosed 'courts' with inadequate or nonexistent ventilation and sanitation.[16] In 1804, shortly before his death, Currie himself complained that 'a pernicious practice has been introduced of building houses to be let to labourers in small confined courts, which have a communication with the street by a narrow aperture, but no passage for air through them'.[17]

DIET: 'THE FRENCH PRISONERS ARE ACTUALLY STARVING'

Currie was a compulsive campaigner, and his activities extended into the political sphere. In 1793, under the pseudonym 'Jasper Wilson', he wrote 'A Letter, Commercial and Political, Addressed to the Right Hon. William Pitt, in which the Real Interests of Britain are Considered, and some Observations are Offered, on the General State of Europe'. This pamphlet, which sold rapidly, argued against war with revolutionary France. It was soon translated into French and German and was published in America, but it failed to achieve its purpose and earned Currie temporary unpopularity in some quarters. It had an unexpected aftermath when Currie became involved with the fate of over a thousand French prisoners of war who had been quartered in the Liverpool town gaol, which had been designed for a fraction of their number. On 12 January 1798 the *Liverpool Courier* reported that 'the French prisoners in the dungeons of Liverpool are actually starving' on a diet of inedible meat, stale bread and brackish water, with inadequate ventilation producing foul air. In 1800 Currie visited the prison and took advantage of his position as a Fellow of the Royal Society to write to its influential president, Sir Joseph Banks, asking him to intervene with the government to improve the conditions in which French prisoners of war were living. Currie argued that their pitiful state was a threat to the health of the community. Banks replied complacently that 'the [food] allowance is sufficient for persons who undergo no fatigue', whereupon Currie answered: 'I have seen many spectacles of human misery but none has struck me so much as that exhibited by the French prisoners at present.'[18] A long correspondence ensued between the two men, together with some ill-tempered exchanges between Currie and the government commissioners who were sent to investigate. As a result of his persistence, the food and clothing allowances were increased, mortality among the prisoners dwindled to almost nothing and Currie, who had made himself *persona non grata* with the authorities, was banned from making further visits to the prison.

AIR AND WATER: 'RIDING AS A CURE FOR CONSUMPTION'

Currie's concern about the lack of fresh air, whether in Liverpool cellars or Liverpool dungeons, was a reflection of an experience he had endured in 1783–4 when he believed he had fought off an attack of consumption (tuberculosis) by riding from Liverpool to Bristol and thence to Matlock, Dumfries and back to Liverpool, mostly on horseback, and thereby benefiting from 'inland air' as distinct from (implicitly less healthy) sea air. His report was of sufficient interest to be the subject of comment in *Zoonomia or the Laws of Organic Life*, published by Dr Erasmus Darwin (1731–1802, grandfather of Charles) in 1796. Darwin, referring to Currie as 'J.C., aged 27', recorded: 'The following case of hereditary consumption is related by a physician of great ability . . . and shows that . . . riding as a cure for consumption is not so totally ineffectual as is now commonly believed.'[19]

Currie's interest in the curative powers of fresh air was soon transferred to those of water, on which he wrote extensively, though his main interest lay in immersion in water rather than the supply of clean water for washing and drinking. The origins of this interest are not clear. An account of Currie's life published twenty-six years after his death by his son, William Wallace Currie,[20] states that Currie's father, the Scottish minister, had resorted to the curative powers of the waters of Bath and Buxton in an attempt to overcome his gout.[21] This would have been about a century before these resorts became fashionable and suggests a precocious interest in water cures.

Another early influence was exercised by Dr William Wright (1735–1819), a noted botanist and surgeon-general to Jamaica whom Currie had met during his American odyssey and who was an advocate of cold douches for conditions such as fever, headache and loss of appetite. Wright attributed the origins of the water cure to Galen.[22] In 1792 Currie presented to the Royal Society, of which he became a Fellow the same year, a paper entitled 'An Account of the Remarkable Effect of Shipwreck on Mariners, with Experiments and Observations on the Influence of Immersion in Fresh and Salt Water, Hot and Cold, on the Powers of the Body'.[23] Currie's titles, like his letters, were rarely brief.

THE EXPERIMENTAL APPROACH: MEDICAL REPORTS ON THE EFFECTS OF WATER

Currie's paper is an account of some alarming experiments he carried out in 1791 on two young men and himself to test the effect of immersion in fresh and salt water. They were inspired by the experience of an American ship that, in December 1790, ran aground in the mouth of the Mersey, the fourteen crew being marooned for twenty-three hours before being rescued. The master, officer and cook had secured for themselves positions on the deck, where they were assailed by snow, sleet and wind. They all died. The eleven seamen, who were immersed for most of the time in the cold salt waters of the estuary, all survived. Currie commented that seamen's folklore held that exposure to seawater was less harmful than to fresh water and he deduced that the experience of the shipwrecked mariners supported the belief. To confirm this hypothesis he conducted ten experiments that involved immersing two young men in tubs of salt water and seawater at temperatures of 40–44° Fahrenheit for about thirty minutes and measuring the fall in their body temperatures. He also subjected himself to the same experiment, though in his case his suffering was confined to partial immersion in a slipper bath. In each case the subject experienced a slightly greater fall in temperature in the fresh than in the salt water. He duly informed the Royal Society that 'the experiment clearly enough confirms the greater danger of being wet with fresh than seawater'.

Five years later he published the first version of a work to which he owed his medical reputation: *Medical Reports on the Effects of Water, Cold and Warm, as a Remedy for Fever and other Diseases, whether Applied to the Surface of the Body or Used Internally*. The book, dedicated to Sir Joseph Banks, consists of a series of case studies illustrating the beneficial (or occasionally fatal) consequences of giving cold or warm douches and baths and of administering liberal 'potations' (drinks) of cold water to patients in various feverish conditions. In 1791 a boy of eight with a pulse of 130 and a temperature of 107° was bled (as was then the custom), douched in cold water and encouraged to drink liberal quantities of cold water. He recovered. In 1795 a group of soldiers from the 30th Regiment of Foot, then billeted in Liverpool, were held in close confinement for misbehaviour. They developed 'coughs, phlegm, bloody stools and blood from the nostrils' and temperatures of up to 105°. The rooms in which they were held were, on Currie's insistence, washed and ventilated, while the men were subjected to cold douches. They all recovered – a testimony perhaps to their underlying fitness – and one suspects that the water applied to their filthy cells was of greater benefit than the cold water poured over their feverish bodies.[24]

Currie was not altogether ruthless in his treatments, advising against the use of cold water when body temperature was below normal or 'when the body is under profuse perspiration', though the term 'profuse' in this context was left to the judgement of the medical practitioner.[25] He was, however, a pioneer in his practice of frequently and accurately measuring the patient's temperature, specifying that only instruments of the greatest accuracy should be used, as manufactured by the famous maker of optical instruments Jesse Ramsden (1735–1800). He insisted that 'the strictest attention was paid to the heat of the patients, without which he who undertakes the treatment of fever seems to me to walk in darkness'.[26] He also became involved in a correspondence with his friend Erasmus Darwin about the role of perspiration in fever, Darwin persuading Currie that it caused the patient's temperature to fall after some initial doubts on Currie's part.

A BROADER STAGE: ROBERT BURNS, WALTER SCOTT AND ADAM SMITH

James Currie's activities extended into many spheres and brought him into contact with some distinguished contemporaries. It is clear from his correspondence with Erasmus Darwin that Darwin, while not always agreeing with Currie's scientific hypotheses, felt admiration as well as affection for his contemporary. Currie also published works of literary criticism, in which field his most notable achievement was his work as the first editor of the poetry of Robert Burns (1759–96). He had met the poet during a visit to his native Dumfries in the summer of 1792,[27] and, following Burns's death in 1796, a mutual friend asked Currie to produce an edition of the works with an account of the poet's life, the aim being to provide an income for Burns's wife and children. Currie accepted the task with some hesitation, but, having first raised a fund of 70 guineas for the widow and her children, he completed the volume by May 1800, including a thorough account of Burns's life amounting to over 250 pages.[28] A congratulatory letter from Walter Scott (1771–1832) led to an exchange of letters on literary matters with that author, and to this was added a further correspondence with the biographer of the great economist Adam Smith (1723–90), Dugald Stewart (1753–1828), to whom Currie had already entrusted the education of his son. Currie was able to offer some anecdotes concerning the life of Smith, whom he had encountered while studying medicine in Edinburgh. Currie's work on Burns led to his being offered more literary commissions, which he declined for lack of time. He did, however, find time to campaign for the repeal of the seventeenth-century Test and Corporation Acts, which excluded Catholics and Dissenters from many offices, and he was an early advocate for electoral reform. As early as 1793, nearly forty years before the Great Reform Bill of 1832, he advocated that all 'fathers of families' should have votes – a far more radical proposal than any of those eventually adopted in 1832.[29]

FINAL CAMPAIGNS

Currie's last years were spent campaigning to improve housing conditions in Liverpool. In 1802 he supported an Improvements Bill that would have enabled the Town Council to eliminate the worst of the housing problems, but the measure was opposed by slum landlords. In the words of James Newlands (1813–71), who was appointed Borough Engineer in 1847 and devised the first effective sewerage programme for Liverpool, 'the old cry of rights of property' overcame more humane counsels and, instead, 'a fever hospital was built to mitigate the scourge and a new cemetery was bought to hide its victims'.[30] In the same year, 1802, that he supported the failed Improvements Bill, James Currie was made a Freeman of the City of Liverpool for his services to the growing community, but he was by now increasingly vulnerable to the ill health that had intermittently afflicted him since his ride from Matlock to Dumfries in 1783–4. A visit to Bath, to take the waters there in 1804–5, failed to restore his health, and in March 1805 he resigned his post at the Liverpool Infirmary owing to poor health. He retired to Sidmouth in Devon, where he died on 31 August 1805, leaving six children, one of whom became a doctor. His epitaph is recorded on a memorial tablet in the south side of the nave of the church of St Giles and St Nicholas, Sidmouth, and some of the closing lines celebrate his advocacy of the curative powers of water:

> Art taught by thee shall o'er the restless frame
> The healing freshness pour and bless thy name.

It is easy to mock Currie's alarming experiments with water douches, but his experimental approach, together with his concern with fresh air, clean water, adequate diet and cleanliness, was instrumental in the improvements in public health that occurred in the century following his death, and among those who carried forward his ideas and his work was his nephew Dr Duncan of Liverpool.

'A STRATUM OF AIR': DUNCAN OF LIVERPOOL

Forty-two years after Dr James Currie's death, in 1847, his nephew and fellow-Scotsman Dr William Henry Duncan (1805–63) was appointed as Liverpool's (and Britain's) first Medical Officer of Health. Assisted by James Newlands, Liverpool's engineer, Duncan set about cleansing the cellars and 'courts' that had so concerned his uncle and thereby subdued the cholera epidemics that afflicted the community in the middle of the nineteenth century. Paradoxically, Duncan was one of the firmest advocates of the 'miasmatic' explanation of epidemic causation, believing that foul air, not polluted water, was the cause of the cholera epidemics that plagued Britain, and especially Liverpool, from the 1830s. We have already traced the slow process by which the true cause of cholera epidemics was eventually traced to polluted water.[31] If Duncan had embraced with sufficient enthusiasm his uncle's advocacy of 'potations' of cold water for those suffering with fever, the cholera epidemics, spread by contaminated water, would, one assumes, have been far worse![32]

Thus, if James Currie was a believer in the curative powers of water, William Henry Duncan was convinced of the infective properties of air and the need for decent housing. William's father, George Duncan, had married James Currie's sister Christian. Duncan was born in Liverpool of parents who came, like Currie, from Dumfries. His birthplace in Seel Street, Liverpool, bears a plaque marking the event. It is now a nightclub called the Blue Angel, which in the 1960s was much favoured by groups like the Beatles, but is now a haunt of young doctors and nurses from the nearby Royal Liverpool University Hospital, where Duncan worked and where a building is named in his honour. Duncan took over from his uncle as the city's principal campaigner for better sanitation and living conditions, especially for the poor. In the interval between Currie's death in 1805 and Duncan's own appointment as Medical Officer in 1847, the city had witnessed further dramatic growth in population but no significant improvements in its infrastructure. Liverpool's proximity to the sea should have made it fairly easy to dispose of its waste, as the distinguished engineer John Rennie observed in 1816. His report 'The Sewers or Soughs of Liverpool' recorded that 'no town in the British dominions is better situated than the town of Liverpool for a complete system of sewers but there are few sewers in the town and these not only very deficient in capacity but ill calculated to perform the purposes for which they are designed'.[33]

A Commission of Sewers had been established, after much procrastination, in 1822, and over the next twenty years it succeeded in building just over 30 miles of sewers. However, these were designed only for surface water drainage. Until 1846 houses were not allowed to connect their drains or cesspools to these street sewers. Instead, nightsoilmen emptied them by hand, in return for payment, and disposed of the contents to farmers as fertiliser. This was the situation that Duncan inherited.

He had qualified as a doctor in Edinburgh in 1829. Edinburgh University was at that time the only institution with a professor of Medical Jurisprudence, a fact that may have influenced Duncan's later career. Upon qualifying, Duncan moved back to Liverpool, the town of his birth, where he entered general practice in Rodney Street, the heart of the city's medical quarter. He became physician to the Liverpool Infirmary (now the Royal Liverpool University Hospital) and immediately began to campaign for improvements to the appalling living conditions that many of his patients endured. He argued particularly that houses should not be built without privies. In August 1840 he delivered a 'Report on the Sanitary State of the Labouring Classes in Liverpool' to Edwin Chadwick's Poor Law Commission, which eventually found its way into Chadwick's seminal 1842 *Report into the Sanitary Conditions of the Labouring Population of Great Britain*.[34] In the same year, the Liverpool Building Act was passed, which outlawed the building of narrow 'courts' of the kind earlier criticised by his uncle James Currie, although those already built remained a hazard.

In 1843 Duncan delivered two lectures to the Liverpool Literary and Philosophical Society entitled 'On the Physical Causes of the High Rate of Mortality in Liverpool'.[35] He used figures compiled by the statistician William Farr[36] for the recently appointed Office of the Registrar-General (1838) to demonstrate that the average age of death in the rural communities of Rutland and Wiltshire was 36½ years while in Liverpool it was 19½. Duncan observed that less than half the street mileage of Liverpool had any sewers at all; that it was common practice to dispose of the contents of privies by spreading them over the courts; and that 20 per cent of the working population lived in cellars that were often deep in sewage.[37] Duncan, who was a strong advocate of the 'miasmatic' explanation of disease propagation, attributed the diseases that arose from such insanitary conditions to foul air rather than polluted water, informing his audience that, 'by the mere action of the lungs of the inhabitants of Liverpool, for instance, a stratum of air sufficient to cover the entire surface of the town, to a depth of three feet, is daily rendered unfit for the purposes of respiration'.[38] His diagnosis may have been mistaken, but he was absolutely right in identifying poor sanitary conditions as the underlying cause. Duncan was assisted in his campaigning by a builder called Samuel Holme, who told the Royal Commission on the State of Large Towns and Populous Districts that there were courts that he could not bear to enter because of their foul smell.[39] Holme joined Duncan and others in forming a Liverpool branch of the Health of Towns Association on 23 April 1845.[40] Duncan was especially concerned, as his uncle James Currie had been, about the conditions of the large number of people living in cellars. In a further lecture to the Liverpool Literary and Philosophical Society in 1844 Duncan gave a horrifying account of the unfortunate families living in windowless cellars, 10 feet square, 6 feet high, with no water, sanitation or fresh air.

THE FIRST MEDICAL OFFICER

As a result of tireless campaigning by Duncan, Holme and others, in 1846 the Liverpool Town Council promoted its own 'Act for the Improvement of the Sewerage and Drainage of the Borough of Liverpool and for making further Provisions for the Sanatory [*sic*] Regulation of the said Borough'. It passed into law in 1847. It laid down some minimum standards for the construction of dwellings, prohibited the building of houses without drains or privies and outlawed the practice of living in cellars. It also used the title 'Medical Officer of Health' for the first time in an Act of Parliament and specified that 'it shall be lawful for the said Council to appoint, subject to the approval of one of Her Majesty's Principal Secretaries of State, a legally qualified Medical Practitioner of Skill and Experience to inspect and report periodically on the sanatory [*sic*] condition of the said Borough, to ascertain the existence of Diseases, more especially Epidemics increasing the Rates of Mortality'. The Act also lifted the restriction on connecting house drains to public sewers.

Duncan was appointed to the post on 1 January 1847. His appointment was initially on a part-time basis, at a salary of £300 a year. *Punch* disapproved of the appointment, regarding it as unnecessary and further arguing that Duncan's new responsibilities would conflict with the interests of his private clients, notably butchers and fellmongers, whose offal contributed much to the pollution of the community. It also suggested that the salary offered would be insufficient to attract a person of the right calibre, who could expect to earn at least £1,000 a year as a professional man. Having spelt out the many qualities required for the post, it asked 'who would for a moment encourage them to expect such a man for their money?'[41] A year later, in January 1848, his position was made full time for an annual salary of £750. By comparison, the town clerk was paid £2,000 and the Inspector of Nuisances £170. The latter, the appropriately named Thomas Fresh, worked closely with Duncan in identifying insanitary dwellings and drawing them to the Medical Officer's attention, so that Duncan could take court action to have them cleansed. In May 1847 James Newlands was appointed Borough Engineer at a salary of £700 and instructed to prepare a comprehensive sewerage plan for the town.[42] An examination of the records in the Liverpool city archives leaves an impression of the overwhelming volume of work that Duncan was called upon to do. The first volume of his letter books, covering the years 1849–53, alone comprises 569 pages of handwritten letters on all aspects of Liverpool's health problems.[43]

DWELLINGS: THE LIVERPOOL 'COURTS'

In Duncan's first year in office over 21,000 people died in Liverpool as he embarked upon his programme of cellar clearances. He had described the scale of the problem in his 1843 lectures to the Literary and Philosophical Society.[44] He quoted statistics from the registrar-general showing that 'Liverpool is the most unhealthy town in England'. In London in 1841 one inhabitant in thirty-seven had died; in Liverpool it was almost one in twenty-nine. An inspection of 1,982 'courts' of the kind that had been condemned by his uncle James Currie fifty years earlier revealed 10,692 separate dwellings containing 55,534 people, more than a quarter of the population. A further 629 courts were closed at both ends, access to them being via the houses. Ironically these particularly unhealthy dwellings were exempt from the provisions of the 1842 Liverpool Building Act. There were 6,294 cellars providing homes for 20,168 people. Up to 20 miles of working-class streets were served by only 4 miles of sewers. As a result, a well of sewage 'four feet deep, filled with this stinking fluid, was found in one cellar under the bed where the family slept'. He compared the conditions with those of the previous century's 'Black Hole of Calcutta', to the advantage of the latter.

Duncan's reports demonstrate that for many years Irish families had been arriving in Liverpool seeking food, shelter and work and filling the cellars that Duncan was trying to empty. This problem was greatly exacerbated by the renewed wave of Irish immigration that had occurred as a result of the Irish potato famine, which had begun in 1845.[45] Forty people were found in one cellar, and it was commonplace to find fifty or sixty people sharing a four-room dwelling. Duncan urged upon the councillors measures that would stem the flow of Irish immigrants. In his lecture to the Literary and Philosophical Society, Duncan had described how the worst living conditions were endured by the Irish, adding: 'It may be said that this is merely the result of their greater poverty which compels them to select the most unhealthy (because the cheapest) localities as their places of residence.'[46]

In this judgement he was more sympathetic to the Irish than his collaborator Edwin Chadwick, who described them as 'the very pests of Society',[47] but in March 1847 Duncan wrote to the Liverpool Health Committee urging them that 'some measure to put a stop to the immigration, if at all practicable, should be immediately adopted'.[48] In June he reminded the committee:

Since Christmas the arrivals have amounted to nearly 300,000 and of these the number I believe now located among us is very moderately estimated at from sixty thousand to eighty thousand occupying every nook and corner of the already overcrowded lodging-houses and forcing their way into the cellars (about three thousand in number) which had been closed under the provisions of the Health [i.e. Liverpool Building] Act, 1842.[49]

The councillors, alarmed by Duncan's memorandum, resolved that there should be 'a Deputation to proceed forthwith to London to represent to the Government the state of the town as detailed in Dr Duncan's letter, to urge on them the necessity of passing the Irish Poor Removal Bill'.

The immediate reaction of the government to this proposal is not recorded, but, given the government's preoccupation with the mounting toll of deaths from starvation in Ireland, it is not surprising that no such Bill was passed. The year 1848 was characterised by Duncan, in his annual report, as the year of 'IRISH FEVER' (his capitals), but the following year was worse and was called by Duncan 'the Year of Epidemic Cholera'. In December 1848 an Irish family, arriving by boat via Dumfries, had brought with them cholera, which spread rapidly through Liverpool's courts and contributed 4,173 deaths to the mortality of 17,047 in that dreadful year of 1849.[50] These cholera deaths amounted to 10 per cent of the national total. London itself, with a population more than ten times that of Liverpool, suffered less than three times as many deaths.[51] Twenty medical practitioners assisted Duncan in making daily house visitations to cholera districts, directing the cleansing and whitewashing of over 3,000 houses. This process was outlined by Duncan in his report to the Health Committee and applauded by a professor of hygiene a century later in unambiguous terms: 'this statement of fundamental principles could hardly be bettered.'[52] The work of Duncan and his fellows in visiting dwellings assaulted by cholera was also very courageous, given that they believed the air they breathed could infect them with the dreaded disease.

CELLARS AND SEWERS

Nevertheless a note of despair is clearly heard in Duncan's report for 1849. He requests a clerk to help him with his office duties so that he can concentrate on visiting the stricken area: '*in so far as it is practicable to do so* [emphasis in original] I should visit every house in the worst-conditioned districts.' The Inspector of Nuisances had referred to Duncan 187 cases of dwellings so insanitary that they were hazardous to health, of which five had had to be taken before magistrates before the owners could be persuaded to take corrective action. In 1851 he renewed his attack on the cellar dwellings, corresponding with the redoubtable campaigner Edwin Chadwick[53] on the subject, and in his report for that year he described the lengths to which some desperate residents would go in order to remain in their cellars: 'To bring a cellar within the provisions of the [1842 Liverpool Building] Act the Magistrates require proof of its being occupied *during the night* and, in order to withhold this proof, the parties are in the habit of removing or concealing in the daytime the beds.'[54]

Despite these difficulties, by 1851 Duncan had made such good use of the legislative powers available to him that 10,000 cellars had been cleared of their inhabitants.[55] At the same time, and with Duncan's enthusiastic support, his colleague James Newlands, Borough Engineer, was building sewers at an unprecedented rate and connecting them to the dwellings. Between 1847 and 1858 Newlands built 146 miles of sewers, compared with the 30 miles built in twenty years in the 1820s and 1830s, for surface water drainage.[56] Other necessary improvements accompanied these measures. In 1848 the borough council bought out two private companies bringing water from Bootle and Toxteth Park, and in 1857 these were augmented by an additional supply from Rivington, helping to ensure a readier supply for cooking, washing and flushing sewers. In 1888, twenty-five years after Duncan's death, Liverpool gained the water supply it needed when water was brought from Lake Vyrnwy in Wales.

Duncan, like most of his contemporaries, continued to believe that cholera was caused exclusively by a polluted atmosphere. In November 1853, as a new epidemic approached, he wrote: 'I believe the disease to be propagated, as a rule, by some atmospheric influence whose nature is as yet undetermined and which requires some predisposing cause as filth, moisture or overcrowding to call it into action.'[57]

The concept of a 'predisposing' cause of illness as an explanation of disease has been noted as the 'orthodoxy' of the Board of Health before germ theory gained acceptance.[58] Nevertheless, Duncan's cellar clearances, house inspections and whitewashing had the desired effect. When cholera returned in 1854, its effects were far less virulent than in the 1848–9 epidemic.[59] In that same year, 1854, a Sanitary Amendment Act gave the borough council stronger powers to charge for constructing house drains in proportion to the houses' linear footage, and over the next twelve years 3,932 orders were made affecting 7,512 houses and 48,828 inhabitants, mostly from the poorer classes.[60] As the situation improved in Liverpool, Duncan became a fierce defender of the community. His letter books include correspondence complaining that Liverpool's record in public health was subjected to unfair comparisons with communities like Ely, which had 'one principal street . . . 6,176 inhabitants, most of whom are engaged in agricultural pursuits'. This foolishness he attributed to 'an understanding among the London men to snub Liverpool whenever opportunity offers'.[61]

'UNTIRING ZEAL AND INTELLIGENCE'

Duncan died at Elgin, in his parents' native Scotland, on 23 May 1863, 'worn down by the uneven contest'[62] of struggling with Liverpool's health problems. He was 57 years old. His obituary in the *Liverpool Daily Post* on 26 May referred to Duncan's 'untiring zeal and intelligence' and concluded that the health of Liverpool had so improved as a result of his exertions that 'there is therefore no longer any occasion for a Medical Officer at a salary of £700 a year'. The newspaper, ever zealous for the interests of the ratepayers, recommended that the post once again become part-time. Fortunately the recommendation that followed the compliment was ignored. A year after Duncan's appointment the City of London had appointed its first Medical Officer, (later Sir) John Simon. Duncan established a pattern that would not be broken. His belief in the harmful effects of 'miasma' may have been mistaken, but by campaigning for cleaner dwellings for the urban poor he was continuing the valuable work of his uncle and predecessor, James Currie. His support for effective sewerage in order to remove foul smells had the more beneficial effect of protecting the community's water supply from pollution, so, while his reasoning may have been faulty, the desired effect was nevertheless achieved.

NOT FORGOTTEN

In the year 2001, 154 years after Duncan's first appointment, the *Liverpool Echo* announced that its forebear, the *Liverpool Daily Post*, was to have its wish granted.[63] The city's Medical Officer's post was to be abolished in favour of a larger health authority covering Merseyside and Cheshire, with local services in Liverpool itself provided by three primary care trusts. But Duncan's memory will be perpetuated by some institutions of widely varying character. In 1997 the leading figures in public health in Liverpool set up the Duncan Society. Its purpose is 'to stimulate debate, discussion and understanding on issues and policies which affect the health and quality of life of the people of Merseyside and Cheshire'.[64] An annual Duncan Memorial lecture is given in the Duncan Building of the University of Liverpool. The Duncan Building is a part of the Faculty of Medicine and adjacent to the Royal Liverpool University Hospital, formerly the Liverpool Infirmary, which Duncan served as physician. Other, less conventional tributes are no doubt more widely appreciated by the people of Liverpool. The Doctor Duncan is one of the city centre's most popular public houses. Formerly situated opposite Duncan's birthplace in Seel Street, it is now in St John's Lane. It serves a special Dr Duncan's India Pale Ale and a seasonal bottled beer called Dr Duncan's Elixir, both produced by the Liverpool brewer, Cains. With such memorials, W.H. Duncan's reputation is sure to survive in the city he served so tirelessly. Duncan's 'stratum of air' may not have been the true cause of Liverpool's epidemics, but the measures he took in emptying foul cellars, cleansing occupied dwellings and campaigning for better sewers set the pattern for his successors in Liverpool and in other communities.

POSTSCRIPT: WATER AS DISEASE, WATER AS CURE

While Duncan was confronting cholera in Liverpool, the grandson of James Currie's friend Erasmus Darwin was visiting Malvern to take a 'cure' whose components Currie would have recognised from his Medical Reports. The treatment was advocated in a book called *The Water Cure in Chronic Disease*, written by Dr James Gully

(1808–83), who was later disgraced in a notorious case of adultery and suspected poisoning. Charles Darwin, not noted for his gullibility in scientific matters, read Gully's book on the recommendation of an old companion from his *Beagle* voyage. Darwin subjected himself to the treatment for sixteen weeks[65] in an attempt to cure himself of a condition that he may have contracted on his famous journey, though the illness that plagued him was neither cured nor diagnosed with certainty. At 5 a.m. the patient was awoken and wrapped in cold, wet sheets for an hour. Upon release, he was placed in a bath, where a pitcher of cold water was poured on him. After this the patient was required to take a short walk, following which he would be entertained by a German band, playing to revive his spirits while he drank copiously of the healing fluid. After this, breakfast was served, consisting of bread, butter, treacle and yet more water. Further baths and exercise followed before dinner was served at the unusual hour of 3 p.m. Darwin was sufficiently convinced of the efficacy of Gully's cure to continue with it after returning to his home, Down House in Kent. The village carpenter built a hut with a huge cistern containing 640 gallons of cold water. The carpenter's son, John Lewis, recalled that Darwin would 'pull the string, and all the water fell on him through a two-inch pipe'. On other occasions Darwin would be wrapped in blankets 'till the sweat poured off him . . . Then he'd get into the ice cold bath in the open air.' Fortunately for the cause of science, Darwin survived.[66]

The idea that 'water cures' were a significant element in medical practice lasted well into the twentieth century. In the years between the wars the British Health Resorts Association was formed to promote the interests of spas such as Malvern and Bath. The organisation, based at 199 Piccadilly, one of London's most expensive addresses, promoted the publication of guides to the facilities of the various spas, which were prepared 'with the assistance of the Medical Officer of Health and the Medical Committees in the localities',[67] a clear endorsement from the medical authorities. It made many confident claims including one that 'Scientific Research has proved that *Gout, Rheumatism, Sciatica etc.* [emphasis in original] can be effectively cured by the Radio-active thermal waters of Buxton'.

In 1924, when the work was first published, the term 'radioactive' did not have the sinister associations that it acquired later, so this highly dubious claim presumably carried some weight.

Despite these efforts, the use of spas continued to decline, though the National Health Service, whose services supplanted those of the spas, continued to make use of spa facilities for many years. Bath continued to supply spa treatments until 1976. More recently, 'water cures' have undergone a revival within recognised medical practice, notably in the management of pain, an application not foreseen by Currie. One of the most successful applications of hydrotherapy in the management of pain is to be found in Bath, the spa to which Currie resorted in his final illness. One of England's leading pain management units has been established at the Royal National Hospital for Rheumatic Diseases in Bath (still referred to locally as the Mineral Water Hospital) in association with the University of Bath. James Currie would surely be pleased.

THOMAS SOUTHWOOD SMITH: 'UNIVERSAL PURITY AND HAPPINESS'

The medieval 'moralistic' view of sickness was represented in Victoria's reign by the physician Thomas Southwood Smith (1788–1861), grandfather of Octavia Hill, who made such efforts to improve housing conditions for working people.[68] Born in Somerset, Southwood Smith qualified as a doctor in Edinburgh in 1816 and, at the same time, became a Unitarian minister. Religion, as well as science, was to form his view of disease in a way that was characteristic of many Victorian reformers. The moral element of his medical theories was illustrated by a work he published upon graduating and whose cumbersome title tells the reader all he needs to know about its arguments: *Illustrations of the Divine Government, Tending to Show that Everything is under the Direction of Infinite Wisdom and Goodness and will Terminate in the Production of Universal Purity and Happiness.* Sin, suffering and, by implication, disease resulted from disobedience to the divine will. Given the stern morality and the pseudo-scientific views that underpinned his beliefs, it is not surprising that Thomas Southwood Smith joined the steadfast band that grouped around the unyielding utilitarian philosopher Jeremy Bentham. Such was his devotion to Bentham that, after the philosopher's death, Southwood kept Bentham's skeleton in his consulting room until he retired in 1850, when it was removed to University College London, its present home.

'AERIAL POISON'

That is not to say that Southwood Smith did not recognise other causes of disease than moral ones. In 1824 he was appointed physician to the London Fever Hospital and also served the London Jews' Hospital. As a result of experience gained at these institutions, he published in 1830 *A Treatise on Fever*, which proposed a link between squalid living conditions and epidemic disease. He followed this with a 'Report on Removable Physical Causes of Mortality', which identified a prime cause of disease as 'aerial poison' arising from the putrefaction of animal or vegetable matter, whose 'virulence is always in proportion to the quantity of animal and vegetable matters present'. He announced that, by condensing vapour from contaminated air and injecting it into dogs, 'it is possible to produce fever of almost any sort', though the methods he employed and the results he achieved by this strange process remain a mystery. In 1840 he was a founding member of the Health of Towns Association and argued, particularly, for better ventilation of workhouses to overcome their 'perfectly stagnant and stifling' atmosphere. In some evidence he produced for a Parliamentary Committee on behalf of the Health of Towns Association, he offered a convincing biological explanation of the processes by which foul air worked on the human body:

> If provision is not made for the immediate removal of these poisons, they are carried by the air inspired to the air-cells of the lungs, the thin delicate membranes of which they pierce, and thus pass directly into the current of the circulation . . . by the natural and ordinary flow of this current, three distinct and fresh portions of these poisons must necessarily be transmitted to every nook and cranny of the system in every eight minutes of time. The consequences are sometimes death within a few hours, or even minutes.[69]

How could any parliamentary committee resist such a precise scientific explanation?

However, in an article in the *Westminster Review* as early as 1825, he came close to a clear and accurate definition of the mechanism by which epidemics were spread:

> A contagious disease is a disease which is capable of being communicated from person to person. An Epidemic disease is a disease which at certain periods prevails generally over the whole, or over a large portion of the community . . . A contagious disease prevails by the communication from person to person of that specific animal poison from which the malady derives its existence. An epidemic disease prevails because of the influence of the atmosphere.[70]

With the exception of the final sentence, this is not a bad description of the causes of epidemics. He then further distinguished between 'pre-disposing causes', such as diet, lifestyle and climate; and 'exciting causes', like the smallpox bacillus or the 'aerial poison' that arose from putrefaction. The primitive science that informed theories of this kind can seem comical to commentators of the twenty-first century, but there was a strange truth underlying them. Some diseases, like tuberculosis, require an 'exciting cause' or disease agent, but they are much more likely to prosper amongst ill-nourished people living in damp, unhealthy conditions that 'pre-dispose' their victims to infection. Southwood Smith could not accept the idea that disease could be caused by infectious agents alone and specifically rejected the suggestion that the bubonic plague of 1665 could have been imported from the Continent on a cargo boat carrying French silk and, of course, flea-ridden rats.

The question of 'predisposition' was central to the miasmatic theory. Thomas Watson (1792–1882), Professor of Medicine at King's College London and later president of the Royal College of Physicians, drew a distinction between *exciting causes* of disease and the condition of the body at the time the exciting cause was applied.[71] This enabled the influence of *pre-disposing factors* to be accommodated within theories of disease causation without excluding other explanations for the immediate causes of infection.

He thereby reflected the conclusions of Edwin Chadwick's 1842 *Report into the Sanitary Conditions of the Labouring Population of Great Britain*, which supposed that poor living conditions, dissipated lifestyles, overcrowding and, in particular, foul air predisposed urban populations to epidemic disease with little if any need for the intervention of external agencies. All that was required was a really nasty smell.

The author of a mid-century text, *A Dictionary of Practical Medicine*, held that *predisposing* causes could themselves be the source of disease without the need for any *exciting* causes. He wrote: 'predisposing causes may, either by their activity, or by their acting in combination or in close succession, of themselves produce disease, without the aid of any of those usually termed exciting . . . the indulgence of the appetites, fatigue, the depressing passions, moist states of the air etc. are often the only causes to which disease can be traced.'[72] This confusing statement mirrors the minds of those who could smell something foul in the air but could see nothing nasty in the water.

DR JOHN SUTHERLAND: 'IRREGULAR AND DISSIPATED HABITS'

Another connection with both Scotland and Liverpool is represented by Dr John Sutherland (1808–91). He was born in Edinburgh, where he qualified as a doctor in 1831. He is chiefly remembered for the work he performed in connection with the health of the army. In 1855 he visited the Crimea at the request of Palmerston to enquire into the health of the troops, alarming accounts of which had reached London from William Russell, *The Times* correspondent. During this visit Sutherland met Florence Nightingale in her hospital at Scutari. Upon his return to Britain he was summoned to Balmoral to give an account to the Queen of what he had discovered. As a result he was appointed to a series of posts that involved visiting military barracks and hospitals in Britain and India and making recommendations, which led to improvements in both. However, his early work was concerned with the causes of cholera. His approach to the problems of disease also showed some moralising tendencies, which, while irrelevant to the problems at hand, was a characteristic tendency among many well-intentioned medical practitioners of the time.

After gaining his MD in Edinburgh in 1831, Sutherland worked on the continent of Europe for over ten years before opening a medical practice in Liverpool in the mid-1840s, as Duncan, with whom he worked, assumed the post of Medical Officer to the growing port. There he first encountered Liverpool's infamous 'courts', which had been condemned by Dr James Currie as early as 1804 for their lack of ventilation, a particular concern of the miasmatists. Currie's concern with the lack of ventilation was reflected in the later work of other physicians, including that of Sutherland himself. In 1848 Sutherland was appointed as an Inspector to the General Board of Health, which had been set up in that year as a result of a long campaign by Edwin Chadwick and others who were concerned with the insanitary conditions in which much of the population lived, particularly those living in towns. It was in this capacity that he made his contribution to the 'Report of the General Board of Health on the Epidemic Cholera of 1848-9', an epidemic that killed 14,137 citizens in London alone.[73]

The evidence that he gave to the board reflects his uncertainty about the causes of epidemic cholera and the measures that could be taken to prevent it. In his opening remarks on 'localising causes' he acknowledges that cholera 'is propagated according to certain fixed laws, although the limits of these laws have not as yet been precisely defined'. He went on to deal with *localising causes*, referring to 'that property which is possessed by certain states of the constitution or by certain well-marked characteristics of special localities', which overwhelmed the individual's resistance to the epidemic. He hesitates to judge whether the 'localisation' occurs in the person or the place. A discussion of the symptoms of the disease is followed by some moralising attempts to explain that 'certain constitutions [are] predisposed by irregular and dissipated habits' to 'rapid and fatal attacks of cholera'.

UNWHOLESOME WATER OR TOO MANY PLUMS?

Finally, in his evidence to the General Board, Sutherland addressed the problem of *unwholesome water* and came close to identifying the real cause of the cholera epidemic, though without making reference to the seminal paper of Dr John Snow that had been published the previous year.[74] Sutherland, in his evidence to the board, was prepared to concede that 'a number of most severe and fatal outbursts of cholera were referable to no other cause than the state of the water-supply'. However, whereas Snow, in his evidence and in later papers, was prepared to identify polluted water as the prime cause of epidemic cholera, Sutherland would allow only that it was the cause of a 'predisposition', albeit 'perhaps the most fatal of all'. In this Sutherland was simply following the orthodox belief of his time. He made reference to the Prussian barque *Pallas*, which nine German seamen had brought from Hamburg, where there was a cholera epidemic, to Hull. Three of the crew died of cholera, but the blame was laid on the cargo of plums on which the crew had over-indulged. 'The eating of a few plums would certainly, under ordinary circumstances, have produced no such fatal results but during an epidemic constitution, such indulgence is well known to be fraught with extreme danger.'[75]

FOUL AIR: 'PUTRID EXHALATIONS'

Finally, Sutherland considered *defective sanitary alterations*, and here he examined the problem of 'putrid exhalations from a number of open conduits', which 'impregnate the whole air both internally and externally with a strong cesspool odour'. The offending buildings to which he was referring were the site of a cholera outbreak in Bristol and were identified as 'courts', similar in design to those he had encountered in Liverpool and, in the case of the Bristol courts, dependent for their ventilation upon the adjacent burial ground. Sutherland drew attention to the fact that 'a death took place in every house under the floor of which a drain passed' and suggests that 'it would indeed be difficult for human ingenuity to contrive and arrange a set of conditions more thoroughly unhealthy, or more likely to predispose the inhabitants to epidemic disease'. Once again, 'predisposition' was allowed without a prime cause being identified. Fellow miasmatists like Chadwick, and Sutherland's former colleague in Liverpool, Dr W.H. Duncan, would have had no difficulty supporting Sutherland's condemnation of foul air. Others were not so sure. William Alison (1790–1859), physician in Scotland to Queen Victoria, inconveniently observed that illnesses were more common in winter, when smells were least offensive.

Four years later Sutherland was asked to comment on the 1853–4 cholera outbreak, and his views are recorded in the report that was sent to Palmerston, the Home Secretary.[76] In this later report Sutherland concluded that 'there is no sufficient proof that water in this [impure] state acts specifically in generating cholera' but acknowledged that 'the use of water containing organic matter in a state of decomposition is one predisposing cause of cholera'. By the time that he wrote this (1855) Sutherland had turned his attention, at Palmerston's request, to the condition of the army, and this led him to investigate epidemics in the garrison communities of Malta and Gibraltar in 1865. In the case of Malta he concluded: 'we must exclude impure water from the chain of causes' and added: 'the hypothesis that cholera is propagated by emanations from excreta receives no countenance . . . the events give no countenance to any hypothesis as to epidemics taking their origin from specific cholera germs.'[77] Foul air, overcrowding and filth were still the favoured explanations as 'predisposing' populations to cholera.[78] John Sutherland died on 14 July 1891. By that date eight years had passed since Robert Koch had identified the cause of cholera as a bacillus carried in polluted water, though not to the satisfaction of sceptics like Edwin Chadwick. In its highly appreciative obituary, the *Lancet* hinted, unintentionally, at Sutherland's equivocal stance on the causes of cholera. It wrote: 'To say that some disease or other was solely attributable to contagion, or depended upon a bacillus, and to stop there, as seems to be so much the tendency of these days, brought little satisfaction and no comfort to practically minded men like Dr Sutherland.'[79]

SIR JOHN SIMON AND THE CITY OF LONDON

In 1848 John Simon (1816–1904) (pronounced *Simone*, the name being French in origin) was appointed Medical Officer to the City of London. He had worked as a surgeon at King's College Hospital and St Thomas's Hospital and knew something of the work of Ignaz Semmelweis in Hungary, and he adopted the practice of boiling his instruments before operating long before the practice was common.[80] He was also ahead of his time in recognising the importance of hospital hygiene, dedicating forty pages to this subject in a report to the Privy Council in 1863, two years before Lister began his experiments with carbolic acid.[81] His appointment occurred a year after that of Duncan in Liverpool, but Simon's proximity to the heart of government gave him a more decisive influence over the government's attitude towards public health. Much of the responsibility for combating the cholera epidemics that struck the capital in 1849, 1854 and 1866 fell upon his shoulders, and, towards the end of his life, he recorded some of the difficulties faced by his colleagues and himself as they sought to combat the problems of urban disease. In 1897 he wrote: 'In 1830, when William IV began his reign, and equally in 1837, when the reign ended, the statute book contained no general laws of sanitary intention. The central government had nothing to say in regard to the public health and local authorities had but the most indefinite relation to it.'[82]

Fortunately for the health of the nation, Simon possessed qualities of diplomacy that were alien to some of his contemporaries, like, for example, Edwin Chadwick, whose battles with his fellow campaigners are recorded elsewhere in this volume.[83] Simon recognised that many of his fellow citizens had misgivings about the continuing intrusion upon private welfare of government agencies. After his appointment as Medical Officer to the Privy Council, Simon commented on this issue. He wrote that, as far as many electors were concerned, the government 'has interfered between parent and child [a reference to vaccination] between employer and employed [over sanitary measures in factories] and between vendor and purchaser [referring to legislation governing the quality of water and the adulteration of food]; has put restrictions on the sale and purchase of poisons and has made it a public offence to sell adulterated food, drink or medicine'.[84] Simon used persuasion more effectively than Chadwick used compulsion. Simon had qualified as a surgeon and became a lecturer at St Thomas's Hospital, but this experience can have been of little value in overcoming the bureaucratic practices that he faced in his new task. His attempts to persuade workhouses, prisons and Poor Law Medical Officers to provide information on diseases and mortality was at first met by refusals, but, when cholera struck in 1849, the year after he had taken office, he made enterprising use of the 'Cholera Bill' of 1846[85] and of the City police force to inspect and suppress insanitary practices in the dwellings of the City. *The Times* carried an account of the results.[86] There were inspections of 15,010 houses, of which over one third, 5,085, were found to be seriously deficient owing to such matters as 'offensive smells', 'water closets in a very offensive state' and 'cellars used as cesspools'. In his first annual report Simon commented that 'animals will scarcely thrive in an atmosphere of their own decomposing excrement; yet such, strictly and literally speaking, is the air which a very large proportion of the inhabitants of the City are condemned to breathe'.[87]

His report was carried in full in *The Times*, the *Morning Post* and other influential newspapers, and such was the importance attached to it that, the following day, 8 November 1849, *The Times* itself declared that 'if any number of this journal ever deserved to be rescued from the usual fate of ephemeral publications and regarded as a possession for all time it is that of yesterday'. The report proposed such measures as slum clearance, improved water supply and better house drainage. Rapid improvements followed, the City authorities enforcing measures against slum landlords, many of whom were also aldermen. Simon also pressed for the filtration of water supplies, a provision that was incorporated in the 1852 Metropolis Water Act with beneficial consequences for the customers of the Lambeth water company, as noted by Dr John Snow.[88]

WATER OR AIR?

As a result of these measures, the cholera epidemic of 1854 recorded fewer deaths in London than that of 1849 – 10,738 against 14,137 – though the population had grown in the intervening five years.[89] Simon, in his explanation of the 1854 epidemic, remained a believer in the 'miasmatic' doctrine that foul air was the cause of the epidemic, though the mounting evidence produced by Dr John Snow was gradually pushing him towards the view that polluted water also played its part. By 1856, in his 'Report on the Last Two Cholera Epidemics of London as Affected by the Consumption of Impure Water', he conceded that 'fecalised drinking water and fecalised air equally breed the poison'.[90] This was a significant concession. However, in arguing for the practice of placing in quarantine ships thought to be carrying the disease, he claimed that the vessels were affected when they sailed through a poisoned-charged layer of air at sea.[91] In 1867, by which time he had served nine years as Medical Officer to the Privy Council, Simon attended a conference on cholera in Germany and reported that 'the person who contracts cholera in this country is *ipso facto* demonstrated with almost absolute certainly to have been exposed to excremental pollution', though he still believed that the pollution was more likely to be communicated via the air than via the water supply.[92] By this time Simon was familiar with Pasteur's germ theories of disease propagation, and by 1874 he was telling the Privy Council that an epidemic of typhoid 'runs its course, as with successive inoculations from man to man, by instrumentality of the molecules of excrement, which man's filthiness lets mingle in his air and food and drink'.[93]

In 1876, in his monograph *Filth-Diseases and their Prevention*, Simon estimated that 25 per cent of recorded deaths could be prevented by effective sanitary measures and made specific acknowledgement of the importance of a supply of clean water. He wrote that 'the question, what infecting powers are prevalent in given atmospheres, should never be regarded as a mere question of stink . . . agents which destroy its stink may yet leave all its main powers of disease-production undiminished' and reminded his readers that the year of 'The Great Stink' itself,[94] when Parliamentarians had suspended their sittings because of the stench from the polluted Thames, had seen a rather low death rate. Later in the century Sir Edward Frankland (1825–99) would develop chemical and bacteriological tests that would enable harmful impurities in water to be identified with confidence, but at the time that Simon was writing such tests for identifying harmful agents were far from perfect and Simon now acknowledged that 'waters which chemical analysis would probably not condemn may certainly be carrying in them very fatal seeds of infection' and that in the cases of diseases characterised by diarrhoea 'every discharge from the bowels must teem with the contagion of the disease'. He had also identified cases of typhoid being spread by dairymen in Marylebone washing pails with water polluted by excrement. He called for effective sewerage to be installed, following the example of Sir Joseph Bazalgette in London, to protect water supplies, but he hedged his bets by arguing for effective ventilation of sewers, just in case the foul-smelling air bore some responsibility for epidemics.[95]

Currie and Duncan had recognised the link between filth and disease without understanding the role of water, rather than air, in promoting epidemics, and Currie had identified some of the problems caused by poor diet. John Sutherland had admitted that polluted water might cause 'predisposition', but preferred 'putrid exhalations' or even indulgence in plums as the 'exciting' cause, while the moralist Southwood Smith identified 'aerial poison' and dissipated lifestyles as the culprits. John Simon identified excrement and poor sanitation as culprits and eventually acknowledged that polluted water had a role, if not the principal one, in creating epidemics. Between them these doctors had assembled all the necessary components of a convincing explanation of the propagation of epidemics: poor food, filthy dwellings and foul water. In the meantime, however, others, especially engineers, were beginning to find solutions to the problems of pollution while trying to solve another – the problem of smells.

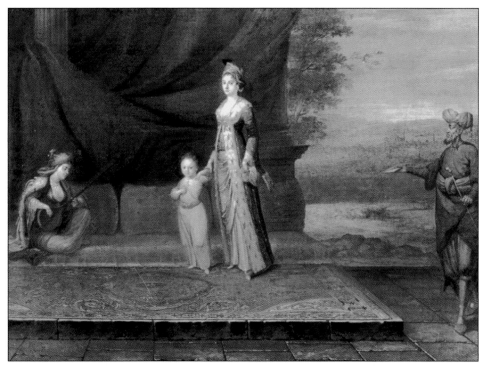

1. Lady Mary Wortley Montagu, who brought inoculation from Constantinople to England. *(By courtesy of the National Portrait Gallery, London)*

2. Cow pock. 'Not everyone viewed with confidence the process of vaccination'. *(By courtesy of the National Portrait Gallery, London)*

3. Angela Burdett-Coutts, whose 'positively distressing and ridiculous' marriage did not prevent her from becoming 'the Queen of the poor'. *(By courtesy of the National Portrait Gallery, London)*

9. Dr William Duncan is remembered in Liverpool not as Britain's first Medical Officer but by the pub and the beer that bear his name. *(Faye Halliday)*

10. Endell Street Lying-in Hospital, founded in 1749, is now a smart restaurant called 'The Hospital'.

11. Rosalind Paget, founding mother of the Royal College of Midwives. *(By courtesy of the National Portrait Gallery, London)*

12. Zepherina Veitch, 'practically the Miss Nightingale of midwives'.

13. Sir Joseph Bazalgette, whose great civil engineering works protected London's river from sewage and its citizens from cholera. *(Thames Water plc)*

14. Thomas Hawksley, who, despite 'trouble with the plumbers', transformed water supply to Britain's cities. *(By courtesy of the National Portrait Gallery, London)*

FIVE

The Public Servants

The sewerage of the Metropolis, though it is a frequent subject of boast to those who have not examined its operations or effects, will be found to be a vast monument of defective administration, of lavish expenditure and extremely defective execution.

(Edwin Chadwick, on London's sewers)

As the air of London is not supplied like water to its inhabitants by companies the air has had the worst of it. For air no scientific witnesses have been retained, no learned counsel has pleaded; so the atmosphere has been freely charged with the propagation of plagues of all kinds; while Father Thames and the water gods of London have been loudly proclaimed innocent.

(William Farr, writing on the 1866 Whitechapel cholera epidemic)

DEFEND THE KINGDOM

To twentieth-century citizens who are accustomed to the idea that almost 40 per cent of national income should be taken and spent by the government for the public good, it is very hard to enter into the minds of Victorian politicians. In the early part of the Queen's reign her ministers had a view of their roles that would have been recognised by Henry VIII, if not Alfred the Great. Government had two tasks: to administer the law and to defend the kingdom. The law was the responsibility of judges and unpaid magistrates, the latter also being responsible for the administration of local affairs, covering matters ranging from the maintenance of roads and bridges to the implementation of the Poor Laws. There was no police force outside London in any modern sense of the word. The defence of the kingdom was entrusted to the Royal Navy, and occasionally, in times of conflict, an army would be assembled to fight on the Continent or in the colonies. When the dispute ended, most of the soldiers would be discharged, and many of the officers were put on half pay. Otherwise the government stood back from the nation's affairs. Education was in the hands of private schools and universities for those who could afford them. Transport between towns was left to turnpikes constructed by entrepreneurs, who charged for their use. Canals and railways were constructed by wealthy individuals or by joint-stock companies. The health of the nation, outside the Poor Law infirmaries attached to the workhouses, was in the hands of hospitals, which were largely dependent upon charitable endowments and upon doctors who charged professional fees that were well beyond the means of most of the population. Even prisons were only just emerging from the sphere of private enterprise. The medieval and Tudor practice of auctioning the office of gaol 'keeper' or governor and leaving the successful bidder to regain his investment by exactions upon inmates was a long time dying and survived, albeit without official approval, into the nineteenth century.[1]

The idea that the government should raise taxes to educate, transport and support the health of the populace was alien to the ministers who held office during much of Victoria's long reign. The forms of taxation inherited by Victoria's ministers were a haphazard collection of emergency measures, protectionism and opportunism rather than a coherent system designed to finance government or promote the welfare of the population. Window taxes had been introduced by William III to finance his wars with Louis XIV and survived until 1851. Excise duties on products like wine, spirits and tobacco were a significant source of both revenue and crime, as they promoted a flourishing trade in smuggling. Rates levied on local households financed what there was of local government and encouraged local councillors and magistrates to minimise expenditure on anything. Stamp duties on legal documents provoked the American War of Independence, while taxes on imported paper, newspapers and pamphlets produced more controversy and evasion than revenue and were abolished in Gladstone's 1861 budget as taxes on knowledge. Income tax had been introduced by Pitt in 1799 as an emergency measure to finance the Napoleonic Wars and were revived in 1842 as part of a tariff reform programme that eventually led to the abolition of the Corn Laws – themselves a system of protection that benefited large landowners and pushed up the price of food for the poor. As late as the 1870s Gladstone made himself very unpopular by trying to fill Victoria Embankment Gardens with offices whose rents, he hoped, would enable him to abolish income tax. In the last year of the century, as the Boer War placed unusual strains upon the national revenue, income tax was still 8*d* (about 3p) in the pound.

The public servants who are the subject of this chapter thus had to fight a long and arduous battle to persuade their political masters that the health of the nation was a good investment. As the century wore on and deaths from diseases such as cholera and typhoid not only affected the impoverished but also reached into the aristocracy and even the royal family, the authorities gradually came to accept a degree of responsibility for public health. This acceptance is reflected in the lives and work of the public servants whose work is the subject of this chapter, but the negative attitude to taxation that was so deeply embedded in the public psyche explains why so many of their arguments were grounded not in morality or the public good but in the belief that such investment would save money in the long run. They were not mean men obsessed with money. They were realists who fell in with the values of their age. One of the earliest influences on their ideas was the philosopher Jeremy Bentham.

THE GREAT UTILITARIAN

Bentham, born in Houndsditch in 1748 to a family of lawyers, studied at Oxford and at Lincoln's Inn, though he never practised as a barrister. His numerous written works expounded what he called 'the principle of utility', also described as 'the greatest happiness principle', the former term borrowed from the Scottish philosopher David Hume. Utilitarianism, the philosophy that became associated with his name, argued that every act, be it legislative, regulatory or judicial, should be judged by its 'utility' – the extent to which it contributed to the sum of human happiness. The concept, though superficially attractive, ran into a number of difficulties. How was happiness to be measured and judged? What happened when people had to be *compelled* to do something for their own good – a good that they could not themselves recognise? These issues became critical after Bentham's death, when, for example, governments began to recognise the need to introduce measures like effective sanitation whose benefits were recognised by most, though not all, of the population but that would require an increase in taxes before the benefits were felt. Bentham and those who followed him, like John Stuart Mill, resorted to philosophical gymnastics such as the 'means justifying principle', which succeeded in convincing them, if not their opponents, that unpopular measures could be adopted if the benefit of, say, good drainage demonstrably outweighed the costs. But demonstrated by whom to whom?

These difficulties did not prevent Bentham and his followers from applying their ideas to a wide range of social problems. Universal suffrage, annual parliaments and prison design were among the subjects to which they turned their attention. During a visit to Russia Bentham had designed a prison he called 'The Panopticon', which enshrined many utilitarian principles and in particular those of *lenity*, *severity* and *economy*. As its name implies, its floors were laid out so that every prisoner alone in every cell could be observed by a warder from a central point, thus minimising the costs of supervision and ensuring economy in operation. The principle of *lenity* required that there should be no cruel punishments, though *severity*, in the form of the treadmill, was designed to promote exercise and occupation in the hope that the habits thus engendered would encourage the prisoner, upon release, to apply his energies to useful ends. *Severity* also incorporated the 'solitary' and 'silent' systems of imprisonment that prevented inmates from having any contact with fellow prisoners, thereby, it was hoped, encouraging them to contemplate the errors of their previous lives and lead them to become useful citizens. This was a time when many believed that disease, including moral turpitude, could be communicated by the air, so that even in prison chapels prisoners were screened from one another to prevent criminal tendencies passing like contagion from one offender to his neighbour.

EDWIN CHADWICK AND THE POOR LAW

One of Bentham's most enthusiastic followers was Edwin Chadwick (1800–90), also a non-practising barrister, who became Bentham's secretary and imposed the full force of utilitarian ideas upon the Poor Law. Chadwick's zeal as a campaigner for praiseworthy philanthropic causes was matched only by his capacity for antagonising others who shared his aims and would have been more useful as allies. He applied his energies to many areas of public life and succeeded in making enemies, as well as some improvements, in each. Thus in 1854 he turned his attention to the reform of the Civil Service. The Northcote–Trevelyan report of that year was addressing the fact that the rapid expansion of the service had not been accompanied by any improvements in methods of recruitment. In 1815, at the end of the Napoleonic Wars, there had been 25,000 civil servants and by 1854 the number had increased by 60 per cent to accommodate the evolving responsibilities of government. However, in its upper reaches it was still the preserve of those with aristocratic or political connections but little talent for administration. Chadwick proposed entry to the Civil Service by examination, following the French model, but his arrogant and condescending style of advocacy made his ideas (and those of other reformers) an easy target for opponents with vested interests in preserving the existing, antiquated system. They clothed their opposition in rational garb, arguing that examinations did not test 'character' and suggesting that, if the senior levels of the civil service were not in the gift of the Prime Minister, the Civil Service could frustrate the intentions of a democratically elected government. Almost twenty years passed before Gladstone's administration introduced many of Chadwick's proposals in the Civil Service Reform Act of 1871, though even after that date the Foreign Office was exempted from entry by examination.

In the sphere of public health, Chadwick scarcely wavered in the dim view that he formed of the medical colleges as being mostly concerned with furthering their own interests, but he did have respect for Poor Law Medical Officers and for men like Thomas Southwood Smith,[2] who laboured for little reward in fever hospitals. Chadwick did, however, have confidence in the role that engineers could play in improving the health of the population. This did not prevent him from entering into several of his customary disputes with some of the most distinguished members of the profession, disputes that are described in Chapter 7. Some groups, however, were beyond the help even of civil engineers. Chadwick was particularly astringent about the Irish who had fled poverty in their native land and were often obliged to settle in the most insalubrious quarters of towns. In 1836 he identified the Irish population of Birmingham as being the original cause as well as the purveyors of epidemics when he wrote: 'The Irish in Birmingham are the very pests of Society . . . they are frequently the means of *generating* [emphasis added] and communicating infectious diseases.'[3]

The Poor Law as it existed in the early nineteenth century was still largely dependent upon the Speenhamland system devised by the magistrates of Berkshire in that county's village of Speen, near Newbury. A meeting of the magistrates, held in 1795 at an inn called The Pelican, decided that payments to the unemployed and destitute would be based upon the price of a loaf of bread. Those in work who were unable to support themselves and their families would receive what was, in effect, a subsidy to their wages from the ratepayers. This encouraged employers, when work was in short supply, to pay their workers wages at less than the subsistence level, in the knowledge that the deficit would be made good from the rates. As a result, the bill for public assistance increased greatly. A system based on that of Speen was widely adopted in the south of England, though with greatly varying rates of payment, while it was more sparingly applied in the north, though the expenditure, which reached £8 million in 1818, was much greater than had been anticipated by its originators. The idea that the public purse would, in effect, make an open-ended commitment to the support of parsimonious employers was deeply inimical to Chadwick's utilitarian philosophy.

In the face of this enormous burden, in 1832 a Royal Commission into the workings of the Poor Law was set up, with Chadwick as one of its most influential members. It resulted in the passing of the

Poor Law Amendment Act of 1834, which replaced the Speenhamland System with one based on a national network of workhouses. The Act was based upon utilitarian principles and in particular that of 'eligibility'. Those entering the workhouse should be accommodated in conditions that were less 'eligible' (that is to say less attractive) than those outside. The quality of the accommodation, the clothing and the food was thus designed to ensure that no one would wish to enter the workhouse who had any choice in the matter. Chadwick became secretary to the Poor Law Commissioners and used the position to campaign for reforms in public policy, particularly in the sphere of sanitation. The system was never popular, and its imposition was resisted in much of the country, especially the north. Poor Law Guardians were elected by ratepayers, those having more highly rated properties being entitled to two or, in some cases, three votes. Parishes were grouped into Poor Law Unions, and in the early days the contribution of each parish depended upon the poor relief it incurred in the previous three years. For that reason the main aim of ratepayers was to minimise poor relief, which ensured that the regimes were even grimmer than Chadwick had envisaged. Public expenditure was as unpopular at parish level as it was in Westminster.

CHADWICK'S REPORT

By this time Chadwick was one of the most ardent and influential advocates of the 'miasmatic' theory of disease causation that was to bedevil the science of epidemiology and that survived in some quarters into the twentieth century. The theory held that epidemics were caused by foul smells, and this was the orthodoxy of the time. In 1838, in the Fourth Annual Report of the Poor Law Commissioners, Chadwick advanced a classical utilitarian argument for sanitary reform on economic grounds: 'all epidemics and all infectious diseases are attended with charges, immediate and ultimate, upon the poor rates.' In the same year government auditors queried the expenditure by some Poor Law Guardians of public money on measures designed to remove, through better sanitation, 'nuisances' that they believed to be the cause of disease. Disease, in turn, caused expenditure on Poor Law relief, so the

Guardians were acting prudently to prevent future wasteful expenditure though there were doubts whether such expenditure was strictly legal. It seems likely that Chadwick prompted the Guardians to act in this way to test the government's attitude to public health measures.[4]

The Home Secretary, Lord John Russell, prevaricated by asking for reports on the matter from the Poor Law Commissioners, which were followed by further reports from three doctors, all of them drawing attention to the link between poor sanitation, disease and Poor Law expenditure. At a time when governments considered that the maintenance of minimal public expenditure was little less than a sacred duty, this should have been a decisive argument, but Russell still delayed, so Chadwick made use of another contact. Charles Blomfield, bishop of London, admired Chadwick's attempts to improve the living conditions of the poor, and it was probably as a result of Chadwick's prompting that, in September 1839, Blomfield moved in the House of Lords that an inquiry be made into the sanitary conditions of the labouring classes.[5] The ruse worked, and the result was Chadwick's great *Report into the Sanitary Conditions of the Labouring Population of Great Britain*, published in 1842, one of the seminal works of nineteenth-century social history.

Chadwick made use of the machinery of the Poor Law to gather the materials for his *Report*. Letters were sent to Poor Law Commissioners throughout Great Britain, and the *Report* also contains evidence of Chadwick's extensive reading of continental and American works on sanitary questions. The *Report* was published in July 1842, under Chadwick's own name as secretary to the Poor Law Commissioners, the Commissioners themselves declining to add their names because of the controversial nature of the document. The *Report*, which runs to over 400 pages of densely argued prose, was extensively and generously reviewed in leading newspapers such as *The Times* and the *Morning Chronicle*, as well as influential quarterlies such as the *Quarterly Review* and *Tait's Edinburgh Magazine*.[6] Chadwick informed the Lord Chancellor, Lord Brougham, that 'upwards of twenty thousand copies have been sold', though this may have been an author's exaggeration, since Sir John Simon estimated that 10,000 were sold or given away, many of them to Boards of Poor Law Guardians.[7]

The *Report* was principally concerned with four major themes. The first was the relationship between insanitary living conditions and disease, and the second was the cost of that disease arising from the creation of widows, orphans and those rendered incapable of work by disease. Thus the initial focus of the work was on the *economic* consequences of poor health, in keeping with the precepts of utilitarian philosophy and public thrift. Bentham would have approved and so, presumably, did Gladstone and other parsimonious politicians. The third theme was the *social* effects of poor living conditions – intemperance and immorality – with their own moral and economic consequences; and the final theme was the need for new systems of administration to eliminate the conditions that the *Report* recorded. This final section reflects Chadwick's distrust of local bodies, operating according to the whims of local citizens with no uniformity of policy or practice. He argued:

> Whatever additional force may be needed for the protection of the public health it would everywhere be obtained more economically with unity, efficiency and promptitude by a single, securely-qualified and well-appointed responsible local officer than by any new establishment applied in the creation of new local boards.[8]

This was to become a recurring theme as Chadwick campaigned for strong executive bodies, appointed rather than elected and furnished with authority and money from central government to undertake the massive task of sanitary reform.

WORKMANSHIP AND CONSISTENCY

The standards of workmanship that were applied to the laying of sewers left much to be desired and were described in detail in the *Report*. Chadwick quoted 'a surveyor of extensive practice' as saying: 'As regards the appointment of surveyors to the Commissioners of Sewers, I would observe that, in my opinion, very few of them are properly qualified by education or otherwise to perform the important duties entrusted to them in an effective and proper manner.'[9] He also referred to the experience of the Holborn and Finsbury Sewers Commission, one of eight sewers commissions that had been established under the Bill of Sewers of 1531 in the reign of Henry VIII:

> When the Commission advertised for a person to act as surveyor to the works who understood the use of the spirit level, the candidates, who were nearly all common house builders, were greatly surprised at the novel demand and several of them began to learn the use of the instrument, in order to qualify for the appointment.[10]

Evidence came from other quarters to support Chadwick's. An engineer called Henry Austin conducted a survey of London's sewers and gave further reasons for anxiety. It was the practice in many areas to build egg-shaped sewers with the narrow end at the bottom, so that, in times of limited flow (for example, at night or in dry weather), the liquid would be concentrated in a narrow area and thus speed the flow. Austin reported that the sewer beneath Cumberland Street, Chelsea, was 'egg-shaped, with the *broad* end down'.[11] Such problems were compounded by the fact that District Surveyors had limited authority to correct faults. John Roe, surveyor to the Holborn and Finsbury Commission, explained that, while he could forbid builders to connect defective house drains to public sewers, he could not *require* them to make connections at all. He gave an account of a case where a house drain was laid so that it flowed *towards* the house.[12]

Chadwick's verdict on the condition of London's sewers is not surprising: 'The sewerage of the Metropolis, though it is a frequent subject of boast to those who have not examined its operations or effects, will be found to be a vast monument of defective administration, of lavish expenditure and extremely defective execution.'[13]

CESSPOOLS AND THEIR CONSEQUENCES

Chadwick's *Report* also drew attention to some of the consequences of London's 200,000 cesspools. Since medieval times these had acted as receptacles for human waste and had, at intervals, been emptied at night by nightsoilmen (often in fact women), who, besides charging the householders for the work, could then sell the contents as fertiliser to the farms close to the City at places like Moorfields and what is now Regent's Park. London's sewers were designed purely for collecting rainfall and emptying it into the network of underground rivers that were used for the purpose intended by nature – conveying rainwater to the Thames. Emptying of waste of any kind into the sewers was thus forbidden, though surreptitiously practised by many householders and trades. The nightsoil trade was profitable work, but by the time Chadwick's *Report* was being compiled the system was breaking down for three reasons. First, the growth of London meant that the fields were retreating, so the nightsoilmen had further to transport their awkward, leaking carts, making the business less remunerative. Secondly, an alternative fertiliser became available. In the early 1840s the going rate for one cartload of human waste sold to a farmer was half a crown (12½p, a good day's wage for a labourer). In 1847 guano, solidified bird droppings, began to be imported from South America. It was a better fertiliser, more easily transported and cheaper, so the market for human waste received a further blow, and the price for a cartload fell to a shilling or less.

However, the reason for the final collapse of the nightsoilmen's trade was the water closet, whose history and consequences are described in more detail in Chapter 7. Unfortunately, the combination of the new water closets and the old cesspools had devastating consequences. When flushed, the WC despatched a small quantity of human waste and a far larger volume of water into the cesspool, which consequently filled up twenty or more times as fast with liquid that was difficult to transport and that no farmer wanted to buy. The nightsoilmen went out of business, and the ageing cesspools leaked and quickly overflowed, with consequences that Chadwick described. He quoted an engineer called Howell who had inspected two houses that were undergoing repairs in the notorious St Giles District, which, in the vicinity of the present site of Centre Point, held London's worst tenements:

I found whole areas of the cellars of both houses were full of nightsoil to the depth of three feet, which had been permitted for years to accumulate from the overflow of the cesspools . . . Upon passing through the passage of the first house I found the yard covered in nightsoil, from the overflowing of the privy to the depth of nearly six inches and bricks were placed to enable the inmates to get across dryshod.[14]

Chadwick had a clear explanation for this state of affairs. He observed that the cost of emptying a cesspool was about one shilling and, 'with a population generally in debt at the end of the week, and whose rents are collected weekly, such an outlay may be considered as practically impossible'. He could have added that, in tenement buildings such as that described in St Giles, the cesspools in the basement were used by all the residents but the burden of emptying them would inevitably fall on those living in the lowest floors, since those in the upper storeys did not suffer directly from the overflow.

The Nuisances Removal and Diseases Prevention Act of 1846 provided a mechanism whereby the Privy Council could insist that existing buildings connect their cesspools to the public sewers. This Act was known as the Cholera Bill, because its enactment was prompted by the approach, across Europe, of the second great cholera epidemic, which duly arrived in 1848. In the same year, the General Board of Health had taken office, with Chadwick as a member. Its brief was to supervise the activities of local boards, which were responsible for monitoring death rates in their communities and raising the standards of sanitation in those localities where, in the opinion of the General Board, they were inadequate. In practice this often meant in the opinion of Edwin Chadwick. Chadwick was to become, in the words of a later writer, 'the most hated man in England, detested alike by the poor, by vestrymen and by local boards of Guardians for his "Prussian" style of operation'.[15] The Poor Law Commission itself was eventually dissolved as a result of the antagonisms aroused by Chadwick's authoritarian methods, a feat he repeated with the General Board of Health itself. By this time, in the face of a second cholera epidemic, it was coming to be widely accepted that public intervention in support of good sanitation was desirable on grounds of economy as well as humanity, but not everyone agreed.

By this time, 1848, Chadwick had become a member of the Metropolitan Sewers Commission, a body established in 1848 to replace the eight neighbourhood commissions that the Victorian metropolis had inherited from Henry VIII. For the next seven years a sequence of commissions, appointed by the Crown, wrestled with the problems of devising a suitable system for ridding the capital of its sewage, each commission being dissolved in turn as it failed to find a solution. Invitations were extended to all to submit proposals; arguments raged over who was to pay for the work; engineers were appointed to the commission's staff, notably the young Joseph Bazalgette, who was eventually to solve the problem; above all the commissioners quarrelled among themselves. One of the most quarrelsome was Chadwick himself, who, however, was matched in animosity by a commissioner called John Leslie, 'a thoroughly unpleasant man, spiteful, offensive and ungenerous'.[16] Each man championed his own scheme and denigrated that of the other. Acrimony descended into farce when each party began to organise meetings attended only by his own supporters at times that were kept from opponents. Eventually the atmosphere became so charged with distrust that the Home Secretary, Lord Morpeth, dissolved the Commission and specified that 'neither of the prominent parties in the late disputes and differences should reappear in the new Commission'. Chadwick and Leslie had been sacked. Chadwick had previously been removed from both the Poor Law Commission and the General Board of Health on account of his remarkable capacity for antagonising people who would have been better as allies, so his dismissal from the Sewers Commission marked a notable treble.

However, in the meantime Chadwick had achieved one of his aims – to empty the capital's sewage into the Thames. As the second great cholera epidemic claimed the lives of London's citizens, *The Times*, on 4 October 1849, quoted Chadwick as advocating a policy of flushing cesspools, house drains and street sewers into the Thames: 'the complete drainage and purification of the dwelling house, next of the street and lastly of the river' summed up by the paper as 'no filth in the sewers, all in the river'. The weakness of this remedy was that, by dispatching human waste to the river, its most harmful elements, typhoid, cholera and other waterborne agents, would return with the tide to pollute the water supply. At high tides the sewage backed up into the tributary streams and into the capital's ageing sewers, leaking into underground springs that fed drinking water supplies such as the Broad Street pump.[17]

This was not, of course, a problem for Chadwick, whose devotion to the miasmatic theory of disease propagation told him that the priority was to remove foul smells from the home. In this belief he was following the prevailing orthodoxy as expressed by Florence Nightingale, who, in her classic text *Notes on Nursing*, criticised the common practice of laying drains beneath houses, arguing that escaping odours would cause outbreaks of diseases, including scarlet fever, measles and smallpox.[18] Chadwick went further. In 1846, in evidence to a Parliamentary Committee that was considering the problems of sewage disposal, he claimed: 'All smell is, if it be intense, immediate acute disease; and eventually we may say that, by depressing the system and rendering it susceptible to the action of other causes, all smell is disease.'[19] He never wavered in the face of scientific evidence. In the last year of his life, 1890, seven years after Robert Koch[20] had identified the cholera bacillus in India, Chadwick, by now Sir Edwin, attended a meeting of the Royal Society of Arts at which he referred to the advantages of an edifice like the Eiffel Tower, recently opened in Paris. The magazine *The Builder* reported the occasion and in its account a note of irony can be detected: 'Sir Edwin concluded his somewhat prolix communication by advocating the bringing down of fresh air from a height, by means of such structures as the Eiffel Tower and distributing it, warmed and fresh, in our buildings.'[21]

Chadwick's advice was not confined to his own capital. His authoritarian tendencies had earned him admirers among some of Europe's more assertive rulers, and one of these, Napoleon III, invited Chadwick to Paris in 1864, where Haussmann was reconstructing the French capital in accordance with the emperor's wishes. Chadwick's sensitive and experienced nose detected deficiencies in the city sewerage, so he offered some advice to Napoleon: 'Sire, they say that Augustus found Rome a city of brick and left it a city of marble. If your majesty, finding Paris stinking, will leave it sweet, you will more than rival the first emperor of

Rome.' The emperor's reply was not recorded. Nor was Chadwick by any means the most extreme exponent of the miasmatic theory. In 1844, as the sewage in the Thames was beginning to worry many observers, a professor of chemistry wrote a reassuring letter to *The Builder*: 'The free currents of air which are necessarily in constant circulation from their proximity to the majestic Thames have been considered (and not improperly) as a great cause of the salubrity of the metropolis.' This pompous claim was made twelve years after the first cholera epidemic and four years before the second, and in the same letter the professor expressed an even more extravagant version of the theory: 'From inhaling the odour of beef the butcher's wife obtains her obesity.' The writer advocated a policy of watering the streets so that the consequent evaporation 'will carry up with it into the atmosphere, and above the reach of mischief, the various decomposing and decomposed organic matters floating about and which, otherwise allowed to remain, would be productive of contagious miasms'.[22] With the support of the formidable Edwin Chadwick, the miasmatic doctrine became the orthodox explanation of epidemic disease (as well as the less harmful incidence of obesity in the butchery trade) for much of the nineteenth century.

ALTERNATIVE EXPLANATIONS: A CAMPAIGNING STATISTICIAN

The comfortable and excusable delusion that epidemics were caused by nasty smells emanating from filth was not accepted by all observers. The work of a campaigning statistician would eventually, and belatedly, deal it a fatal blow. William Farr (1807–83) was born in the village of Kenley, Shropshire, the son of parents of modest means. At the age of two he went to live with Joseph Pryce, a local squire noted for his charitable works, who virtually adopted the young William and paid for his education. Between the ages of nineteen and twenty-one William travelled each day the 10 miles to Shrewsbury, where he worked as a 'dresser' in the infirmary and studied medicine there with a doctor called Webster. On his death in 1828 Squire Pryce left William a legacy of £500, which enabled the young man to pursue his studies in Paris and Switzerland. It was during a visit to Switzerland with a fellow student called Bain that William Farr, who had no training in mathematics, first gave evidence of the interest in medical statistics that was to determine his future career. While visiting the small town of Martigny, in the Swiss Alps, Farr observed that the community had an exceptional number of people suffering from an unusual deformity (later known as *cretinism* and associated with a diet deficient in iodine). He persuaded the landlord of his inn to assemble a number of them for inspection. When Bain returned from a walk in the mountains, he recorded what he saw: 'Mr Farr was standing with a table and numerous large sheets of paper before him on which he was marking the shapes of the different heads of which he had previously taken the contours, vertically and horizontally, by means of a leaden tape. That evening we dined late.'[23]

In 1831 Farr worked for six months as an unqualified surgical locum at Shrewsbury and then studied at the newly opened University College London, where he became a licentiate of the Society of Apothecaries, the only medical qualification he ever gained by study and later the means by which Elizabeth Garrett Anderson entered the medical profession.[24] In 1833 he married a farmer's daughter who died of consumption four years later and in 1842 he remarried, a union that produced eight children, of whom three died in infancy. Perhaps these early and tragic encounters with premature mortality influenced his later career.

In 1833 he set up as an apothecary in Bloomsbury, which was then in the process of being transformed by Thomas Cubitt from a swamp into a fashionable residential area for those employed in the City of London. He supplemented his income by writing for early editions of the *Lancet*, which had been founded in 1823. His first article, in 1835, was on hygiene, which was to become a regular theme of his work, and this was followed by further articles on quack medicine, life assurance (a reflection of his growing interest in statistics) and cholera, the disease whose cause he later, somewhat belatedly, identified.

Farr was fortunate in his benefactors, since, in 1837, he was the recipient of a further legacy of £500 from his former Shrewsbury mentor Dr Webster, who also bequeathed him a large library. In the same year Farr contributed an article on 'Vital Statistics' to a volume called *McCulloch's Account of the British Empire* and at about the same time he became acquainted with Queen Victoria's physician,

Thomas Cubitt (1788–1855) made a contribution to the health of Victorian London by turning foetid swamps into fashionable residential areas. He was trained as a ship's carpenter and travelled in that capacity to India, saving enough money from his labours to set himself up as a builder upon his return. He was the first large-scale builder to employ a permanent (as distinct from jobbing) workforce of tradesmen embracing diverse crafts: carpenters, glaziers, tilers, bricklayers, etc. In order to maintain a steady flow of work for these employees he became engaged in speculative building and was thereby responsible for developing into attractive residential areas Bloomsbury, Belgravia and Pimlico (all previously swamps) as well as Highbury and Clapham. He modified and extended Osborne House on the Isle of Wight for the royal family and rebuilt Buckingham Palace. At the request of Prince Albert he negotiated the purchase of the land on which the South Kensington museums were built with the profits of the Great Exhibition of 1851. He left over £1 million in his will, which, at 386 pages, is the longest on record. The Duchess of Cornwall is one of his descendants.

Sir James Clark (1788–1870), a Fellow of the Royal Society. It may have been though Clark's influence that Farr obtained the position of Compiler of Abstracts (chief statistician) to the Registrar-General, though the ubiquitous Edwin Chadwick also claimed to have recommended him.[25] The Registrar-General's office was created in 1838 with the task of registering births, marriages and deaths as part of the campaign waged by Chadwick and his fellow utilitarians to bring order into public affairs. Before utilitarian principles could be applied, it was first necessary to know how many people of varying ages and degrees of dependency lived in each community, what their needs were and how long they lived. The first Registrar-General was a soon forgotten popular novelist called Thomas Lister, who had strong political connections. The dominant figure in the new service, however, was William Farr, who remained in the post of compiler until his retirement in 1880 and used his office to campaign for better sanitary conditions, especially in urban areas. Each annual report of the Registrar-General was enlivened by a series of essays on public health, written by Farr and drawing attention to the devastating consequences of poor housing, inadequate sanitation and other factors that contributed to epidemic disease and other sources of premature mortality. He was particularly critical of the reluctance of governments to concern themselves with matters that would benefit poorer members of society, arguing in his fifth report in 1843: 'Over the supply of water, the sewerage, the burial places, the width of streets, the removal of public nuisances, the poor can have no command . . . and it is precisely upon these points that the Government can interfere with most advantage.'[26]

Farr quickly recognised that 'diseases are more easily prevented than cured and the first step to their prevention is the discovery of their exciting causes'.[27] This statement was even truer in 1838 than it is now, since the cures available to medical practitioners were, in the absence of modern drug treatments or much understanding of the causes of disease, both few and ineffective. Farr set about forming a firm statistical foundation for his work, though he was not the first person to use statistics to identify causes of mortality. A pioneer in the field was William Heberden (1710–1801), a lecturer from Cambridge who made a study of the bills of mortality and tabulated causes of death according to his own categories. Many of these now seem strange, such as 'suddenly' and 'killed by several accidents'.[28]

Farr's approach was more systematic. He approached the Presidents of the Royal Colleges of Surgeons and Physicians and the Master of the Society of Apothecaries and persuaded them to write to their members throughout the kingdom urging them 'to give, in every instance which may fall under our care, an authentic name of the fatal disease'.[29] These would be recorded in local registers from which Farr compiled his statistics and from these Farr created what he called a 'statistical nosology', which listed and defined twenty-seven fatal disease categories to be used by local registrars when recording causes of death. Thus dysentery ('bloody flux') was distinguished from diarrhoea ('looseness, purging, bowel complaint'). He also gave the 'synonymes' (*sic*) by which the conditions might be known in local dialects. The same instructions were issued to ships' captains, who might encounter a death among crew or passengers. He used the term *zymotic*, from the Greek word meaning 'ferment', to describe diseases that could contribute to deadly 'miasmas'.

It was Farr's practice, from the first reports, to tabulate causes of death by disease, parish, age, sex and occupation. London was the subject of a separate report each year, and thirteen provincial cities were also frequently the subjects of such analysis. He regularly included essays on related matters, such as the one he wrote in 1842 on the statistical practices of fifteen European cities and the USA. He often included essays on life assurance. He quickly established a reputation as an effective advocate of reform, using his gifts as an exceptionally lucid writer to draw attention to public health issues that concerned him.

'DISEASE MIST . . . AN ANGEL OF DEATH'

However, like many people who hold strong views, including his mentor Edwin Chadwick, Farr was sometimes noted for the consistency of his beliefs rather than their scientific probity. In the words of his mostly benign entry in the *Dictionary of National Biography*, 'he was not always well advised in holding to his opinions in the teeth of contradictory evidence',[30] a particularly culpable trait in one who based his beliefs on the precepts of mathematics. This paradox is illustrated by his obstinate attitude towards the great cholera epidemics of the nineteenth century and itself illustrates the strength of orthodoxy in the face of evidence. Farr produced impressive statistical evidence demonstrating that the disease was spread by polluted water, yet he long shrank from reaching that conclusion, clinging instead to the orthodox view of his mentor, Edwin Chadwick, that the culprit was foul air.

Thus, in the fifth annual report, covering the year 1842, he drew attention to the wide variations in mortality between different areas and particularly emphasised the high death rates occurring in London, a problem he attributed to the 'miasma' in which much of the population lived and which he described in the following terms:

Every population throws off insensibly an atmosphere of organic matter . . . this atmosphere hangs over cities like a light cloud, slowly spreading, driven about, falling dispersed by the winds, washed down by showers . . . to connect by a subtle, sickly medium, the people agglomerated in narrow streets and courts, down which the wind does not blow and upon which the sun seldom shines.[31]

In the tenth annual report, that of 1847, compiled as the second great cholera epidemic approached from Europe, he estimated that, in one small area of London, 'at least thirty-eight people died in excess of the rate of mortality which actually prevails in the immediate neighbourhood' and followed this with an even more emphatic 'miasmatic' explanation for this state of affairs:

This disease mist, arising from the breath of two millions of people, from open sewers and cesspools, graves and slaughter-houses, is continually kept up and undergoing changes; in one season it was pervaded by Cholera; in another by Influenza; at one time it bears Smallpox, Measles, Scarlatina and Whooping Cough among your children; in another it carries fever on its wings. Like an angel of death it has hovered for centuries over London.[32]

FARR AND THE BROAD STREET PUMP

In 1855 Farr served on the Committee for Scientific Inquiry into the cholera epidemic of the previous year that had killed more than 10,000 citizens of London alone. The strange and contorted logic that Farr and his fellows used in their determination to cling to the 'miasmatic' doctrine is the best possible illustration of the strength of that belief. The committee observed that 'in the Southwark and Vauxhall [companies'] water evidence of unfiltered contamination reaches its highest degree, revealing to the microscope not only swarms of infusorial life but particles of undigested food referable to the discharge of human bowels', but did not conclude that any harmful results would proceed from these discharges. Furthermore Farr used the data gathered by his office to draw a diagram illustrating the relationship between the incidence of mortality from cholera and the elevation above sea level of the affected districts. His diagram, which was published by a Parliamentary Committee,[33] clearly demonstrated that, the further removed a district was above the level of the polluted Thames, the lower the mortality. The most striking exception to this inverse relationship between mortality and height was shown by Farr's diagram to lie in the vicinity of Golden Square, Soho, close to the pump that John Snow had identified as the source of the infected water that was killing the local people who drew water from it. Farr's table revealed the following:

Elevation in feet	Cholera deaths per 10,000 population
0	137
15	50
25	40
35	25
45	20
55	13
65	36*
75	19

* The height of the Broad Street pump.

The committee, in response to the persuasive arguments of Dr John Snow, whose study of the Soho outbreak had connected it with water from a pump in Broad Street,[34] made a detailed study of the Broad Street outbreak. The committee's report observed that, on the south side of the street, 48 houses out of a total of 49 were affected by cholera, while, from a resident population of 860 in the street as a whole, 90 had died together with 25 others who worked in the street but lived elsewhere. The committee had to resort to some strange logic to explain this anomaly in 'miasmatic' terms. They suggested that 'the outbreak arose from the multitude of untrapped and imperfectly trapped gullies and ventilating shafts constantly emitting an intense amount of noxious, health-destroying, life-destroying exhalations' and comforted themselves that the incidence of death had been lower in corner houses than others, concluding that the wind blew harder on corners! They were not troubled by the fact that deaths among workers at a nearby brewery (where the occupants drank beer rather than pump water) were very few indeed, despite the fact that they were breathing the same air. Referring to Dr John Snow's attribution of cholera to the polluted pump water, they added: 'After careful enquiry we see no reason to adopt this belief.' Snow had observed that a lady living in Hampstead had died after sending her maid to collect water from Broad Street, and, faced with such evidence, the committee felt obliged to refute it in some detail:

> If the Broad Street pump did actually become a source of disease to persons dwelling at a distance, we believe that this may have depended on other organic impurities than those actually referred to and may have arisen, not in its containing choleraic excrements, but simply in the fact of its impure waters having participated in the atmospheric infection of the district . . . on the whole evidence it seems impossible to doubt that the influences which determine in mass the geographical distribution of cholera in London, belong less to the water than to the air.[35]

This report, written by Farr and his fellow committee members in July 1855, for the first time allows some modest role for water in the phrase '*less* to the water than to the air', but within twelve months Farr himself was beginning to change his views. In an appendix to the 1854 Report of the Registrar-General, written in late 1855 or 1856, Farr made a careful analysis of the incidence of cholera among the customers of ten London water companies. He noted that the Lambeth company, which had moved its intake to Teddington, above the tidal reach of the polluted Thames, had seen a rapid fall in mortality compared with that of the 1849 epidemic, when it had drawn water from the tideway. Farr referred to Snow's hypothesis that cholera was transmitted in water and acknowledged that 'the cholera matter, where it is most fatal, is largely diffused through water, as well as through other channels'. Farr is here hedging his bets, but for the first time the emphasis is on water as the principal means of infection.

THE EAST LONDON EPIDEMIC AND THE CONVERSION OF WILLIAM FARR

It was, however, the failure of the East London water company to protect its water from contamination, together with the attempt of the company's directors to conceal that failure, that finally converted Farr from an increasingly hesitant advocate of the miasmatic theory to a very angry campaigner against polluted water. On 27 June 1866 a labourer called Hedges and his wife both died from cholera. The Hedges' water closet at 12 Priory Street, Bromley-by-Bow, discharged into the River Lea at Bow Bridge, half a mile below the East London water company's reservoir at Old Ford. The incoming tide would carry the infected sewage back upstream towards the reservoir. This should not have mattered, since the company had installed filter beds for its new covered reservoirs and supposedly isolated these from its old, uncovered reservoirs, which had pervious bottoms. Nevertheless, Farr observed the degree to which the outbreak was concentrated in a small area of Whitechapel served by the East London company. Previous cholera epidemics had affected the whole metropolis, with mortality striking rich and poor alike in all quarters. In the Whitechapel epidemic 5,596 deaths from cholera were recorded in a very small area.

On 1 August 1866 *The Times* carried a report that 924 people had died in one week in districts served by the East London company. On the same day, on Farr's recommendation, notices were displayed in the affected area advising that 'the inhabitants of the district within which cholera is prevailing are earnestly advised not to drink any water which has not previously been boiled' – advice previously given by John Snow in the 1854 epidemic. The effectiveness of the advice may have been vitiated by the fact that, according to the local Medical Officer, temperatures in direct sunlight were reaching 160°. Faced with such public criticism, the engineer to the company, Charles Greaves, wrote to *The Times* on 2 August, at the height of the epidemic, to refute the suggestion that contaminated water had been allowed to enter the supply, claiming that 'not a drop of unfiltered water has for several years past been supplied by the company for any purpose'.[36] The following day Farr visited Old Ford and asked for an analysis of the company's water. He observed that, despite Greaves's reassuring letter to *The Times*, two customers of the East London company claimed that they had found eels in their water pipes.[37] Farr also wrote to Joseph Bazalgette, chief engineer to the Metropolitan Board of Works, to ask about the possibility of sewage waste entering the water pipes.[38] Since 1859 Bazalgette had been constructing the system of main drainage that intercepted London's sewage before it reached the rivers and conducted it to treatment works at Barking and Plumstead, beyond the metropolitan boundary. Most of the system was in operation by this time, but Bazalgette replied to Farr:

> It is unfortunately just the locality where our main drainage works are not complete. The low level sewer is constructed through the locality but the pumping station at Abbey Mills will not be completed until next summer . . . I shall recommend the Board to erect a temporary pumping station at Abbey Mills to lift the sewage of this district into the Northern outfall sewer. This can be accomplished in about three weeks.[39]

In September, as temperatures dropped, the number of deaths fell, but twenty-nine residents signed a 'memorial' to the Board of Trade in which they alleged that their water supplies were being contaminated by water from the River Lea, despite the assurances of the company. A Captain Tyler was appointed to report upon the matter and he found evidence that the company's reservoirs were not effectively protected from contamination by surrounding groundwater, which might itself have become polluted. More damning evidence was forthcoming from the company's employees, whom he questioned at some length. They revealed that, on three occasions in the spring and summer of 1866, a 24-year-old carpenter had allowed water from an old, unprotected reservoir to pass into the company's closed reservoir, from which drinking water was drawn. This was a clear breach of the law and was no doubt the source of the contamination. Captain Tyler estimated that 4,364 deaths had occurred in July and August, of which 93 per cent had occurred in areas served by the East London company. In reference to the complaints of the 'memorialists' Tyler wrote:

I am of the opinion that the allegation has been proved and that the water of the Lea finds its way into these covered reservoirs . . . the use of such unfiltered water so stored in an uncovered water is indefensible and was a distinct infringement of the Metropolitan Water Supply Act of 1852 . . . a case of grave suspicion exists against the water supplied by the East London company from Old Ford.[40]

A chorus of disapproval now descended upon the East London company. The *Lancet* was particularly censorious, commenting: 'the companies in whose hands that supply [of water] is a monopoly secretly infringe the law, trusting to the difficulties by which discovery is virtually rendered next to impossible . . . [it is] greatly to be regretted that a heavy penalty has not been exacted for the infraction of the law.'[41] The *British Medical Journal*, which at this time was one of the most ardent supporters of the miasmatic theory. was also highly critical of the company. It had carried out its own investigation and concluded that the company's covered reservoirs had regularly been polluted for the previous three years. It asked: 'Who has been brought to account for the terrible result of the day's work in East London.'[42]

Farr made his customary statistical evaluation of the 1866 outbreak and drew attention to the results of attaching a piece of modern technology, the water closet, like that of the unfortunate Hedges family, to a medieval system of cesspools:

Almost co-incidentally with the appearance of epidemic cholera, and with the striking increase of diarrhoea in England, was the introduction into general use of the water-closet system, which had the advantage of carrying night-soil out of the house, but the incidental and not necessary disadvantage of discharging it into the rivers from which the [water] supply was drawn.[43]

In his summary of the evidence one can detect not only a change of heart as to the relative responsibility for air and water in transmitting cholera but also the anger that he directed at the East London company for trying to suppress the truth about its operations:

As the air of London is not supplied like water to its inhabitants by companies the air has had the worst of it. For air no scientific witnesses have been retained, no learned counsel has pleaded; so the atmosphere has been freely charged with the propagation of plagues of all kinds; while Father Thames and the water gods of London have been loudly proclaimed innocent. Dr Snow's theory turned the current in the direction of water . . . the theory of the East wind, with cholera on its wings, assailing the East End of London ignores all past experience. The population in London probably inhaled a few cholera corpuscles floating in the open air and the quantity thus taken from the air would be insignificant in its effects in comparison with the quantities imbibed through the waters into which cholera dejections had found their way and been mingled with sewage by the churning tides. An indifferent person would have breathed the air without any apprehension; but only a very robust scientific witness would have dared to drink a glass of the waters of the Lea at Old Ford after filtration.[44]

This damning verdict, with its acknowledgement of John Snow's earlier diagnosis, did not prompt Farr to abandon altogether the belief that London's foul air was to blame for some cases of the disease. His examination of meteorological records led him to believe that the northerly winds of July and August had carried the cholera to other parts of the capital not supplied by the East London company and that washerwomen had caught the disease 'to some extent carried up from warm liquids by watery vapour'.[45] Nevertheless, Farr's contribution to improvements in public health was generously acknowledged by the *British Medical Journal* in its lengthy obituary following his death in April 1883: 'Farr and John Simon stand side by side as the foremost figures of their time among the heroes of preventive medicine'. though the journal also deplored the fact that he had received no public honour commensurate with his work.[46]

SCEPTICS REMAIN

Over the years that followed, the debate moved irresistibly in the direction of John Snow's explanation. The *Lancet* commented that

Farr's 'elaborate array of facts' had rendered 'irresistible the conclusions at which he has arrived in regard to the influence of the water-supply'.[47] Not all were convinced. A chemist called Henry Letheby, Medical Officer for the City of London, assured the Parliamentary Select Committee on East London Water Bills that he had heard nothing in proof of the statement that the prevalence of cholera in East London was due to the water supply and concluded that there was so much mystery attaching to the subject of cholera that they were not justified in forming any conclusion as to its origin or propagation. As late as 1894 two equally eminent chemists were assuring a Royal Commission that cholera germs would be *destroyed* by sewage.[48]

However, not even the discovery of the cholera bacillus by Robert Koch, a future Nobel Prize winner, in 1883 was sufficient to convince the real sceptics. As previously observed,[49] Edwin Chadwick, in the last year of his life, 1890, remained convinced that fresh, warm air from London's answer to the Eiffel Tower would solve the problems of epidemic disease. It is perhaps more surprising that the distinguished English epidemiologist Charles Creighton was still displaying a note of scepticism in 1894, in which year he published his definitive *History of Epidemics in Britain*. He wrote of the Broad Street pump: 'The whole incident was seized upon and worked up by Dr Snow who had written a speculative essay in 1849 upon the probability of cholera being conveyed by water . . . he had enthusiastic followers at the time and has probably more now.'[50] It would seem that the 'followers' did not include Charles Creighton any more than it included Edwin Chadwick or Florence Nightingale. Such is the power of orthodoxy!

THE RATIONAL DRESS SOCIETY

Moreover, the 'miasmatic' idea, though mistaken, did have some beneficial results. In 1887 Dr Gustav Jaeger of Stuttgart published *Essays on Health Culture* in which he drew attention to the harmful effects of the cumbersome couture that had been imposed on fashionable young women since the Prince Regent had adopted the habit of wearing corsets to hide his massive girth. Jaeger asserted that:

If at any point underclothing or lining intervene between the body and the outer atmosphere, an obstacle is set up to the free passage of the exhalation from the skin, with the result that the noxious portion of the exhalation settles in the vegetable fibre, which consequently becomes malodorous; and everything malodorous is prejudicial to the health.[51]

From the 1820s, when the Prince Regent ascended the throne, women adopted the practice of wearing multiple petticoats and, later, crinolines, so the unnaturally corseted waist, which impeded breathing, was joined by several pounds of horsehair, whalebone and frames of wire and wood, which offset the narrow waist and promoted the pale, sickly appearance that fashion demanded. In 1859 a young lady was reported to have died as a result of her ribs being pierced by whalebone stays. In the same decade Amelia Bloomer, editor of a temperance magazine in the United States, gave her name to loose-fitting trousers that could be worn under a skirt, and in 1881 Viscountess Harberton founded the 'Rational Dress Society', which sought 'to promote the adoption of a style of dress based upon considerations of health, comfort and beauty' and whose publication, the *Gazette*, opposed designs that restricted or contorted the female form. Dr Jeager's assertion that the cumbersome fashions bequeathed by the Prince Regent prevented exhalation of noxious odours helped to curtail the reign of the corset among the middle classes and promote looser-fitting clothing such as split skirts suitable for the new pastime of bicycling. So Chadwick's 'noxious vapours' did some good after all!

In the meantime, moreover, the forces of commerce, in the form of water companies, and of science, in the form of engineering, were pressing relentlessly forward with the provision of piped, filtered water and sewerage, which would advance the health of urban populations more than the medical profession was equipped to do.[52]

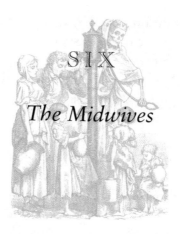

SIX

The Midwives

Contrary to expectations, the advantages these institutions offered were over-balanced by one dread drawback; the mortality of mothers was not diminished; nay it became in some cases excessive; in others appalling.

(William Farr, writing on the effects of childbirth in hospitals in 1870)

Doctors are gentlemen and gentlemen's hands are clean.

(Obstetrician Dr Charles Meigs resisting the proposal that doctors wash their hands between examining patients)

We never mentioned the word midwife in those days without a blush.

(Rosalind Paget, advocate of midwifery as a profession, giving voice to Victorian prudery on the work it involved)

CHILDBED FEVER

Childbed fever, also known as *puerperal fever* or *puerperal sepsis*, leading to blood poisoning, was responsible for a greater number of deaths in Victorian England than the great cholera epidemics, whose sporadic progress across Europe was closely followed by a fearful press. Yet, while the great waterborne epidemics were brought under control in the latter part of Victoria's reign, the annual death toll from childbed fever actually increased. In 1850 the total number of deaths from this condition was 3,478; by 1900 this had risen to 4,455.[1] After 1900 the death rate steadily declined to its present level of about five deaths a year. This improvement owed much to the work of a small number of determined women who fought relentlessly, often against male opposition, to improve the standards of care in childbirth. It is tempting to reflect that the condition received less attention than it deserved because, unlike cholera, typhoid and smallpox, childbed fever killed only women. The medical profession was almost exclusively male. Some of its victims, admittedly, were women whose deaths were tragic not only for their immediate families but for many others as well. Jane Seymour, third wife of Henry VIII, died from the condition after giving birth to the future Edward VI. Had she survived, the king's urgent desire for more male heirs would perhaps have been satisfied, with beneficial consequences for some of his later victims. Mary Shelley was left motherless by the death of her mother, the early feminist Mary Wollstonecraft, the first of many tragedies to mark the life of the author of *Frankenstein*. The French writer Voltaire was left distraught when his companion Émilie du Châtelet, translator into French of the works of Isaac Newton, died of puerperal fever in 1749.

It was not only the medical profession whose concern with the subject left much to be desired. Martin Luther's pronouncement on the subject was notably unsympathetic: 'If a woman die in childbed that does no harm. It is what they were made for.' Thus the pangs of childbirth, unrelieved by anaesthetics until the 1840s, when they were introduced in the face of much medical and theological opposition, were likely to be followed by the greater agonies of childbed fever. The condition inflicted unbearable pain on the sufferer that no treatment could relieve, and there were reports of women crying out in pain for days before the arrival of merciful death.

The increase in deaths that occurred during the nineteenth century was, paradoxically, caused by well-intentioned attempts to improve the standards of maternity care by encouraging women to give birth in hospitals. It appears, from the small amount of evidence available, that death following childbirth (usually at home) was uncommon in medieval times, even though the condition is referred to in the works of Hippocrates. The seventeenth century saw the establishment of maternity, or 'lying-in', hospitals in many continental cities, and the first epidemic of childbed fever recorded in Europe occurred at the Hôtel Dieu hospital in Paris in 1646. It was not unknown for deaths following childbirth in hospital to reach one woman in four from that date onwards.[2] Many observers attributed these deaths to a 'miasma', that pervasive explanation for all manner of diseases, which has been discussed in earlier chapters.[3] Others thought it was due to the labouring woman's disturbed state of mind. Yet another held that it was caused by putrefied breast milk being carried via the bloodstream to the genital regions. As late as 1883 correspondents to the *Lancet* were blaming it on the proximity to the mother of stagnant ponds, sewer gas and pig sties.[4] Dozens of epidemics were reported in Britain from 1770 onwards, with mortality levels as high as 80 per cent in some cases – higher than for smallpox or the Black Death. One midwife, in the months of December 1830 and January 1831, was reported to have delivered thirty women of whom sixteen died.[5]

OLIVER WENDELL HOLMES

Immediately after childbirth the placental site is an open wound vulnerable to infection by bacteria such as staphylococcus and streptococcus. These are easily transmitted from one mother to another on the unclean hands and instruments of midwives and doctors. However, in the nineteenth century the idea that infections could actually be *caused* by doctors was deeply offensive to their profession, even after Pasteur had evolved his germ theories and Lister had expelled infections from his patients and operating theatres with the aid of carbolic acid.[6] One of the first to recognise that infections could be transmitted by doctors was the American Oliver Wendell Holmes (1809–94), whose reputation as a writer and wit has eclipsed his earlier role as a doctor and scientist. Born in Cambridge, Massachusetts, he attended Harvard, where he studied first law and then medicine, later studying also in Paris. He practised in Boston and became professor of anatomy and physiology at Harvard Medical School in 1847. However, his only notable contribution to medical science was an essay he published early in his career, in 1843, entitled 'Contagiousness of Puerperal Fever'.[7]

He had come across a paper by a Scottish physician, Dr Alexander Gordon, who, in a paper published in 1795, had observed that childbed fever 'seized such women only as were visited or delivered by a practitioner, or taken care of by a nurse, who had previously attended patients affected with the disease'. Gordon had added: 'I myself was the means of carrying the infection to a great number of women' – an astonishing admission from a doctor of that time. Furthermore, wrote Gordon, 'I arrived at that certainty in the matter that I could venture to foretell what women would be affected with the disease, upon hearing by what midwife they were to be delivered, or by what nurse they were to be attended, during their lying-in; and in almost every instance my prediction was verified'.[8] He added, in specific refutation of the 'miasmatic' theory, that 'the cause of the puerperal fever was a specific contagion or infection, altogether unconnected with a noxious condition of the atmosphere'. Gordon's claims were very controversial and provoked so much criticism that when, in 1799, he was called upon to join the Royal Navy as a surgeon, he did so with some relief in order to escape the unpopularity he had brought upon himself in professional circles in his native Aberdeen. Unfortunately he contracted consumption while serving with the fleet and died later the same year.[9] Gordon's experiences supported the evidence of Holmes's own observations when he witnessed the deaths of a medical student and a physician who had performed an autopsy on a mother who had died from puerperal fever. This experience led him to conclude that 'the disease known as Puerperal Fever is so far contagious as to be frequently carried from patient to patient by physicians and nurses', though he declined to speculate whether 'the particular mode of infection be the atmosphere he [the physician] carries about him into the sick-chamber or by the direct application of the virus to the absorbing surfaces with which his hand comes into contact'. He thus sidestepped the 'miasmatic' debate. He added: 'the existence of a private pestilence in the sphere of a single physician should be looked upon not as a misfortune but as a crime.' Holmes thereby brought upon himself the wrath of his colleagues. Thomas Watson (1792–1882), whose view of the *exciting causes* of disease has already been observed,[10] had written in 1842, the year before Homes published his paper, that 'wherever puerperal fever is rife, or when a practitioner has attended any one instance of it, he should use most diligent ablution', and went on to recommend handwashing with chlorine solution and changes of clothing. At the same time the statistician William Farr[11] congratulated a Doncaster surgeon called Robert Storrs for publishing facts that it was in the interests of the medical profession to conceal. In *Observations of Puerperal Fever* Storrs had suggested that, after conducting a post-mortem, a surgeon should attend to 'the most careful ablutions of the hands and for the surgeon to avoid attendance on a labour in any part of the dress in which such operations have been performed'.[12]

The opposition to Holmes's suggestion that doctors could actually cause infection was led by one of America's most distinguished and influential obstetricians, Charles Meigs, whose attitude towards childbirth and, indeed, to women tells us much about the opposition that confronted those who wished to make childbirth safer and less of an ordeal. Meigs was lecturer in obstetrics in the School of Medicine, Philadelphia, and had no hesitation in dismissing Holmes's hypothesis, declaring that 'doctors are gentlemen and gentlemen's hands are clean'.[13] Meigs's view of the female sex was similarly unflattering. He informed his students that a woman 'has a head almost too small for intellect and just big enough for love'.[14] He had misgivings about the indelicacy involved in the examination of pregnant women by male doctors (there were, of course, no female doctors when he wrote) and informed his students: 'I am proud to say that, in this country generally, there are women who prefer to suffer the extremity of danger and pain rather than waive those scruples of delicacy which prevent their maladies from being fully exposed.'[15]

He also opposed the use of anaesthetics in childbirth, thereby voicing views that were widely held and supported by much of the religious establishment in America as well as Britain. A belief that the agonies of labour were some kind of retribution on the female sex for Eve's disobedience in the Garden of Eden was held by some influential clergy, who were, of course, exclusively male. Contemporary fashions actually added to the difficulties and dangers of labour among the wealthier classes. The wasp waist achieved by tight corsets marked one's middle- or upper-class status, but could lead to deformities that were inimical to childbirth. Many physicians campaigned against these practices without success until the advent of the Rational Dress Society began to liberate women from them later in the century.[16] Dr James Simpson used chloroform to ease the pains of childbirth for one of his patients in Edinburgh in 1847 and later commented that 'he had to reply to the objections of religious spokesmen for having removed Eve's curse'.[17] The theologians, however, were no match for Queen Victoria, who requested chloroform for the birth of Prince Leopold, her sixth child, in April 1853. It was administered by John Snow, who had contributed to the conquest of cholera,[18] and the Queen's example, which was widely reported, was swiftly followed by other women, despite the reservations of churchmen.

DR IGNAZ SEMMELWEIS

Five years after Thomas Watson issued his advice, a decisive advance was make by the Hungarian doctor Ignaz Semmelweis (1818–65). Semmelweis, the son of prosperous parents who may originally have come from Swabia in Germany, was born and schooled in Buda and went on to study at the University of Pest, the two cities, not united as Budapest until 1872, then being part of the Austro-Hungarian empire. He later studied in Vienna with Dr Joseph Skoda (1805–81), a pioneer in diagnostic methods, and was then appointed to a post in an obstetric clinic in Vienna's General Hospital. Semmelweis's clinic, which was used for teaching medical students, had an appalling record of deaths from childbed fever, with almost one woman in ten suffering this fate. Many of the medical students were thereby involved in autopsies. A second obstetric clinic, in the same hospital, had a mortality rate less than half that of the first.[19] That clinic was run by midwives, who carried out no autopsies. The year after he took up the post a colleague died from an infection contracted while carrying out an autopsy on a woman who had died from childbed fever. Semmelweis concluded that some unidentified 'cadaveric material' spread the infection among doctors and patients. He later wrote: 'the fingers and hands of students and doctors, soiled by recent dissections, carry those death-dealing cadavers' poisons into the genital organs of women in childbirth.'

He immediately instituted a regime of hand-washing in chlorinated lime, as recommended by Thomas Watson, for doctors examining patients. The mortality rate in Semmelweis's clinic immediately dropped to that of the midwives' clinic.

Semmelweis's theories and practices were not well received by colleagues, who were as reluctant as Charles Meigs had been to acknowledge that doctors could actually be the cause of infection and death. It was further argued that it simply was not practical for doctors, midwives and nurses to wash their hands between examinations of patients. Semmelweis's mentor, Joseph Skoda, tried to persuade the imperial Ministry of Education to order an official investigation into Semmelweis's theories, but a mixture of bureaucratic and Conservative opposition to Semmelweis (who was an active supporter of the Liberal interest in politics) led to his departure from Vienna. He returned to his native Pest, where he took charge of the maternity ward of St Rochus's hospital, whose mortality rate he reduced to less than 1 per cent. It was not until 1861 that Semmelweis published a long-winded, repetitious and turgid account of his theories under the cumbersome title *The Aetiology, the Concept and the Prophylaxis of Childbed Fever*, running to 543 pages, so it is perhaps not surprising that he received less credit than he was due. He did, however, include the perfectly unambiguous statement that 'the lying-in hospitals are called "murder-dens" not only by physicians but also by administrative officials'.[20] His ideas were widely adopted in Hungary but continued to be rejected in Vienna, one of his most prominent critics being Rudolf Virchow,[21] and towards the end of his life he was a rather bitter figure. Semmelweis died in an asylum in Vienna in 1865, possibly suffering from Alzheimer's disease. Ironically, the immediate cause of his death was a form of sepsis similar to puerperal fever following an infection contracted during surgery.[22] His death was largely disregarded beyond the Austro-Hungarian empire, no obituary appearing even in the *Lancet*. A later writer suggested that Semmelweis's nationality was a disadvantage, commenting: 'Operating from a politically suppressed and scientifically backward country with a second-rate university, Semmelweis was effectively hampered in the promulgation of his ideas.[23] Paradoxically, the *Lancet* did refer to Semmelweis in its obituary of Louis Pasteur thirty years later, bracketing Semmelweis with Lister and Pasteur himself as among the pioneers of antiseptic surgery.[24]

At the time of Semmelweis's death, Louis Pasteur was developing the theory that living organisms, germs, could cause infection, and shortly afterwards Joseph Lister instituted the antiseptic practices that reduced mortality in operating theatres, practices closely related to those of Semmelweis. In 1879 Pasteur himself identified streptococcus bacteria in the blood of a woman with childbed fever. Semmelweis thus posthumously won his argument, but further battles had to be fought with the medical profession before childbirth became a relatively safe process, and one of the fiercest of those battles was fought in Great Britain.

ENGLISH MIDWIVES: THEIR HISTORY AND PROSPECTS

In 1872, seven years after Semmelweis's death, Dr James Aveling published a book entitled *English Midwives: Their History and Prospects*.[25] Dr Aveling, an obstetrician, had been a lecturer in midwifery at the Sheffield School of Medicine and had co-founded the Jessop hospital for women in that city. He later established a medical practice at 1 Upper Wimpole Street, London, and co-founded the Chelsea Hospital for Women in the King's Road, the first hospital in London dedicated to the treatment of women. He was a founding fellow of the Obstetrical Society of London and wrote numerous articles on the practice of midwifery and the education of midwives.[26] His attitude towards women as doctors was ambiguous. Thus he nominated Elizabeth Garrett Anderson for membership of the Obstetrical Society in 1874, but added: 'I am not standing up to plead the cause of women as obstetricians because I think that if there is one occupation for which they are less fitted than another it is that of attending the emergencies of obstetric practice.'[27]

Despite this lukewarm attitude to women in the medical profession, Aveling was a steadfast supporter of proposals to improve the training and status of midwives. Ten years earlier the Obstetrical Society had carried out a survey, which estimated that less than one third of births were attended by a trained practitioner (a doctor or a midwife). In the 1881 census 2,646 women described themselves as midwives, though less than a tenth of that number had

Elizabeth Garrett Anderson (1836–1917) was the first Englishwoman to qualify as a female doctor in England. This clumsy preface is necessary, since James Barry (*c.* 1795–1865) succeeded in working as a doctor in the British army by posing as a man; and Elizabeth Blackwell (1821–1910) was born in Bristol but qualified as a doctor in New York before returning to England. Elizabeth Garrett Anderson, the daughter of an Aldeburgh corn merchant, failed to gain entry to a medical school but trained as a nurse at the Middlesex Hospital. She learned that the Society of Apothecaries did not exclude women from taking their examinations, which she took and passed (whereupon the Society changed its rules to prevent other women from following her). She obtained a medical degree in Paris and established a dispensary for women in London, which later became the Elizabeth Garrett Anderson Hospital. In 1872 she opened the New Hospital for Women in London, staffed exclusively by women. In 1876 the General Medical Council finally agreed to admit women to the profession. In 1902 she retired to Aldeburgh and was elected mayor – the first female mayor in England. Her sister, Millicent Garrett Fawcett, after whom the Fawcett Society is named, was a notable campaigner for women's causes.

undergone some kind of formal training involving hospital work, and a Parliamentary Committee estimated that between 10,000 and 20,000 women, mostly with no qualifications at all, were working as midwives. The comparatively safe practice of giving birth at home, which had been the practice in earlier centuries, was partially supplanted from about 1700 onwards by the establishment of specialist hospitals like those adopted on the Continent, and with the same unfortunate consequences.[28] Confinements took place in prestigious teaching hospitals, like Queen Charlotte's, founded in 1752, or 'lying-in' (maternity) hospitals, like the British Lying-in Hospital in Endell Street, Covent Garden, opened in 1749. However, the cross-infection that occurred in these establishments had unforeseen and tragic consequences. In his analysis of their performance, William Farr, who was a seminal influence as a campaigning statistician,[29] wrote in 1870: 'Contrary to expectations, the advantages these institutions offered were over-balanced by one dread drawback; the mortality of mothers was not diminished; nay it became in some cases excessive; in others appalling.'[30]

He later put the problem in more dramatic terms when he compared the lying-in hospitals with the warning over the entrance to Dante's *Inferno*, suggesting that 'Lasciate ogni speranza voi ch-entrate' (abandon hope all ye who enter here) would have been as appropriate over their open doors as it was over the gloomy underworld of the great Italian poet. He also added his own considerable weight to the growing campaign for the proper training of midwives, commenting that 'until lately it was assumed that midwives were born, not made'.[31] At about the same time an even more influential voice was arriving at similar conclusions. Florence Nightingale's record as a nurse has overshadowed her remarkable achievements as a statistician. As a young woman she received an excellent mathematical training from her father and aunt and made use of this knowledge to campaign for sanitary improvements in hospitals, including maternity services. In 1858 she became the first woman to be elected to the Royal Statistical Society and herself invented a type of histogram, a *polar area chart* to highlight sources of patient mortality. In 1871, in her *Introductory Notes on Lying-in Institutions*, she demonstrated that there was a close relationship between the number of surgical cases in a hospital and the number of cases of puerperal fever; and, moreover, that the greater the number of births in a hospital, the greater the *proportion* of cases of the fatal condition. The clear implication was that puerperal fever took advantage of opportunities for cross-infection both where surgery was taking place and where the number of births was high.[32]

The figures spoke for themselves. The mortality in English maternity clinics mirrored those that Semmelweis had encountered in Vienna. In the 1860s in King's College Hospital the figure was 33 per 1,000 births; in Queen Charlotte's it was 42 per 1,000 births; while for a lying-in hospital it was only 14 per 1,000 births. In the hospitals, as in Semmelweis's clinic, doctors passed from patient to patient, spreading infection as they did so. In the lying-in hospitals, midwives had contact with fewer patients and did not perform autopsies. For births at home, where there was little danger of cross-infection, supervised by one of the very few qualified midwives, the figure fell to less than 2 per 1,000 births.[33] In the words of a later author:

> The safest way for a woman in London to be delivered, *regardless of social class*, was at home by a trained member of the Royal Maternity Charity or a trained midwife. The most dangerous by a long measure was in the wards of a prestigious hospital such as Queen Charlotte's, where the mortality was ten or more times as high.[34]

The idea that cleanliness was an essential feature of hospitals was not new. Florence Nightingale's principal contribution to the reduction of mortality in her hospital at Scutari during the Crimean War was to ensure that, as far as her resources allowed, the wounded rested between clean linen, in clean wards, with clean dressings. To these measures her fellow-nurse and rival Mary Seacole added adequate nutrition, but it was many years before a wide acceptance of Louis Pasteur's germ theories of disease propagation led doctors to acknowledge that their hands needed to be as clean as a hospital's linen.

Dr Aveling's research revealed that the first proposals to license midwives dated from medieval times and arose from the fact that midwives were often called upon to baptise infants, especially if the babies were in danger of dying before they could be taken to a priest. The church allowed this, though midwives were enjoined not to use 'witchcraft, charms, sorcery or prayers' unless they were approved by the Catholic Church.[35] In 1552, in his *Breviary of Health*, a former Carthusian monk called Andrew Boorde proposed that bishops be given the authority to license midwives. An Act of 1511 had authorised bishops to license physicians and surgeons. Boorde (*c*. 1490–1536) had studied medicine on the Continent and was a confidant of Henry VIII's minister Thomas Cromwell, to whom he sent some rhubarb seeds he collected during his continental travels, thereby introducing the plant to England. One of the first bishops to issue licences to midwives was Edmund Bonner (1500–69), bishop of

Mary Seacole (*c.* 1805–81) was born in Jamaica in about 1805, the daughter of a black Jamaican woman and, according to her own autobiography, *Wonderful Adventures of Mrs Seacole in Many Lands* (1857), a Scottish soldier called Grant. Her mother ran a boarding house for British soldiers and sailors and was a 'doctress' or practitioner of traditional local medicines, knowledge she passed on to Mary. Mary married Edwin Seacole, a godson of Lord Nelson, in 1836. Edwin died in 1844, after which Mary visited her brother in Panama, where she was credited with combating a cholera epidemic by the application of herbal remedies. In 1855 she offered her services as a nurse in the Crimea, and, when her offer was turned down by Florence Nightingale (who seems to have regarded her as not much more than a brothel-keeper), Mary travelled to the Crimea itself at her own expense. There she often braved the gunfire of the front line while running her 'British Hotel' near Sebastopol, which provided clean accommodation and nourishing food, much of it given free of charge to those who could not afford to pay. Bankrupted by this enterprise, she returned to Britain a heroine, her efforts applauded by William Howard Russell of *The Times*, who wrote the preface to her autobiography, and by *Punch*, which composed verses in her honour. She was rescued from bankruptcy by an appeal orchestrated by *The Times* and died in 1881, the subject of laudatory obituaries. A Blue Plaque marks her residence at 157 George Street, London W1.

London, commonly known as 'Bloody Bonner'. His zeal for opposing Catholic doctrines during the reign of Henry VIII was exceeded only by his enthusiasm for upholding them during the reign of Mary and for burning heretics who disagreed with him. In 1567 a midwife called Eleanor Plead was thus licensed, having taken an oath in which she undertook not to dismember babies, pull off their heads or substitute one child for another – an interesting reflection on the practices of the time. She also agreed to baptise in the name of the Father, the Son and the Holy Ghost. At this time such instructions as existed on the subject of midwifery were written in Latin. The nature of the subject was thought to be too delicate for an English translation to be made, since such a text might fall into the hands of male readers and inflame their passions in an inappropriate way!

Forty years after Bloody Bonner, Peter Chamberlen, who attended James I's queen, Anne of Denmark, petitioned the King 'that some order may be settled by the State for the instruction and civil government of midwives'. Chamberlen was one of a family of 'men-midwives' who were doubtfully credited with the invention of a secret device, possibly a forceps of some kind, which supposedly aided deliveries in difficult cases.[36] Such was the mystery surrounding this instrument that, during delivery, the mother was shrouded in sheets so that the device was hidden from her and the secret remained safe within the family.[37] One cannot help reflecting that the precautions may have been unnecessary, since the mother presumably had other things on her mind at the time. Chamberlen's nephew, also called Peter, was a physician who in the 1640s tried to organise midwives into a 'company' headed by him, but his initiative was frustrated by the opposition of his fellow-physicians. During the Commonwealth period he looked forward to the restoration of bishops with the authority to license midwives as Bonner had done. The practice of licensing by bishops resumed after the Restoration of Charles II and continued into the eighteenth century. Similar proposals to create a formal organisation for midwives followed in the next 200 years, none of them drawing on official support and most of them arousing the hostility of the medical profession, who saw the establishment of midwifery as a respectable, knowledgeable profession as a threat to their livelihoods.

In his 1872 text Aveling had recommended that a course of lectures and supervised practice should be undertaken by midwives, who would then be required to pass written and oral examinations administered by the Obstetrical Society of London, commenting rather condescendingly that women must pass the same examinations as men. The Society was one of the products of the 1858 Medical Act, which was passed to govern entry into the medical profession and, in particular, to exclude the quack doctors who preyed upon unsuspecting patients. For the first time a regulatory body, the General Medical Council, was set up to maintain standards and to strike from its register any practitioners who failed to meet them. Aveling further argued that, once the midwives had reached the required standard, they should be registered by the General Medical Council, thereby ensuring that this doctor-dominated body would exercise control over entry to the profession. In the words of the GMC's resolution: 'Midwives were practitioners *to a certain extent* of a branch of surgery and medicine' (emphasis added). Aveling concluded: 'The state will not allow a man who knows nothing of navigation to have the management of a ship at sea, but a woman who is utterly ignorant of midwifery is permitted to take charge of another during labour – a period in her voyage through life in which fatal accidents are most likely to occur.'[38]

Sophia Jex-Blake (1840–1912) was the daughter of a successful barrister who was, with difficulty, persuaded to allow his daughter to attend a teacher training college and to teach in Germany and the United States, where she was impressed by experiments with co-education and by the fact that women could work as doctors. She attended Edinburgh University medical school with her friend Edith Pechy, where they passed the examinations but were refused admission to the degrees they had earned. The British Medical Association therefore refused to register them as doctors. A change in the law in 1876 encouraged medical schools to award to women the same qualifications as men, and, by this means, Sophia qualified as a doctor through the Irish College of Physicians. She joined Elizabeth Garrett Anderson and Thomas Huxley ('Darwin's bulldog') to establish a medical school for women in London and later moved to Edinburgh, where she built a successful medical practice. She joined the campaign for women's suffrage, in which she remained active until her death in 1912.

Four years after Aveling's book had been published, in 1876, the Royal College of Surgeons introduced a Diploma in Midwifery. The formidable feminist Sophia Jex-Blake and her friend and fellow-campaigner Edith Pechy applied to follow the programme, whereupon the examiners resigned. Nevertheless the General Medical Council agreed to register suitably qualified women, and by 1880 the names of sixteen women had been entered on the British Medical Register.

ZEPHERINA VEITCH

In the years that followed, the cause of trained, registered midwives was to be taken up by a number of determined women. The most prominent of these was Zepherina Veitch (1836–94), who was born in Sopley, near Christchurch, Hampshire, the daughter of a Scottish clergyman called William Douglas Veitch, who had originally come from Sanquhar, near Dumfries in Scotland. She was descended from James Veitch, Lord Elliock (1712–93), a Scottish judge who had been a confidant of Frederick the Great of Prussia.[39] Zepherina's father served as a curate in the parish of Sopley from 1832 to 1841. She later told a Parliamentary Select Committee that her interest in midwifery had been aroused by her experiences of visiting the poor in her father's parish and observing that many women dated the onset of lifelong ill health to the experiences undergone in childbirth.[40] Painful vaginal infections, prolapsed uterus and embarrassing urinary conditions could lead to lifelong illness and social isolation.

Zepherina's family had a substantial estate at Eliock House[41] just outside Sanquhar, Dumfries, where Zepherina may have spent some of her childhood, but she also spent some of her early years in Palestine, where her father worked as a clergyman.[42] In 1862 the family moved to London, when the Revd Veitch became the incumbent at St Saviour's, Paddington, and it was shortly after this that Zepherina began to train as a nurse, working at University College Hospital, King's College Hospital and St George's Hospital, which was at that time near Hyde Park Corner. While working at Kings College Hospital she met Professor Henry Smith, a distinguished surgeon whom she married in December 1876, and she also met Dr James Aveling, who was to become strongly associated with the movement to create midwifery as a profession. She worked as a Red Cross nurse during the 1870–1 Franco-Prussian war and wrote of her experiences during that grim campaign in a series of letters to her sister, which were published after her death.[43] Her years in Palestine appear to have involved some straitened circumstances, since her sister observed after her death that they had prepared her for the rigours of the battlefield.[44] However, the experience of war seems to have sharpened Zepherina's appetite, since in one of her letters from France she explained that she and her colleagues were eating heavily 'all day on the principle of the Australians'!

By 1871 she was a sister at Charing Cross Hospital, where she observed that expectant mothers had to choose between paying the substantial sum of a guinea to have their baby delivered by a doctor or entrust themselves to a 'midwife' – a title that could be assumed with no qualifications. At this time she wrote a *Handbook for Nurses for the Sick*, which contained the stern advice: 'Do not undertake the work with any romantic ideas of being a ministering angel.' She was also a very early follower of the ideas of Ignaz Semmelweis and Joseph Lister on hygiene in hospitals, writing in 1870 that sponges used in operating theatres 'should be well washed in a strong solution of carbolic acid to free them from all impurities' and stressing that a sponge should be used only once during an operation unless it was thoroughly washed.[45] This was only three years after Lister had announced the results of his use of carbolic acid in operations and at a time when his ideas were not accepted by most of his fellow-doctors. This emphasis on hygiene was to be critical in the conquest of childbed fever.

Zepherina moved from Charing Cross to the 'British Lying-in (maternity) hospital' at 24 Endell Street, which had been opened in 1749 for 'the distressed poor – married women only' near Covent Garden, a voluntary hospital where she worked and trained as a midwife.[46] In January 1873 she became the tenth diplomate of the Obstetrical Society of London, the diploma declaring that she was 'a skilled midwife, competent to attend natural labours', for which she had had to complete a course of study involving formal lectures, a written and oral examination and attendance at twenty-five births.

The 1858 Act required medical practitioners to have knowledge of obstetrics as well as medicine and surgery and had the perverse outcome of encouraging doctors to safeguard their obstetric practices by excluding experienced and qualified midwives from practising their skill. The fact that, after a long struggle by women like Elizabeth Garrett Anderson, the General Medical Council had admitted women to the profession did not mean that they were ready to see their guinea fees diluted by the intrusion of Zepherina and her followers.

While working from the Endell Street hospital, Zepherina described the circumstances in which she delivered a baby in one of the poorest districts of the capital: 'The mother was in the direst poverty and there was nothing in the house larger than an Australian meat tin in which the baby could have its first wash.'[47] In the meantime the great majority of women, who could not afford the doctors' fees, were attended by women with no qualifications at all, who were often little more than well-meaning charlatans and often much worse. The profession was lampooned by Charles Dickens in the person of the gossiping, gin-swilling Mrs Gamp of his 1843 novel *Martin Chuzzlewit* and her friend the pipe-smoking Betsy Prig, but they were not the worst of their kind. That honour falls to Elizabeth Brownrigg, who was executed at Tyburn in September 1767 for torturing to death her female apprentices. In the early part of the nineteenth century a midwife was often a widow, with children of her own, who would attend the woman in labour with concoctions of herbs and a drink called *caudle*: a drink of warm wine or ale, sweetened with herbs or sugar, which were reputed to promote labour. She would be accompanied by *gossips*, women who witnessed the birth and attested that the baby was the mother's and not a changeling.[48] These women, if they could read, might be guided by *The Ladies' Dispensatory, or Every Woman her own Physician*, published in 1739, which recommended the administration to the mother of a cordial containing liquid laudanum (a derivative of opium) after birth, following which the baby should be washed in small beer and butter. Warm wine should be poured down the baby's throat or squirted up its nostrils, and laudanum should be given to the baby if it was peevish.[49] In the middle of the nineteenth century the status of midwife was summed up by the writer Harriet Martineau. Writing in the *Edinburgh Review* in 1851, she commented that 'the stigma attached to the profession was such that educated entrants to it were rare indeed'. The universities of Oxford and Cambridge declined to teach obstetrics as part of their medical degrees until the 1840s, since anything connected with midwifery was 'an occupation degrading to a gentleman'.[50]

WOMEN AND WORK

The campaign to improve the standards of care in childbirth must be seen in the context of the broader movement to improve the status and the employment prospects of women in Victorian England, a movement in which Louisa Hubbard (1836–1906) played a central role. Louisa was born in St Petersburg to a wealthy merchant. Resisting marriage, in her own words she 'gradually drifted into the position of wishing to champion the cause of the unmarried woman, and from the first I refused to apologise for her existence'.[51] Her independent means enabled her to devote her life to campaigning for women whose circumstances were less fortunate than her own, particularly women of education whose career options were limited by the conventions of the time to marriage or to the role of governesses, in which capacity they would be impoverished gentlefolk dependent upon the patronage of well-to-do families.

In October 1875 she had founded, and largely financed, the *Woman's Gazette*, which was, in the words of the editor's first leader, 'primarily intended to furnish the latest information upon all work, remunerative or otherwise, needing the services of women and upon the ways and means of obtaining employment therein'.[52] The *Gazette* changed its name in 1880 to *Work and Leisure*, but both titles were devoted to promoting the cause of employment for educated, middle-class women. Every issue of the *Gazette* explored nursing as a career for educated women, the emphasis being on the word *educated*, since, despite the activities of people like Florence Nightingale, nursing, like midwifery, was still not regarded by many such women as altogether respectable. In February 1879 women were also encouraged to take up chiropody. Educated, middle-class women were particularly welcome as asylum nurses, since, in the

Harriet Martineau (1802–76) was the daughter of a textile manufacturer from Norwich who resisted the attempts of her parents to marry her off but benefited from her father's decision to give her a better education than was offered to most of her contemporaries. From an early age she suffered from deafness. Her father's death in 1826 encouraged her to support herself by writing articles for the *Globe* and other publications. She first came to public notice as the author of an article entitled 'On Female Education' and later turned to writing books on such subjects as politics and economics. Her text *Illustrations of Political Economy*, published in 1834, was a popular success and gave her the financial security that enabled her to turn her attention to campaigning for such causes as the abolition of slavery; the rights of trade unions to organise and to take strike action; and the entitlement of women to receive an education. Her 1837 treatise *Society in America* was critical of the United States and made her very unpopular there. In 1845 she moved to Ambleside in the Lake District, where she was to be seen smoking a pipe, brandishing her ear trumpet and walking the fells. In 1855 she wrote a *Complete Guide to the English Lakes*. She found herself in opposition to her neighbour and contemporary William Wordsworth over the future of the Lake District. He had written his own *Guide to the Lakes* and opposed the coming of the railway to Windermere, which would, he feared, lead to the invasion of his beloved lakes by day trippers from Yorkshire and Lancashire. She believed that the railways would bring much-needed prosperity to the rural poor, arguing that the Lake District landscape brought 'rock for foundations, the purest air and the amplest supply of running water; yet people live in stench, huddled together in cabins and almost without water'.

words of the chaplain of one of the establishments, 'good breeding and refinement would exercise beneficial influence' on the inmates.[53]

A series of articles explained what was involved in nursing and how qualifications were obtained. The process was expensive as well as arduous, as set out in May 1876, when the magazine ran a feature on nurse training at the Royal Free Hospital, then in Gray's Inn Road. Nurses would pay a fee of £30 a year (excluding board and lodging) and would work a fourteen-hour day shift or a ten-hour night shift, with short meal breaks. 'No cooking or scrubbing' was required, but they did have to attend church on Sundays. After one year a certificate of competence would be issued.[54] The £30 fee ensured that only middle-class women would be able to afford the training. The articles provoked a lively correspondence on nurse training, one of the correspondents being Zepherina Veitch, who in April 1876 wrote to reassure a previous correspondent that 'the results of prolonged and severe study' upon young ladies' brains would not be harmful!

This exchange of letters is an interesting reflection upon contemporary views of women's intellectual capacity, which was echoed in a later article entitled 'A Few Thoughts on the Recreations of Girls' Schools'. At a time when the concept of muscular Christianity and the code of games were in the ascendant at public schools like Rugby, the *Woman's Gazette* reflected anxiously on the effects of outdoor activities for girls, with the attendant 'risk of catching cold'. Badminton, tennis, croquet and rounders were considered suitable, while the *Lancet* was cited as an authority for the fact that skating was also recommended, though it was ruled out for 'delicate girls', whose exercise should take place only indoors. It is hard to avoid the conclusion that women (at least middle-class women) were really regarded as a separate species from men. Two years later an even more extraordinary (to twenty-first-century readers) article headlined 'Intellectual Education as a Preparation for Domestic Duties' asked 'how far such an education unfits for the domestic duties?' The article concluded that 'intellectual education does not disqualify a woman for domestic duties' BUT 'it may indeed, if carried too far, prevent her from acquiring competent skill for humbler duties or create a distaste for them'. How far was 'too far' was not specified.

The 1870 Education Act had made the first serious attempt to provide universal elementary education. It is therefore not surprising that the *Woman's Gazette* encouraged women to train as teachers with articles like 'Elementary Teaching: A Profession for a Gentlewoman',[55] and to this end Louisa Hubbard founded Bishop Otter's teacher training college in Chichester. She also supported the Ladies' Dwelling Company, which, in 1887, purchased Sloane Gardens House in Lower Sloane Street and converted it into flats where single, middle-class women could live unchaperoned yet respectably.[56] A Kindergarten training school in Tavistock Place was recommended as offering instruction, leading to the examinations of the Froebel Institute. The magazine also contained many advertisements for employment in girls' public day schools – forerunners of the more ambitious foundations like Roedean, Queenswood and Berkhamsted, which were founded in the 1880s with the aim of providing something more than an elementary education for the daughters of middle-class families. The headmistress of a girls' school could earn the respectable salary of £250 plus a capitation fee for pupils in excess of 100.[57] In October 1875 a more exotic note was struck when an advertisement appeared for an English teacher at a girls' school in Beirut at a salary of £30 per annum with bed and board provided. Applications were to be made to Mrs Henry Smith (formerly Zepherina Veitch), so the contact may have arisen from contacts made during Zepherina's childhood in the Middle East.[58] A more ambitious establishment still was the London School of Medicine for Women, which had been founded in 1874 by a number of determined women, including Elizabeth Garrett Anderson and Elizabeth Blackwell, both of whom lectured there. It offered a three-year lecture cycle with a view to enabling women to achieve the qualifications that Elizabeth Garrett Anderson had gained in the face of such difficulties a few years earlier. In January 1878 the magazine was delighted to report that women would henceforth be admitted to the degrees of London University on the same terms as men 'a truly historical [*sic*] epoch in the history of female education'.[59]

Besides the *Gazette* itself, Louisa Hubbard also published, from 1875, the *Year Book of Women's Work*, which was prefaced by the slightly puzzling dedication 'To the Men of England, in full reliance upon their Chivalry as Men and their Justice as Englishmen', and included a list of occupations suitable for women at all levels of skill and class from 'cigar rolling' and 'collier women' to book-keeping and the medical profession, though Louisa added that 'great efforts have been made to exclude women from entering the medical profession on the same footing as men'. If all else failed, emigration was recommended. This was followed by an article extolling the 'London School of Medicine for Women'.[60] Midwifery was particularly recommended as being 'more remunerative than nursing', and the Endell Street hospital where Zepherina Veitch had trained was one of the establishments recommended. The pupil midwife paid a fee of ten guineas plus fifteen shillings a week bed and board and would attend lectures and births for three months under the supervision of the Matron before undergoing an oral examination before two physicians. However, this notice was followed by another to the effect that the full year's training offered at La Maternité hospital at Port Royal, Paris, offered a more thorough training for the French equivalent – *une sage femme de la première classe.*

'WE NEVER MENTIONED THE WORD MIDWIFE'

One of the regular correspondents to the *Woman's Gazette* was Zepherina Veitch, who commented regularly on the training of nurses and in December 1876 contributed a long article on her experiences in obtaining qualifications in midwifery. Louisa Hubbard's interest in the cause of midwives arose from a belief that midwifery offered another outlet for the talents and energies of educated women. In the autumn of 1881 James Aveling, Zepherina Smith and Mrs Evans, Matron of Sheffield's Jessop Hospital for Woman founded by Aveling, met and discussed the problems associated with unqualified midwives. The meeting took place at the London offices of *Work and Leisure*, whose editor, Louisa Hubbard, was also present. The doctor, the matron, the midwife and the journalist agreed to form the Matron's Aid or Trained Midwives Registration Society, whose prospectus was published in the October 1881 edition of *Work and Leisure*. It explained that: 'Out of 1,250,000 births which take place in Great Britain annually it is calculated that only about three in ten are at present attended by medical men', the rest being 'attended by women only. These women are under no control or regulation whatever in England.'

As previously observed, more than 4,000 mothers died in childbirth annually, while as many as 16 per cent of babies died shortly after birth. The writer of the prospectus, almost certainly Louisa Hubbard herself, estimated that 10,000 qualified midwives would be needed if each birth were to be attended by a qualified person, whereas 'only eighty women at present hold a certificate of any value'. Coincidentally, the figure of 10,000 was the same as had been estimated by the London Obstetrical Society in 1862 and, even more strangely, the same as the deficit in numbers of midwives calculated by the Royal College of Midwives in 2005.

This was not the first occasion on which attempts had been made to improve the training of midwives or to restrict entry to the midwifery profession to those who were suitably qualified. In 1861 Florence Nightingale, whose concern for better practices in maternity care was noted earlier,[61] had opened an annex to Kings College Hospital to train midwives who would work among the poor. Candidates paid for board and lodging but the training was free, paid for from the proceeds of the Nightingale Fund, raised by Florence following her work in the Crimea. The school flourished for a while, helped by the fact that wealthy landowners paid for women from their communities to train as village midwives, but it closed in 1867 following several outbreaks of puerperal fever.[62] A Ladies Medical College had also flourished in Little Portland Street from the 1860s and had been welcomed by Dr William Farr, Chief Statistician to the Registrar of Births, Marriages and Deaths, who wrote in the *Lancet* welcoming the prospect of young, educated women replacing 'ignorant old women' in bringing children into the world.[63] Farr had long campaigned to reduce the high incidence of mortality associated with poor medical practices and insanitary conditions. However, the cost of following the Ladies Medical College's courses (£80 a year) was beyond the means of most who wished to qualify, and the eventual success of women in gaining access to the medical schools of the teaching hospitals rendered it no longer necessary.

The cumbersome title, Matron's Aid or Trained Midwives Registration Society, was due to embarrassment over the use of the word 'midwife', which, despite its innocent Anglo-Saxon etymology ('with women'), was associated with the process of childbirth, and therefore regarded as being little short of obscene. Louisa Hubbard herself, despite her robust attitude to other matters concerning women, and her regard for midwifery as a profession, shared these fine feelings. On one occasion she told a midwife: 'My dear, I wish there was another word for you; it would be so awkward if we used it just when the footman came in to put on coals.'[64] In the early days the society's magazine, *Nursing Notes*, was posted to subscribers in stout brown envelopes in case any man or child in the subscriber's household should inadvertently see the offending word 'midwife' on the cover of the publication. In the words of the society's first secretary, 'We never mentioned the word *midwife* in those days without a blush', and in its early days it was referred to as the Matrons Aid Society or the MAS.

One of the earliest supporters of the founders of the society was Florence Nightingale herself, who wrote to Zepherina on 1 September 1881: 'I wish you success from the bottom of my heart if, as I cannot doubt, your wisdom and energy work out a scheme by which to support the *deadly* want of training among women practising midwifery in England.'[65]

Florence Nightingale had herself encountered the kind of opposition that Zepherina and her colleagues would now face when, on her return from the Crimea, she had set about improving the standards of education for nurses. Her celebrity had enabled her to raise the enormous sum of £45,000 to fund the Nightingale training school at St Thomas's Hospital, but her reputation did nothing to protect her from the suspicions of doctors who were worried that trained nurses might threaten their status and livelihoods. Mr J.F. South, senior consultant surgeon at St Thomas's, declared that nurses were 'in the position of house-maids' and that 'this proposed hospital nurse training scheme has not met with the approbation or support of the medical profession'. Despite such opposition, the Nightingale School opened on 24 June 1860 with fifteen candidates who followed a year's course including lectures from a professor and practical work under the direction of a head nurse ('sister'), who had been taught how to train. Training, board, lodging, washing facilities and uniform were paid for from the Nightingale fund, which also made a grant of £10 a year for personal expenses. The Nightingale School is still training nurses in the twenty-first century, but the initial hostility towards it of the medical profession was a harbinger of the problems that would be faced by the determined band of women who now set about turning midwifery from an occupation into a profession. ﹅

THE MIDWIVES' INSTITUTE AND TRAINED NURSES' CLUB

Twenty-six women joined the Matron's Aid or Trained Midwives' Registration Society, whose first secretary, Rosalind Paget (1855–1948), a young, newly qualified midwife, began to organise monthly lectures and to establish a library, first at 22 Berners Street and later in Buckingham Street in houses earlier occupied by Peter the Great, Samuel Pepys and Charles Dickens and, in fiction, by David Copperfield. Rosalind Paget was a major influence in the establishment of the society in its first difficult years and subsidised its early publications from her own pocket. She was the very attractive daughter of a barrister who, contrary to the wishes of her father, trained as a nurse at Westminster Hospital and the Royal Liverpool Infirmary. It was in Liverpool that her uncle, William Rathbone, had worked with Florence Nightingale to found Britain's first school of nursing. Like Zepherina Veitch, Rosalind Paget had worked at the Endell Street hospital and gained the certificate of the London Obstetrical Society. She had attended an early meeting at Zepherina's house in Wimpole Street, where she had not been impressed either by the ambitions of the society or by the euphemisms associated with its activities. Rosalind made it clear that she was interested in joining the society only if it had some declared educational purpose, so when the founders agreed to organise a course of lectures and invited her to become the first secretary, she could hardly refuse. The objects of the society were to raise the standards of midwifery; to petition Parliament for the regulation of the profession and the compulsory registration of midwives; and to support these aims with lectures and a library.

The lectures would be followed by a discussion of the issues raised, and both the lecture and the discussions would be published in *Nursing Notes*, financed by Rosalind herself – the first such journal in the world aimed specifically at female medical practitioners. This was the pattern followed by other learned societies of the time, such as the Institution of Civil Engineers, whose lectures and debates were published in the Institution's *Proceedings*. However, the continuing opposition of the medical profession made itself felt early. On 8 February 1888 a Dr Allchin wrote a letter to the *Lancet* observing that 'it would seem that there exists in this city a midwives' institute and trained nurses' club' and complaining that the publication of the institute's lectures in *Nursing Notes* amounted to advertising, a practice contrary to medical ethics. Perhaps Dr Allchin was right to be alarmed about the 'advertising', because the membership of the society rose rapidly to 170 and changed its name to the Midwives' Institute and Trained Nurses' Club. It is the ancestor of the Royal College of Midwives, which gained its royal charter in 1947.

Following one of the early meetings, *Nursing Notes* observed that 'England remains notorious for being the only civilised country where unlicensed and uncertificated women can practice midwifery' and added that veterinary surgeons were better regulated than were midwives. A later edition reported the views expressed by James Aveling, who was one of the strongest advocates of trained midwives. It nevertheless recorded that 'Dr Aveling appeared to be in favour of the employment of an inferior class of women as midwives, especially in country districts, one of his reasons being that a more educated woman would object to perform such humble household services as might be required in a cottage household'.[66]

The publication acknowledged the support the profession had received from Dr Aveling while noting that his proposal would 'combine the two professions of charwoman and midwife'. Despite this somewhat condescending attitude from one of its warmest supporters, in 1890 the institute announced that it would offer its own courses for the examinations of the Obstetrical Society, and within a few years a thousand people had obtained the qualification. The candidates had to provide a 'certificate of moral character', supervise twenty-five labours, complete a course of lectures and pass written and oral examinations, a blueprint that is recognisable in the training of midwives in the twenty-first century.

Attempts to improve the quality of midwifery care would have limited success as long as unqualified women could exercise the calling, so a campaign now began to exclude the Sairey Gamps who had given the profession a bad name. A start of sorts was made in 1813, when the Society of Apothecaries, whose members were able to practise medicine, petitioned Parliament for midwives to be licensed by doctors: a proposal that would have raised the standards of the profession while ensuring that the practitioners remained firmly under the control of the medical profession.

In May 1889 Louisa Hubbard organised a meeting that was attended by a number of titled ladies and by other prominent women such as Mrs Oscar Wilde with a view to promoting a Parliamentary Bill to require that midwives be trained and registered. Hannah de Rothschild, Lady Rosebery, wife of the future Prime Minister, sent her apologies, but the group had sufficient political influence to ensure that, later that year, *Nursing Notes* was able to report that the institute was supporting a Parliamentary Bill for the registration of midwives. It was introduced to Parliament by Henry Fell Pease, Liberal MP for Cleveland, as a Private Member's Bill. It was the first of eight such bills that were drafted and that failed. Pease's Bill had the support of the General Medical Council, and the consultant obstetricians of the London teaching hospitals, though some members of the medical profession would continue to view registered midwives as a threat to their livelihoods. The bill was debated on 21 May 1890 and was opposed by Dr Tanner, MP for Cork, who spoke for his profession when he complained that 'if the Bill passes into law it will deprive many a medical man of the conduct of these cases of midwifery'.[67] At least Dr Tanner was being honest about his motives. Opposition came too from other quarters. When the formidable Mrs Bedford Fenwick founded the British Nurses' Association in 1887 she described midwives as a 'historical curiosity'. Her main aim in life appears to have been to ensure that no other organisation would present any obstacle to her own attempts to maximise recruitment to the organisation she had founded. Charles Bradlaugh (1833–91), the radical MP who had recently won his long struggle to be admitted to the House of

Commons as an atheist, opposed the measure on the strange grounds that it was interfering with 'the liberty of the subject' and eventually the bill foundered owing to lack of parliamentary time.

Similar attempts failed throughout the 1890s, including one promoted in 1890 by the British Medical Association itself, whose tone reflected the misgivings still felt by doctors, especially among provincial GPs. The bill would have allowed 'midwifery nurses [to] act under the supervision of a doctor', thus ensuring that doctors would remain paramount in the processes of childbirth. Zepherina Veitch and Rosalind Paget went before the Select Committee that was considering the Midwives' Registration Bill in May 1892 and told its members of the consequences of using untrained midwives, arguing that the title 'midwife' should be restricted to qualified practitioners.[68] Rosalind explained that in France only qualified practitioners were allowed to act as *sages femmes*, the best of these being 'a very superior article to anything we have in England', and claiming that many unqualified midwives in England 'bury, as stillborn, children that are nothing of the kind'. Moreover, in France the services of a doctor cost much less than in England. The French writer Hippolyte Taine, in his *Notes sur l'Angleterre* published in 1872, commented with surprise that a visit from a doctor in London cost one guinea (a week's wage for a working-class family) – about five times the cost of a doctor in Paris.[69] In an attempt to placate the anxieties of doctors who feared loss of fees, Zepherina argued that a qualified midwife would be much more likely to recognise problems and to send for a doctor than would an unqualified one, citing in evidence her own experience of having recognised a case of Bright's disease. Dr Aveling told the committee that the cost of a doctor was beyond the means of poorer families, a situation made worse by the fact that a nurse would also have to be engaged 'to wash the baby', which was beneath the dignity of a doctor. Moreover, a midwife would charge a fee of between half a crown and ten shillings, a sum, in Dr Aveling's words, 'quite inadequate to remunerate the services of educated gentlemen' – that is to say doctors.[70] The Registrar General the previous year had recorded 4,255 deaths of women in childbirth, the rate being 1 in 200 for all births but only 1 in 650 when the women were attended by trained midwives.

'AN UNQUALIFIED EVIL'

Dr Robert Rentoul was the principal opponent of the Midwives' Registration Bill, arguing 'the existence of this class of [certificated] practitioners of midwifery to be an unqualified evil' and suggesting that they be replaced by trained nurses, who would, of course, have to work under the guidance of a doctor at all times. A member of the committee, Dr Farquharson, who had been persuaded by the arguments of Rosalind Paget, drew attention to the superior training in childbirth that midwives received compared with that of doctors: 'I should rather trust my wife to a woman who had attended twenty cases [i.e. births] and three months' lectures than to a man who had attended only six cases and three months' lectures.' Despite the strictures of Dr Rentoul, the committee concluded that there was 'serious and unnecessary loss of life and health, and permanent injury to both mother and child in the treatment of childbirth'. Proposals for legislation swiftly followed but were lost when Parliament was dissolved.

Further arguments raged over whether midwives should be registered by local authorities or by a central, national body and, if the latter, whether midwives should be represented on it. In 1898 *Nursing Notes* recorded, with a hint of despair, that 'a sort of triangular duel is going on between those who desire to see midwives under proper regulations, those who desire to see them suppressed and those who pay a very strong respect to the liberty of the subject. It is impossible to please everybody.' An attempt was made by some doctors to substitute the term 'obstetric nurse' for that of 'midwife', since nurses traditionally worked under the direction of doctors whereas midwives, for normal births, worked independently, but this late rally by the medical profession was repelled.[71] Altogether eight bills were drafted and failed before, on 31 July 1902, the Midwives Bill received the royal assent. It specified that, from April 1910, no woman should attend a birth for payment unless she was certified, having followed a course of study similar to that of Zepherina Veitch: a course of lectures, written and oral examinations, and attendance, under supervision, at a specified number of births. This pattern is still followed today. The eight-year interval was intended to allow a sufficient number of midwives to be trained. *Bona fide* midwives would be allowed to practise in the meantime, these being women who had no formal training but had satisfied a local Medical Officer that they had practised successfully for at least one year. Certificates were to be issued by a central Midwives Board, on which doctors would be in the majority but on which midwives would be represented. The certificates continued to emphasise, as advocated by Zepherina Veitch,[72] that midwives were qualified to attend *natural* labours, anything untoward requiring the services of a doctor. The board, with its majority of doctors, further specified in its first guidelines that midwives should not be taught treatment for haemorrhages or the feeding of infants after ten days: they were to remain the preserve of doctors. The recently established boards to regulate dentists and nurses did not have a predominance of doctors, presumably because doctors did not regard these practitioners as being such a threat to their incomes.

In 1905, three years after the Midwives Bill had become law, it was estimated that there were almost 10,000 midwives who had received certificates either from the Obstetrical Society of London or from hospitals and 12,000 *bona fide* midwives. The Midwives Bill was too late for one of its strongest advocates. Zepherina Veitch had died in February 1894 at her home at Summerhill, Horsell, near Woking in Surrey, leaving one daughter. Her obituary referred to her long campaign for the training and registration of midwives, which had led her to give lectures on the subject at many places, including the Universities of Oxford and Cambridge. The writer described her as 'practically the Miss Nightingale of Midwives'.[73] The effects of her campaign may be seen in the decline in the number of deaths attributable to childbed fever,[74] and in the infant mortality rate in the years that followed the passing of the bill. Death rates in the population as a whole had declined steadily from 39 per 1,000 in 1840 to 12 per 1,000 in 1903. Among infants, the mortality rate had remained obstinately at about 15 per 1,000 throughout this period and did not fall below the 1840 level until the five years following the passage of the bill, when it reached 13.8 per 1,000. From then it was downhill all the way. The work of others like Sir John Simon and other campaigners for sanitary reform in helping to achieve this had, of course, been very influential, but the improvements in midwifery care that resulted from the campaigns of Zepherina Veitch and her colleagues to ensure appropriate training and registration for midwives were a decisive influence.

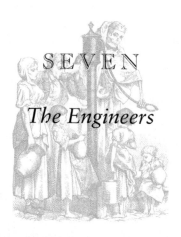

SEVEN

The Engineers

The engineers have always been the real sanitary reformers, as they are the originators of all onward movements; all their labours tend to the amelioration of their fellow-men.

(William Cubitt, Presidential Address to the Institution of Civil Engineers, 1850)

There were great difficulties with the plumbers.

(Obituary of water engineer Thomas Hawksley, 1893–4)

Although great differences of opinion existed, and continue to exist, as to the causes of the disease, yet an inspection of the houses in which deaths occurred was sufficient to show that, however occult might be the connection between death and defective drainage, the places formerly most favourable to the spread of disease became quite free from it, when afterwards properly drained.

(Joseph Bazalgette in an address to the Institution of Civil Engineers)

THE SCIENCE OF THE CIVIL ENGINEER

Previous chapters have indicated how modest was the contribution that the medical profession could make to improvements in the health of the population during Victoria's reign. In the absence, until late in the century, of any clear understanding of the causes of disease, physicians, with the exception of a few pioneers like John

Snow, did not even know what was making their patients ill. Moreover, even when the theories of John Snow, William Budd, William Farr, Robert Koch and Louis Pasteur had revealed the true causes of some epidemic diseases, doctors were still lacking in effective remedies for their patients. But, while the medical profession was relatively helpless in the face of disease, especially epidemic disease, there was another professional group who, by providing an adequate supply of fresh water for drinking, washing and cooking, and by protecting that water from contamination by sewage, were able to make a significant contribution to the health and welfare of their fellow humans. These were the civil engineers. The Victorian period is often celebrated for the spectacular achievements of engineers such as Isambard Kingdom Brunel and Robert Stephenson. But, while these were building the Great Western Railway or designing *The Rocket*, others, equally accomplished, were carrying out less visible but even more valuable work in protecting their fellow citizens from deadly diseases born of filth, squalor and pollution. This chapter will consider the work of these men, some of them almost forgotten by history, though they were not lacking in confidence, as is shown by the first of the quotations that head this chapter and that no doubt would have been warmly applauded by William Cubitt's audience. They may conveniently, if not quite legitimately, be divided into two categories: those who laid on the fresh water and those who made sure it stayed clean. The qualification stems from the fact that some of them were involved in both activities.

THE NEW RIVER

Sir Hugh Myddleton (*c.* 1560–1631) has a claim to be one of Britain's first water engineers, though he would be better described as an entrepreneur. He was certainly a precursor to the great Victorian water engineers. Before the Tudor period, London had depended for its water supplies on springs, wells and rivers like the Walbrook and Fleet. In the thirteenth century, a lead pipe was constructed to take water from Tyburn, near the present site of Marble Arch, to the Great Conduit in Cheapside, a considerable feat of engineering for its time. From the Great Conduit water was distributed in elm pipes, shaped like funnels so that the narrow end of one pipe fitted into the broad end of the next. In the centuries that followed, other conduits were built, their names still remembered in names like Conduit Street in Mayfair and Lambs Conduit Passage in Holborn. The conduits themselves became sociable places where citizens gathered to collect their water and chat to neighbours as they waited to draw their water, fisticuffs occasionally following as the conduit closed, usually at six o'clock, while people were still queuing. The conduits were later supplemented by ingenious devices designed to draw water from the river. The first of these was a waterwheel within an arch of London Bridge, built by a Dutchman (possibly a German) called Peter Morice. The wheel powered a pump that drove Thames water to premises in the City of London. In 1594 it was followed by a horse-driven pump installed just east of the present site of the Millennium Bridge by Bevis Bulmer, a mining engineer. It pumped water to London's first water tower, from which it, too, provided water throughout the City for any prepared to pay for the connection.

By the reign of Henry VIII it was clear that further supplies were required, but it was only in 1605 that the City Corporation secured the passage of the New River Act, which authorised the construction of a channel to bring water from chalk springs in the Chiltern Hills at Amwell, near Ware in Hertfordshire, to New River Head, close to the present site of Sadler's Wells Theatre. The construction of the New River was entrusted to Hugh Myddleton, a dealer in metals and MP for his native Denbighshire. Myddleton was chosen because his wealth and City connections enabled him to raise money to start the project, though to complete it he eventually had to sell some shares to King James I (known as 'the Crown Clog'), one of the few wise investments made by that improvident and usually impecunious monarch. The New River is 10 feet wide, 4 feet deep and 40 miles in length, as it follows a meandering and slowly descending contour from Amwell to Islington.

The terminus of the river, New River Head, was opened in a grand ceremony in September 1613, when water was first admitted to the company's reservoirs to be pumped through elm pipes to premises whose owners had paid for the connection. The elm pipes, similar in design to those used for the mediaeval Great Conduit, remained in use into the nineteenth century, and customers were supplied for a few hours each day, cisterns within houses being used to store water when the water was not flowing. One of the first customers to pay his 5s (25p) connection fee and the quarterly rate of 6s 8d (33p) was the father of John Milton. The company always enjoyed a reputation for good, clean water, despite well-founded suspicions that citizens whose dwellings were situated on its banks used it for doing their laundry, and it enjoyed a separate existence until 1902, when it passed into public ownership as part of the Metropolitan Water Board.

Competitors followed, quite slowly at first. In 1675 the York Buildings company constructed a water tower close to the present site of Charing Cross station from which to supply the royal quarter of St James and the West End, and in 1722 the Chelsea company began to supply customers in Westminster from an intake close to the present site of Chelsea Bridge. The Grand Junction, Lambeth, West Middlesex, Kent, Southwark and Vauxhall companies followed, the last two supplying premises south of the river, but it was not until 1806 that the New River company faced direct competition in its own bailiwick from the East London company. Price wars and worse followed as the two companies fought for each other's customers and occasionally damaged each other's pipes. In 1815 the two companies came to an agreement to divide their territory between them and eliminate destructive competition, but by this time concerns were beginning to emerge about the quality of London's water, especially that drawn from the Thames itself.

In that same year, 1815, a former prohibition on connecting house drains and cesspools to the public sewers was lifted, ensuring that from that date an ever-swelling tide of human waste would enter the sewers, the underground rivers such as the Fleet and the Thames itself. The processes by which the capital's drinking water was eventually protected from its own sewage will be discussed later in this chapter, but suffice it to say that, by the late 1820s, the situation was of sufficient concern to have attracted the attention of an MP and a pamphleteer. In 1828 a campaigner called John Wright published an inflammatory pamphlet of which we need only to read the lengthy title to understand its message: 'The Dolphin or Grand Junction Nuisance Proving that Several Thousand Families in

Westminster and its Suburbs are Supplied with Water in a State Offensive to the Sight, Disgusting to the Imagination and Destructive to Health'.[1] The pamphlet was dedicated to Sir Francis Burdett, MP, who informed Parliament that 'the water taken from the river Thames at Chelsea, being charged by the contents of the great common sewers, ought no longer to be taken up by any of the water companies'.[2] Burdett suggested, for the first time, that public

Sir Francis Burdett (1770–1844), a seasoned agitator, married wisely into the wealthy Coutts banking family, which gave him a degree of financial independence to pursue the causes that he embraced. He campaigned against the wars with revolutionary France, the suspension of Habeas Corpus and the treatment of 'political' prisoners. So effective was his activity in this area that he was barred from visiting any prisons. He was elected MP for Middlesex in 1802 and deprived of his seat after objections from opponents. Despite swearing to have nothing more to do with politics, he returned as MP for Westminster in 1807 after a duel with a rival whose candidature he had originally promoted. In 1809 he was committed to the Tower of London for supposedly infringing Parliamentary privilege and later gaoled for three months for agitation in connection with the Peterloo massacre of 1819, when a peaceful assembly in Manchester had been charged by cavalry on the orders of magistrates. He also advocated Catholic emancipation and Parliamentary reform, but, once these had been achieved, in 1829 and 1832 respectively, Burdett decided that things had gone too far. His reactionary views then caused him to be rejected by his Westminster constituents, whereupon he was adopted by a Tory constituency in Wiltshire. His daughter Angela Burdett-Coutts was also a reformer and is credited with the construction of model housing for working people in Bethnal Green and the establishment of drinking fountains in London to encourage temperance. Her activities are described in Chapter 2.

ownership of the companies was the only solution to London's water problems. The time for this novel idea had not yet come. Instead, the government of the day appointed a Royal Commission, the first of many that wrestled with the problem over the following decades.

Following Burdett's claims, the government asked the distinguished engineer Thomas Telford, aged seventy-one, to consider the problem, assisted by a chemist and by Dr Roget, a physician better known for his *Thesaurus*. The committee concluded that the Thames was no longer a safe source of drinking water and proposed that water be brought from the River Wandle in Surrey and from the Ver in Hertfordshire. The New River was identified as a supplier of safe water and Telford suggested that it be permitted to draw more water from the Lea and from wells on the Chiltern slopes. The cost of these measures was estimated, with confident precision, as amounting to £1,177,840, 16s 5d. No suggestions were forthcoming as to how this huge sum might be raised.

JAMES SIMPSON

In the meantime some more practical steps were being taken to clean up the existing water supply. In 1823 an engineer called James Simpson (1799–1869) succeeded his father Thomas as engineer to both the Chelsea and Lambeth water companies. In 1828 he built for the Chelsea company the world's first 'slow sand filter bed'. This consisted of a layer of fine sand beneath which were further layers of coarse sand, sea shells, gravel and bricks. At the bottom were pipes with small holes. Water was released on to the filter and made its way through the sand, the top inch of which filtered out impurities. The shells were designed to prevent the sand being washed into the pipes. The water then made its way through the gravel and bricks until it entered the pipes from which it passed to the reservoirs, cleansed of 95 per cent of its impurities. Virtually all the pollutants were trapped in the top inch of the sand layer (referred to as 'the slime layer'), which would regularly be removed and replaced with fresh sand. Simpson regarded his novel device as a physical filter, which it was.[3] It was not for many years that advances in chemistry and biology by scientists like Sir Edward

Frankland (1825–99) revealed that the bacteria in the bed made it a biological filter as well. Filter beds that are recognisably descended from Simpson's are still used. Simpson also persuaded both the companies he served to remove their reservoirs to Seething Wells, near Kingston-upon-Thames. There, in 1852, he installed sand filter beds, which ensured that the companies' water supplies were as safe as science could then make them. In both respects he anticipated the Metropolis Water Act of 1852, which required that, by 1856, all companies should move their water intakes to a point above Teddington weir, the upper limit of the tidal river. Beyond that point, London's sewage could not pollute the upper reaches of the river. The Act also followed Simpson's example in requiring filtration. The beneficial consequences of these measures for the customers of the Lambeth company, as revealed by Dr John Snow, are described in Chapter 3.

THOMAS HAWKSLEY

Simpson's greatest rival as a water engineer was Thomas Hawksley (1807–93). He was also involved in designing schemes for sewerage and the supply of gas, but here we are particularly interested in his contribution to clean water supply. He was born near Nottingham and educated at the local grammar school before being articled to a local architect at the age of fifteen in 1822. In 1830, aged only twenty-three, he undertook to construct new waterworks for the rapidly growing town, building a pumping station adjacent to the river at Trent Bridge, where the water was naturally filtered through beds of sand and gravel: it was a similar process to that adopted by James Simpson two years earlier, though on this occasion nature provided the filter. Hawksley remained engineer to the Nottingham Waterworks company until it was taken over by the corporation in 1880. He was associated with his place of birth throughout his long life, his other contributions to the welfare of his fellow citizens including the construction of a cholera hospital to meet the first epidemic, in 1832.

Towards the end of his life he claimed to have been involved in the construction of 150 water supply schemes throughout Great Britain and abroad, the latter including places as diverse as Denmark,

Sweden, Austria, Brazil and Poland. The last of these was particularly eventful. In 1863, while overseeing the construction of waterworks in Warsaw, he was attacked by some of the local inhabitants who harboured grievances against their own government, and the discontented would-be revolutionaries were driven off by a posse of gendarmes. He received honours from Emperor Franz-Jozef II of Austria and the Emperor of Brazil, though in his own country he was content to be elected President of the Institution of Civil Engineers (ICE) in 1871, an office he held for two years, and Fellow of the Royal Society in 1878. He had no doubts about the value of his profession, informing the ICE, in his presidential address in 1872, that the recent triumph of the Prussians over the French in the Franco-Prussian War of 1870–1 was due to the superior use of engineering techniques by the Prussian forces.[4] He founded a dynasty of civil engineers, his son Charles following him into the profession and himself becoming President of the ICE. The engineering consultancy that Thomas Hawksley founded in 1852 at 30 Great George Street, close to the institution, survives into the twenty-first century as part of the multinational consultancy MWH, formerly known as Watson Hawksley. In London he designed the small pumping station at the northern end of the Serpentine, in Hyde Park, thought by some to be modelled on the *Petit Trianon* at Versailles.

In Great Britain hazards such as he encountered in Warsaw were not unknown. During a demonstration by Chartists in 1848 he drove an invading mob from a gasworks by directing a tongue of flame at them, and his career was not without controversy in other ways.[5] He was one of the first and most insistent advocates of the principle of 'constant service' – the continuous provision of piped water into homes, under pressure. Most of his colleagues, including James Simpson, regarded this as unrealistic and favoured the system of intermittent supply for a few hours each day, which the New River had adopted since the early seventeenth century. These engineers argued that the system of constant service would lead to much loss of water, because plumbing accessories like taps and valves were of such poor quality that more water would be lost than used. Hawksley replied that constant service under pressure would have two beneficial results. First, it would make it difficult and even hazardous for thieves to make off with the precious lead piping in which the water was conveyed. Any attempt to remove any part of it would result in an immediate and conspicuous flood. Moreover, by creating a constant supply system, the water company would oblige suppliers of equipment to improve their quality and durability, if they were to avoid incurring the wrath of their customers. In this way Hawksley brought about a permanent improvement in quality standards in the industry. In the words of Hawksley's obituary, his insistence on constant supply in his systems meant that 'there were great difficulties with the plumbers, but Mr Hawksley's plan was to begin by getting them under reasonable control, when all else became easy'.[6] Hawksley himself contributed to the improvement in equipment by working with the engineer William Armstrong to devise a valve that would shut off a pipe when the velocity of water flow exceeded the prescribed maximum. The Nottingham waterworks supplied 35,000 people in 8,000 homes with a constant supply at the cost of a penny a week and managed to pay a respectable dividend of 5 per cent.[7]

William Armstrong (1810–1900) was one of Victorian England's most successful, innovative and wealthy engineer industrialists. He was born near Newcastle and abandoned his articles to a solicitor in favour of engineering. In 1842 he constructed a hydro-electric generator and became interested in the possibilities of using water in engineering. But first he devised the hydraulic cranes at the port of Newcastle. His factory is commemorated in the Geordie anthem 'Bladon Races' in the words: 'We flew past Armstrong's factory'. After the Crimean War Armstrong became involved in arms manufacture, his guns being ordered by armies and navies throughout the world. Towards the end of his life he built the mansion of Cragside, near Rothbury in Northumberland, which was especially noted for the fact that it was the first residence in the world to be lit by hydro-electric power supplied by the reservoirs and turbines he constructed for the purpose.

One of Thomas Hawksley's most important contributions to Britain's water supply network was made at Liverpool. The health problems of Liverpool have been discussed in Chapters 2 and 4. In 1846, as the council prepared to appoint Dr W.H. Duncan as its (and Britain's) first Medical Officer, the corporation invited Hawksley to propose methods by which the water supply to the town could be improved. Hawksley recommended bringing water by gravitation from five reservoirs at Rivington, where the foothills of the Pennines merge into the lowlands of Lancashire, 30 miles from Liverpool. The extensive correspondence on Hawksley's 'Rivington Pike scheme' in the Liverpool City archives is an indication of the controversy it aroused. Many engineers, prominent among whom was James Simpson, advocated bringing water from Lake Bala in Wales, and others favoured the drilling of more artesian wells. After much argument the celebrated railway engineer Robert Stephenson was called in to arbitrate upon the project and adjudicated in favour of Hawksley's proposals, which were completed in 1857. Four acres of sand filters were built to ensure the purity of the supply, and the system remains in use in the twenty-first century.

Almost twenty years later, in 1874, the councillors of Liverpool called upon Hawksley again when further supplies were required by the rapidly growing city. On this occasion Hawksley recommended one of the most ambitious schemes ever devised, bringing water from Lake Vyrnwy in Wales. Again there was some controversy over the scheme, this time over an alternative proposal to bring water from the headwaters of the River Severn. The scheme involved constructing an aqueduct 68 miles in length and a huge dam, designed by Hawksley as engineer in chief to the scheme. It was completed in 1888, the resulting reservoir submerging the village of Llanwddyn. This continues to supply Liverpool with water that is among the softest enjoyed by any city in Britain.

PUBLIC AFFAIRS

Besides his work as an engineer, Thomas Hawksley was a major public figure whose eightieth birthday in 1887 was marked by a flattering article in *The Times* headlined 'A Veteran Engineer'.[8] His high public profile owed much to the time he had spent as an expert witness before parliamentary and other committees concerned with the effective supply of water, sewerage and gas. He was particularly noted for his meticulous preparation for these events and would arrive armed with capacious files, maps, diagrams and statistics on such matters as evaporation rates from reservoirs. These frequently dismayed both his opponents and those whose questions had elicited these clear, comprehensive but above all lengthy responses: His obituary recorded:

> Mr Hawksley might be described as an invincible witness. His appearance in a case was heralded by the introduction of piles of statistics and other data which he had sent before him . . . out came a mass of figures which appalled the opposing counsel and made the younger members of the committee groan in secret.[9]

This aspect of his work also brought him into contact with the ubiquitous Edwin Chadwick, and, as with most people drawn into that great man's circle, the two soon quarrelled. Hawksley first came to Chadwick's notice when giving evidence to a Parliamentary Commission that was inquiring into the health of towns. He described the conditions that could arise in insanitary dwellings:

> The most cleanly and orderly female will invariably despond and relax her exertions under the influence of damp, filth and stench and probably sink into a dirty, noisy, discontented and perhaps gin-swilling drab. The moral and physical improvements certain to result from the introduction of water and water-closets into the houses of the working classes are far beyond the pecuniary advantages.[10]

Chadwick was convinced by Hawksley's arguments for constant service and invited him to join him as engineer to the British, Colonial and Foreign Drainage, Water Supply and Town Improvements Company, an organisation whose comprehensive title reflected the ambitions of Chadwick – it was soon mercifully shortened to the Town Improvements Company. The distinguished board of directors included the economist Nassau Senior and the future inventor of the penny post, Rowland Hill. Chadwick was installed as managing director. The plan was to raise £1 million in capital and to provide, at affordable cost, water, drains and sewage disposal to dwellings so that 'even baths [will be] introduced into the houses of labouring men for the use of themselves and their families'.[11] Further profits would be made from the recycling of sewage as manure, an issue that was to bedevil engineers for decades, so that a dividend of 6–10 per cent was confidently predicted by the directors, who registered the company on 7 August 1845. Unfortunately, the promoters never managed to raise the £1 million they required, since their attempts to do so coincided with the great railway boom of the 1840s led by George Hudson (a boom that would soon end in disaster), so the Town Improvements Company never traded.

In the meantime, Hawksley and Chadwick had fallen out. Hawksley was annoyed that Chadwick had paid him nothing for the work he had done to promote the venture, and Chadwick was offended because Hawksley continued to do private work – understandably, since Hawksley needed an income. Further conflict followed over the activities of the Board of Health, which, since its establishment in 1848, had been used by Chadwick to try to bully local boards into supplying water to households, causing much local resentment and very little progress. Hawksley wrote a pamphlet entitled 'The Privileges of Parliament Endangered and the Rights of the People Violated', which complained that Chadwick's inspectors had it within their power to impose their own designs for sewerage and water supply on local communities and that they were then in a privileged position to secure the work for themselves: 'The grossest jobbing prevails. Able professional men are wrongly injured, both in reputation and profit, for the gain of the government inspectors.'[12]

Hawksley resigned the post and was briefly replaced by another distinguished water engineer, John Frederick la Trobe Bateman, who attracted Chadwick's temporary approval as a result of a lecture he gave when Chadwick was in the audience.[13] This was the first but by no means the last of Chadwick's disputes with the engineering profession, whose active cooperation was, of course, absolutely essential if Chadwick's plans were ever to be realised.

J.F. la Trobe Bateman (1810–89) was born near Halifax, the son of an unsuccessful inventor, and apprenticed in 1825 to a surveyor in Oldham with whom he worked on the construction of reservoirs for mills and canals. Later he collaborated with Robert Stephenson on the London to Birmingham railway. In 1844 he devised a scheme to bring water to the rapidly growing community of Manchester from the Pennines, and three decades later he designed and began the construction of the system that still brings water to that city from Thirlmere in the Lake District. Glasgow was supplied from Loch Katrine in the 1850s. He worked on systems for Buenos Aires, Naples, Colombo, Majorca and Constantinople as well as almost thirty British towns. In 1854 he redesigned the Bilberry dam near Huddersfield, which had collapsed in 1852, causing much loss of life, and in 1869 he proposed a 'Channel railway' crossing between England and France in an iron tube. He replaced Hawksley on the short-lived Town Improvements Company when Hawksley fell out with Chadwick. Bateman shares with James Simpson and Thomas Hawksley much of the credit for creating the modern water supply network and was elected a Fellow of the Royal Society in 1860 in recognition of the innovative nature of much of his work. In the twenty-first century, one of Bateman's descendants works for MWH, which incorporates the company founded by Hawksley.

In the years that followed, a number of increasingly extravagant schemes were proposed. A Royal Commission of 1866 listened to Bateman, who proposed to bring water 180 miles from Wales to a reservoir at Stanmore, whence it would flow by gravity to buildings throughout the capital. The commissioners were not convinced, fearing that over such a long route the supply would be vulnerable to sabotage by an enemy. They came to the same conclusion about an even more ambitious scheme to bring water from Ullswater, Thirlmere and Haweswater in the Lake District.

PUBLIC OWNERSHIP

In the middle of the century water companies charged about £4 to connect a small house to their supply, with an annual charge of about 3s (15p) per room.[14] For this the householder would receive piped water about two hours per day (except on Sundays), unless he was fortunate enough to be connected to one of Thomas Hawksley's systems, such as at Nottingham or Liverpool, where constant supply was the rule. Households were expected to store water in cisterns during the days and hours that water was not being piped and, since the cisterns were often polluted by bird droppings (and occasionally dead birds), this was not conducive to health. The East London company was the first, in 1887, in the metropolis to introduce constant supply. As late as the 1890s 31 per cent of Londoners had no access to a permanent supply of water.[15] In the meantime, access to water for those not supplied by one of the companies was becoming more difficult, since local authorities were gradually closing pumps and wells that they suspected of being tainted by pollution. By 1872 161 wells had been sealed and 36 remained open, two of these being accessible only by keyholders.[16]

The Public Health Act of 1848 had permitted local authorities to take over water companies, with the agreement of the latter, but Chadwick's bullying attempts to raise their enthusiasm for doing so was singularly unsuccessful, as was the desire of the companies to go along with the idea. Advocates of public ownership redoubled their efforts after the failure of the Royal Commission of 1866, and further measures ensured that, by 1880, about half of local authorities were running their own waterworks. London was not among them. Paradoxically, the great sewerage works of Sir Joseph Bazalgette (1819–91), which are described later in this chapter, by protecting London from its own waste, may have encouraged complacency. A half-hearted attempt was made by Disraeli in the 1870s to consider buying out London's water companies, but the government's heart was not in it and the idea was abandoned. A proposal by the City of London in 1884 to conserve water supplies by metering them was denounced by the increasingly erratic Lord Randolph Churchill as 'the wildest socialist doctrine'.

The London County Council (LCC), which took office in 1889, showed more determination and in 1895 presented to Parliament bills that would enable it to buy out the companies. The companies, which were skilled in the arts of procrastination, argued for and obtained yet another Royal Commission, but the LCC mounted its own guerrilla campaign. It criticised the companies for failing to maintain constant supply during the long, hot summers of the 1890s and showed no sympathy when, in the 'year of the great frost', January to March 1895, its customers made the supply situation worse by leaving taps running to prevent the pipes from freezing. It also exerted its influence to hold down rate rises, depress the companies' profits and thus demoralise the directors and shareholders to prepare them for takeover.

The decisive moment came in 1902 with the creation of the Metropolitan Water Board by the Metropolis Water Act of that year. Its members were appointed by local authorities, including the LCC, and the shareholders were bought out by the new body for £47,000,000, of which £6,534,000 was paid to the shareholders of the New River company, Sir Hugh Myddleton's descendants being among them. The 'Crown Clog' remained an obligation, until it was finally bought out for £8,230 following a ruling by the House of Lords. In the years that followed, the supply of clean water to London's dwellings was gradually improved and extended so that by the outbreak of the First World War virtually all enjoyed constant supply. In 1989 the responsibility for London's water was taken over by Thames Water PLC, so that it is now back in private hands. Sir Hugh Myddleton, whose statue stands at the south end of Islington Green, would no doubt approve. His New River continues to supply drinking water to London, though it now terminates at Stoke Newington, where it feeds into the London Ring Main.

PIPES OR BRICKS?

In the meantime Edwin Chadwick had embarked upon yet another dispute with the engineering profession, which was to bedevil the creation of an effective sanitary system for many years. This concerned the question of whether sewers and drains should be built of brick or manufactured in factories as pipes, and it is hard now to understand the passions that were expended on this apparently mundane matter. The critical role assigned by Chadwick to engineers in the improvement of urban sanitation (as against the humble one allocated to physicians) was reflected in his public pronouncements many times. In 1842, the year that his *Report into the Sanitary Conditions of the Labouring Population of Great Britain* was published, he summed up his views of the two professions, and of local opinion, in bringing about sanitary reform in a letter he wrote to a Scottish lawyer called Macvey Napier:

> The chief remedies consist in applications of the science of engineering, of which the medical men know nothing; and to gain powers for their applications, and to deal with local rights which stand in the way of practical improvements, some jurisprudence is necessary, of which the engineers know nothing.[17]

Doctors, he thought, were of little use, and, given the rudimentary state of medical knowledge at the time, this wasn't far from the truth. Engineers had their uses provided they knew their places and didn't become involved in 'jurisprudence' (which we might call politics). Local rights were something to 'deal with'.

Chadwick had become acquainted with Frederick Doulton (1822–72), who, at his works in Lambeth, had founded the company that was eventually to produce Royal Doulton china but that, for the moment, was more concerned with producing glazed ceramic pipes of high quality and larger diameter than had previously been possible. Doulton's interest arose from a realisation that the demand for such pipes would be greatly increased by the movement, led by Chadwick, to install sewers and house drains in towns and cities. Chadwick was convinced that Doulton's pipe sewers provided a much cheaper alternative to the traditional brick sewers favoured by engineers, many of whom believed that Doulton's pipes would not prove to be strong enough to stand up to the pressures of being buried deep in the earth with substantial quantities of waste flowing through them. There was also a widespread belief that main sewers needed to be large enough for a man to enter and clean them when they became blocked, and even Doulton's designs were not large enough for that. Robert Stephenson declared of pipe sewers that 'he hated the very name of them and felt inclined never to mention the word again'.[18] Chadwick argued that the smoother surface of glazed pipes would achieve a more ready flow of sewage. The engineers countered that the layer of slime that would form on bricks would do the job better. Chadwick's intolerance of disagreement developed into paranoia when he became convinced that engineers were opposing pipes and advocating bricks, not because of any technical issues but because brick sewers were more expensive to build and therefore more profitable for engineers and contractors. Two years after he had written to Macvey Napier, expressing a favourable view of engineers, he wrote: 'A more ignorant or more jobbing set of men, less to be trusted than the common run of men who dub themselves with the title of engineer and pretend to science I have rarely met with.'[19]

Chadwick had attempted to force the Metropolitan Sewers Commission, which in the early 1850s was struggling vainly with the problems of improving London's sanitation, to make their sewers from pipes rather than bricks. When he was a member of one of the early sewers commissions, he took the precaution of interviewing all the engineers employed by the commissioners to ensure that they followed the Chadwickian code of glazed pipes and constant supply. One of the first to be appointed was (later Sir) Robert Rawlinson, who was himself to make a significant contribution to the supply of clean water to Britain's towns and cities.

Chadwick was removed from the sewers commission by the Home Secretary because of his quarrels with others. The commissioners who succeeded him, who, like many others, had resented Chadwick's interference, commissioned their engineer, Joseph Bazalgette, to produce a report on the relative merits of the two systems by checking their effectiveness in London and five other towns.[20] Bazalgette, who seems to have understood what his masters expected of him, produced a report that came down strongly in favour of bricks. A subsequent inquiry revealed that his inspections had been hurried, biased and even surreptitious, one inspection

Sir Robert Rawlinson (1810–98) was born in Bristol, son of a stonemason, worked first in the engineer's office in the rapidly expanding Liverpool Docks, and was later responsible for completing the city's famous St George's Hall when the original architect became ill. Rawlinson later worked under Robert Stephenson on the construction of the London to Birmingham railway, but his growing reputation in the relatively new discipline of public health and sanitation led to his appointment as one of the first public health inspectors of the Board of Health, set up in 1848. He later became Chief Inspector for that body and for the Local Government Board that took over its responsibilities. In 1855 he was sent by the government to the Crimea, where he was wounded, but instituted a number of sanitary reforms that reduced deaths from poor hygiene both in the Crimea itself and in Constantinople. During the American Civil War, when unemployment was rife in the Lancashire Mills, he visited almost 100 towns and devised, with support from the Treasury, a scheme for spending over £1 million to create jobs building urban sewerage and water supply systems, with very beneficial results for the health of their inhabitants. He was presumably a man of placid temperament, since he managed to work harmoniously with Edwin Chadwick through the 'pipe sewer' controversy and to do so without antagonising other members of his profession. He was knighted in 1888 for his work with the Local Government Board and as chairman of the Royal Commission on the pollution of rivers. He shares with Sir Joseph Bazalgette much of the credit for improving the sanitation of Victorian towns and cities.

being conducted at night without the knowledge of the local engineer. It reflected no credit on a man who was shortly to play the critical role in the cleansing of London and many other communities, but it confirmed Chadwick's cynical view of the profession. When Bazalgette came to build his system of main drainage, he made extensive use of pipes for street sewers, but his intercepting sewers were so large that no pipe that could then be made would have been large enough.

FOUL WATER

In June 1859 a Dr J. Strang, Glasgow's City Chamberlain, published a learned paper in the *Journal of the Statistical Society* entitled 'On Water Supply to Great Towns'.[21] The paper included some figures that were, at face value, very encouraging to those who believed that a regular supply of clean water was essential to health. They showed a significant increase in the usage of water in London in the period 1850–6:

1850: 270,581 houses used on average 160 gallons each per day
1856: 328,561 houses used on average 244 gallons each per day

Taking the figures together, this showed that, in a six-year period, the usage of water in London had increased from 43 million gallons to nearly 80 million gallons each day. On the face of it, this was excellent use for the sanitarians, but the bare figures failed to draw attention to the uses to which the water was being put. Much of it was being flushed down the newly fashionable water closets, which, when attached to a medieval system of sewage disposal, had disastrous consequences for public health.

In the medieval period human waste was normally deposited in cesspools, situated in the basements of dwellings to which the residents repaired when they needed to relieve themselves. One of the first decrees issued by the first Mayor of London, Henry Fitzalwyn, concerned the construction of the 'necessary chamber' and specified the materials from which it should be made and the distance that should be interposed between it and any neighbouring building. This early example of building regulations indicates that, even in the twelfth century, the possible impact of human waste on public health was clearly understood. It was forbidden to dispose of waste in any rivers, sewers or ditches, a prohibition that was made explicit in a statute enacted during the time that Richard Whittington was Mayor of London.

Richard Whittington (died 1423) was Mayor of London three times in 1397, 1406 and 1419. He came from the hamlet of Pauntley, near Gloucester, and rose from relative obscurity to great wealth as a mercer, or cloth merchant. He advanced substantial loans to Henry IV and Henry V and so earned the trust of the latter monarch that Henry entrusted him with funds to rebuild the nave of Westminster Abbey and decreed that no building was to be demolished within the City except by permission of Whittington and two other leading public figures. He paid from his own pocket to improve the City's water supply and was so concerned about the foul and disease-ridden condition into which Newgate prison had fallen that he left a legacy from which it was completely rebuilt. The new gaol became known as 'The Whit' and a niche in its wall contained a statue of Whittington, accompanied by a cat.

The public sewers and the rivers into which they emptied were reserved for the use intended by nature: the draining away of rainwater. Some of these rivers, which still flow mostly underground beneath the streets of the city, were substantial watercourses. The River Fleet, which rises on Hampstead Heath, flows beneath the Farringdon Road and enters the Thames close to Blackfriars station, where it can be seen at low tide. The Westbourne also rises on Hampstead Heath, surfaces as the Serpentine in Hyde Park, crosses Sloane Square underground railway station in a metal culvert above the trains and joins the Thames in Chelsea. It is certain that these and other rivers were used surreptitiously for other purposes, since royal decrees from the reign of Edward III to that of Charles II and beyond upbraided the City authorities for allowing the sewers and rivers to become polluted, but the great majority of human waste was extracted from the cesspools by 'nightsoilmen' (often women or children) and carted away to be sold as fertiliser to farmers in the fields that lay outside the city walls, like those at Moorfields. In the absence of chemical fertiliser, there was a ready market for the contents of the cesspools, so the work was well paid and the entrepreneurs who ran the nightsoil businesses often became wealthy men. The system worked tolerably well until the early decades of the nineteenth century.

THE WATER CLOSET

Reference has already been made, in previous chapters, to the speed with which the English population was urbanised in the nineteenth century and to the problems that arose in disposing of human waste.[22] Nowhere were the effects of this more pronounced than in the capital itself. In 1801, at the time of the first census, London's population was 959,000, but by the time of the Great Exhibition of 1851 it had increased almost two and a half times to 2,362,000.[23] As the population grew, the fields retreated, obliging the night-soilmen to travel a greater distance in search of their markets, and the importation of guano (solidified bird droppings) from South America from 1847 struck a further blow at their trade. However the greatest problem of all lay with the growing popularity of the water closet.

The WC had been invented in the reign of Queen Elizabeth by Sir John Harington, but this courtier's device was expensive to make and not very efficient. Only two were made: one for Harington's own house at Kelston, near Bath, and the other for the Richmond palace of the Queen herself, his godmother. The device was virtually forgotten for two centuries, until, in 1775, a Bond Street watchmaker called Alexander Cumings improved the design. However, the decisive breakthrough was made by a Yorkshire carpenter called Joseph Bramah (1748–1814), who, when asked to install a water closet in a private house, realised that he could improve the design in such a way as to make it both more effective and easier to mass produce. He patented the mechanism in 1778, and by 1797 had made over 6,000 of the devices. The company he founded continued to produce them until 1890, and in the meantime another entrepreneur had entered the market. This was Thomas Crapper. His name was a fortunate coincidence, since the word 'crap', with its modern meaning, had been in use since the sixteenth century. He founded his business in Chelsea in 1861 and promoted it so successfully with the slogan 'a certain flush with every pull' that it continued to trade from 120 Kings Road until 1966. However, the most enterprising businessman of all was George Jennings, who, in 1851, arranged to install his own designs in the 'Crystal Palace', which housed the Great Exhibition of that year, where 827,000 visitors were exposed to the device upon payment of one penny, thus promoting the new apparatus while adding the phrase 'spend a penny' to the language.

Even before the impact of the Great Exhibition, the effect of the water closet had been noted by the London builder Thomas Cubitt in evidence to the Select Committee Health of Towns. He told the MPs: 'Fifty years ago nearly all London had every house cleansed into a large cesspool . . . Now sewers having been very much

Joseph Bramah (1748–1814) was a Yorkshire farmer's son whose name was originally spelt Bramma. After apprenticeship to a carpenter he travelled to London to start his own business, where, in 1778, he was asked to install a water closet in a private house. He realised that he could improve the design so that the mechanism worked better and lent itself to mass production. He patented the resulting mechanism, the first of eighteen patents, and at the same time he changed the spelling of his name. He began to manufacture WCs in large numbers, their widespread adoption having devastating consequences for the antiquated cesspools and sewers to which they were connected. He also invented an unpickable lock, offering a prize of £200 to anyone who could pick it. The prize was eventually claimed by an American called Hobbs, who took up the challenge at the Great Exhibition of 1851. Bramah's other inventions included a hydraulic press, a machine for numbering banknotes and a screw mechanism for propelling ships.

improved, scarcely any person thinks of making a cesspool but it is carried off at once into the river. The Thames is now made a great cesspool instead of each person having one of his own.'[24]

Cubitt was referring to the disastrous consequences of attaching a modern device, the water closet, to the medieval system of cesspools. The latter were designed to receive and store for collection relatively small quantities of human waste, much of it solid. When a water closet was flushed, it dispatched to the cesspool a small quantity of human waste accompanied by a much larger volume of water – perhaps ten or twenty times as much. The cesspools were rapidly filling with liquid waste that no farmer wanted to buy and that would leak into neighbouring watercourses, thereby polluting wells, streams and, ultimately, the Thames itself. The large increase in water consumption between 1850 and 1856, noted with satisfaction by the Glasgow City Chamberlain,[25] was thus due at least in part to the increasing popularity of the water closet and must be laid to the account of George Jennings's enterprise in approaching the organisers of the Great Exhibition.

The authorities were not unaware of the consequences of the increasing adoption of the water closet. In 1815 the prohibition on connecting house drains to sewers was lifted so that henceforth householders could bypass their cesspools and empty their house waste into the public sewers and thence into the river. In 1844 the Metropolitan Buildings Act decreed that, henceforth, all new buildings *must* be connected to the common sewer, and the imaginative use of this and other Acts extended this, over the next few years, to existing buildings. Thus in a period of about thirty-five years, from 1815 to 1850, London had moved from a position in which *no waste* could be emptied into the common sewers to one in which *almost all waste* should be thus disposed. Chadwick's slogan for these moves, as reported in *The Times* – 'No filth in the sewers, all in the river' – had consequences for the underground streams and the River Thames that may scarcely be imagined.[26] In 1816, the year after the prohibition on connecting house drains was lifted, fourteen salmon, the litmus test for water purity, were caught in the Thames at Taplow. Four years later, in 1820, no salmon were caught, and they were not to return until Sir Joseph Bazalgette had completed his system of intercepting sewers.

The consequences of this waste disposal were made clear in a letter published in *The Times* on 9 July 1855, which included a description of a journey along the Thames. The most significant feature of the letter was the identity of the writer, then the most famous scientist in the world:

Sir,

I traversed this day, by steam boat, the space between London and Hungerford Bridges . . . The appearance and the smell of the water forced themselves at once upon my attention. The whole of the river was an opaque, pale brown fluid . . . The smell was very bad, and common to the whole of the water.

The condition in which I saw the Thames may, perhaps, be considered as exceptional, but it ought to be an impossible state, instead of which, I fear, it is becoming the general condition. If we neglect this subject we cannot expect to do so with impunity, nor ought we to be surprised if, 'ere many years are over, a hot season gives us sad proof of the folly of our carelessness.

I am, Sir, your obedient servant,

M. Faraday, Royal Institution, July 7th 1855

Three years later Michael Faraday's warning took shape in the form of what the press called 'The Great Stink' of 1858. A long, hot, dry summer ensured that a more than normal proportion of the contents of the Thames consisted of sewage and that the smell was particularly vile. This concentrated the minds of the Parliamentarians in the Palace of Westminster, which had recently been rebuilt on the banks of the river after being destroyed in the fire of 1834, and they were the more concerned because they believed, with Edwin Chadwick, Florence Nightingale and most other authorities, that they could contract cholera and other fatal diseases from the smell itself. They were, of course, mistaken, but at high tides the polluted Thames would empty its contents into tributaries like the Fleet, Westbourne and Walbrook, whence the fatal organisms could make their way into other streams, aquifers and drinking wells.

The effect of the Great Stink was beneficial. In 1855 Parliament had passed the Metropolis Local Management Act, which created the Metropolitan Board of Works, with authority across the capital as a whole to undertake major improvements to the infrastructure such as roads, bridges, parks and, above all, sewers. Within a few months the board's engineer, Joseph Bazalgette, had devised a system of intercepting sewers, running parallel to the Thames, which would collect waste from street sewers and conduct it, by gravity, assisted by four pumping stations, to outfalls at Beckton, on the north bank of the river and Crossness, near Abbey Wood, on the south. There it would be stored in huge reservoirs until high tide, so that, as the tide turned, the sewage's first movement would be out to sea, taking with it both the smell and the harmful microbes of cholera, typhoid, dysentery and other waterborne diseases.

Unfortunately, the Metropolis Local Management Act, which created the board, also reserved to the government, in the person of the Chief Commissioner of Works, the right to approve or veto Bazalgette's plans. Two years passed, 1856–8, during which Bazalgette, the board and the government bickered about the quality of Bazalgette's design. Were the sewers long enough? Did they have sufficient capacity to accommodate the sewage and the rainfall of London as it existed and as it might be in the future? Above all, did the sewers take their contents far enough downstream or was there a danger that, with a really high tide, the sewage could be brought back into the centre of London, causing another 'Great Stink' and bringing down humiliation on the head of the Chief Commissioner himself. This gentleman was Sir Benjamin Hall, and, though he has been much criticised for his part in causing the delay, it is easy to sympathise with him. He had presided with some success over the later stages of the rebuilding of the Palace of Westminster and is even credited with having the famous bell in the parliamentary clock named after him: Big Ben. (There is a rival claimant, Ben Caunt, a heavyweight boxer, who had recently retired.) His hard-won reputation for competence could easily have been forgotten if a faulty design, approved by him, led to another great stink.

In the circumstances it is forgivable that he did what many later politicians were to do when faced with such a dilemma: he appointed consultants to advise him. One of these was James

Simpson, whose eminence as a water engineer has already been noted and who recommended that the board's outfalls be sited some 15 miles further downstream, not far from Canvey Island. This would have involved very great additional expense, so a further conflict now arose over who would pay. Would the metropolitan ratepayers bear the additional cost or would the 'Imperial Parliament' foot the bill to the fury of MPs from outside the capital? The debate dragged on for two years while Bazalgette produced additional plans and the Parliamentarians, led by the increasingly hapless Sir Benjamin Hall, argued about designs, capacities, tidal flows and, above all, cost. A further complication arose from the fact that ratepayers could, under the provisions of the Metropolis Local Management Act, appeal against the rates levied for the construction of the main drainage, usually on the grounds that one parish benefited from the system less than another. This led to endless litigation, cost and delay in the Courts of Quarter Sessions, where the cases were heard.

The Great Stink concentrated minds wonderfully. A new government, in which Benjamin Disraeli was leader of the House of Commons, was urged by *The Times* to act, as temperatures mounted and tempers shortened. On 18 June the newspaper declared:

> What a pity that the thermometer fell ten degrees yesterday. Parliament was all but compelled to legislate upon the great London nuisance by the force of sheer stench. The intense heat had driven our legislators from those portions of their buildings which overlook the river. A few members, bent upon investigating the matter to its very depth, ventured into the library, but they were instantaneously driven to retreat, each man with a handkerchief to his nose. We are heartily glad of it.

The writer was glad because he supposed that, faced with their own discomfiture, the MPs would take decisive action. They were further encouraged to do so when the engineer Goldsworthy Gurney, who was responsible for the lighting and ventilation of the house, had informed the Speaker that he 'can no longer be responsible for the health of the house'. In this case the miasmatic belief that the smell was poisoning them had the beneficial effect of prompting the MPs to take the action they had avoided for the previous two years. On 15 July Disraeli introduced a bill to amend the powers of the Metropolitan Board of Works and its engineer, Joseph Bazalgette. It removed the Chief Commisioner's veto on the board's plans and authorised the Board to borrow £3 million, underwritten by the Treasury, to begin work. The right of appeal of ratepayers was also removed. 'The Great Stink' had achieved more in a few uncomfortable days than parliamentary debates had managed in two years.

'THE MOST EXTENSIVE AND WONDERFUL WORK OF MODERN TIMES'

Bazalgette, who had already prepared many of the plans for his system of intercepting sewers, began work almost immediately. Joseph Bazalgette, like Sir John Simon and Isambard Kingdom Brunel, was of French descent. His grandfather, Jean Louis Bazalgette, had been born in the small town of Ispagnac, in the Department of Lozère, in 1750. This is the Auvergne, the most remote and thinly inhabited part of France, and nearby is the village

Sir Goldsworthy Gurney (1793–1885) was born in Cornwall and practised as a surgeon at Wadebridge before moving to London and delivering a series of lectures on chemistry that impressed the young Michael Faraday. Gurney developed the process for producing *limelight*, the very bright light used in theatres; and a steam jet that was used by the Stephensons to power *The Rocket*. Gurney also patented a steam carriage in which he travelled from London to Bath and back in 1829 at an average speed of 15 mph. He was responsible for designing and installing the heating, lighting and ventilation system in the rebuilt House of Commons – hence his anxiety over the health of the Members during 'The Great Stink'.

of La Bazalgette, now desolate. Jean Louis came to England in the 1770s, quickly established himself as a prosperous tailor and dealer in cloth in Mayfair and married at the fashionable church of St George's, Hanover Square, in 1779. His capacity for earning money was matched by his ingenuousness in making unwise loans to the Prince of Wales (the future George IV), the prince's equally spendthrift brothers and the playwright R.B. Sheridan, whose capacity for spending other people's money was exceeded only by his friend the prince. Jean Louis, like many other creditors of the Prince, was eventually repaid only after the intervention of Parliament. Jean Louis was denizened (naturalised) as a British citizen in 1792 and had a son, Joseph William Bazalgette, who served in the Royal Navy and was granted a lifetime pension for wounds received in action. His son was Joseph Bazalgette the engineer, born in 1819 at Enfield and articled to the engineer (later Sir) John MacNeill, with whom he worked on land drainage and reclamation projects in Northern Ireland. After a short period working as a consultant, mostly on railway projects during the railway boom of the 1840s, he was appointed as an engineer to the Metropolitan Sewers Commissions, which struggled vainly with London's problems between 1848 and 1855 and, in the latter year, he became Chief Engineer to the Metropolitan Board of Works. He was by now very well connected and much admired in the civil engineering profession. His referees for the latter post were Robert Stephenson, designer of *The Rocket*, and Isambard Kingdom Brunel, who both gave reassuring accounts of his competence.

Between 1859 and 1875 Bazalgette designed and constructed 1,100 miles of new street sewers beneath the streets of the capital, which collected sewage and surface water from buildings and streets and delivered it to the 82 miles of intercepting sewers, which, running parallel to the Thames, conducted their contents to Beckton and Crossness, whence it was discharged into the river. The system worked mostly by gravity at a fall of at least 2 feet per mile, but, since the Thames, in its passage through London, falls at a rate of only 3 inches per mile, it was necessary to build four pumping stations to lift the sewage into outfall sewers so that it could resume its gravitational flow. The largest of these were at Crossness itself, on the southern bank of the river, and at Abbey Mills, near West

Ham, on the northern bank. Crossness was opened, amid much ceremony, by the Prince of Wales, in April 1865, after which there were no further cholera epidemics south of the river. The engineering works on the more populous northern side were more complex, and it was not until July 1868 that Abbey Mills was opened, thereby protecting the water supply to the residents north of the Thames from their own sewage. Unfortunately they remained vulnerable to the final cholera epidemic, which struck Whitechapel in 1866.[27]

The reason for the longer time taken to complete the works on the northern bank was their massive scale. Two-thirds of London's population lived north of the river, and the sewers had to weave their way beneath congested streets and crossroads, canals and railway lines, some of the last having to be raised or lowered to allow the sewers to proceed at a steady rate of fall from west to east. To accommodate the northern low-level sewer, Bazalgette reclaimed from the Thames over 40 acres of land to build the Chelsea and Victoria Embankments. Of these the most complex was the Victoria Embankment, which, alone, created 37 acres of reclaimed land from the previously sewage-stained northern shores of the river. The Embankment runs from Westminster Bridge to Blackfriars Bridge, and, besides providing a channel for the low-level intercepting sewer, the river's last line of defence against the capital's sewage, it also furnished many other much-needed amenities to London. The Embankment road itself was an alternative route from Westminster to the City, relieving the appallingly congested Strand–Fleet Street–Ludgate Hill route. The Victoria Embankment also accommodated the new underground railway (now the District and Circle Line), provided a service tunnel for gas, water and later electricity pipes and, in the form of Victoria Embankment Gardens, gave that part of London a much-needed green space. As described above, Gladstone attempted to appropriate the last of these amenities in the hope that, by building and renting out offices, he would be able to abolish income tax.[28] This worthy but hopeless aim was frustrated by the stationer and MP W.H. Smith, who successfully argued that London's need for fresh air took precedence over fiscal policy. Bazalgette himself, late in life, described some of the difficulties involved in constructing London's main drainage:

I get most credit for the Thames Embankment but it wasn't anything like such a job as the drainage . . . the fall in the river isn't above three inches a mile; for sewage we want a fall of a couple of feet and that kept taking us down below the river and when we got to certain depth we had to pump back up again. It was certainly a very troublesome job. We would sometimes spend weeks in drawing out plans and then suddenly come across some railway or canal that upset everything and we had to begin all over again. It was tremendously hard work. I was living over at Morden then and often used to drive down there at twelve or one o'clock in the morning.[29]

The quality of the work and its significance in the life of the capital was soon recognised by public and press. In April 1861 the *Observer* informed its readers that 'it is two years since the most extensive and wonderful work of modern times was commenced'[30] and later the same year the *Marylebone Mercury*, which had been following the works closely, added that 'to Mr Bazalgette no tribute of praise can be undeserved'.[31]

WHAT TO DO WITH THE SEWAGE

There remained some controversy over what to do with the sewage once it reached the outfalls. Bazalgette's plan to release it at high tide, so that its first movement would be out to sea, was criticised on two grounds. First there were those who, like Edwin Chadwick and Justus von Liebig, believed that sewage was a valuable fertiliser that should not be allowed to go to waste. So many shared their views that in 1857 a Royal Commission was set up 'to Inquire into the Best Mode of Distributing the Sewage of Towns and Applying it to Beneficial and Profitable Uses'. Numerous schemes were devised by entrepreneurs who confidently anticipated that huge profits were to be derived from the sale of London's sewage to farmers. One was from Thomas Ellis, an Irish solicitor, who proposed to pump the northern sewage to Hampstead Heath and the southern sewage to the top of Shooters Hill, near Woolwich, from which points it would flow in all directions to create half a million acres of rich farmland. At that time Hampstead was not quite yet the fashionable district it later became and would no doubt have remained in that innocent state had Thomas Ellis's scheme been carried out. An alternative scheme, put forward by the Hon. William Napier and Lieutenant-Colonel William Hope, VC, proposed to construct an open channel of sewage from Beckton to the Maplin sands off the Essex coast, which would themselves become rich fields. Farmers on the route of the canal would be encouraged to fertilise their own fields by drawing off sewage from the canal as it passed their holdings. To these economic benefits were added restorative ones, since Hope argued, in support of the scheme, that 'London beauties might come out to recruit their wasted energies at the close of the season and, attired in a *costume de circonstance*, with coquettish jack-boots, would perhaps listen to a lecture on agriculture from the farmer himself while drinking his cream and luxuriating in the health-restoring breeze'.[32]

Bazalgette and the Board wisely asked for a bond of £25,000 to be paid by the Hope–Napier enterprise, but Hope's promise of health as well as money failed to arouse the enthusiasm of investors, and, though some work was begun, the enterprise lapsed. Despite this failure, the idea of the 'sewage farm' continued to appeal to many authorities, and much of Edinburgh's sewage continued to be emptied on to surrounding farmland until well into the twentieth century. The expression is still in use in the twenty-first century, though most 'sewage farms' are in fact better described as sewage treatment works. In these increasingly sophisticated installations, solid sewage is separated from liquid, the former being burned in incinerators whose output frequently generates electricity, which is fed into the national grid. Liquids are treated by a procedure known as the activated sludge process, which involves stimulating microbial action by pumping oxygen into the liquid, thereby sharpening the appetites of microbes, which break down the complex molecules of the pollutants into their harmless constituents such as carbon dioxide and water, leaving clean, odourless water that is fit to be returned to rivers and canals.

The second source of criticism of Bazalgette's system arose from those living near the storage and release points at Beckton and Crossness. Bazalgette had chosen those sites because they were a good distance from the centre of London and in areas where very few people lived. In the years that followed, as London expanded, these communities became more densely populated and the residents objected to the smell from the river when the sewage was released. Petitions to the Home Secretary by the inhabitants of Barking, close to the Beckton site, produced an indecisive inquiry, but the dispute was given a sharper edge in September 1878 when a collision occurred between a pleasure steamer, the *Princess Alice*, and a freighter, the *Bywell Castle*. The *Princess Alice* sank with much loss of life, and it was alleged that the death toll was exacerbated by the fact that the accident occurred at high tide, as the sewage was released. The implication was that many had been poisoned. The government inquiry that followed was indecisive, but the point had been made that the river was still polluted with harmful sewage, albeit at a different point from that which had so alarmed the Parliamentarians in 1858. The Great Stink had moved downstream to Essex and Kent.

Bazalgette therefore redesigned the system, so that, in 1887, precipitation channels were built at Beckton and Crossness, at which the solids would be separated from the liquid sewage. The liquid was treated with chemicals to dilute the smell, and the solids, or sludge, were loaded on to specially constructed vessels, which dumped them in the North Sea. The first sludge-boat, the SS *Bazalgette*, arrived in June 1887, and this system remained in use for over a century, until 1998, when Thames Water PLC began to use a system whereby solids are separated from liquid sewage, the former being burned in incinerators, the power thus generated being turned into electricity. The remaining liquid is treated by the activated sludge process.

THE CHOLERA EPIDEMIC THAT DIDN'T HAPPEN

In 1892 cholera stuck Hamburg, causing great anxiety in Britain, since cholera epidemics had always arrived from the continental seaports with which Britain traded. There were 8,605 deaths in a city one-seventh the size of London, so if comparable mortality had occurred in Britain the epidemic would have been of unprecedented ferocity. Robert Koch, who had identified the cholera bacillus in India nine years earlier, was given such dictatorial powers by Kaiser

Wilhelm II that the Burgomeister of Hamburg complained that 'it was the Imperial Health Office and professor Koch who ran things here'. Hamburg's sewerage system had itself been designed by an English engineer, William Lindley, but 20,000 inhabitants remained unconnected to the system, and the sewage discharged into the River Elbe too close to the city, so that it returned with the incoming tide. So great was the alarm in Britain as the deaths mounted that the *Illustrated London News* devoted three successive issues to the epidemic, which was daily expected to reach the capital.[33]

There was no epidemic in Britain. There were 135 deaths from a 'disease reputed to be of the nature of cholera' spread across sixty-four towns, with 17 occurring in London, mostly among people returning from abroad. Bazalgette had died the previous year, but the system he had constructed protected the citizens of London from the scourge of cholera, as did those he and Robert Rawlinson had designed for other communities like Glasgow, Cambridge and Norwich. The day after his death, *The Times*, in its obituary, summed up his contribution:

> When the New Zealander comes to London, a thousand years hence, to sketch the ruins of St Paul's, the magnificent solidity and the faultless symmetry of the great granite blocks which form the wall of the Thames Embankment will still remain to testify that, in the reign of Victoria, 'jerry-building' was not quite universal. Of the great sewer that runs beneath Londoners know, as a rule, nothing, though the Registrar-General could tell them that its existence has added some twenty years to their chance of life.[34]

By the time this obituary was written, Joseph Bazalgette, Robert Rawlinson and others had ensured that many other English towns and cities were equipped with sewerage that protected their residents from waterborne disease. Bazalgette himself was involved in designing systems for Cambridge, Norwich, Glasgow and many other British communities, as well as others further afield in Budapest and Port Louis, Mauritius. He died a wealthy man, his estate being valued at a figure in excess of £100,000 after his death – a very large sum for the time.

Bazalgette himself remained aloof from the 'miasmatic' controversy. It has to be remembered that the system he designed was intended mainly to remove offensive smells from the capital. He did, however, allow himself one oblique comment on the controversy as it affected cholera in an address to the Institution of Civil Engineers in 1864. He wrote:

Although great differences of opinion existed, and continue to exist, as to the causes of the disease, yet an inspection of the houses in which deaths occurred was sufficient to show that, however occult might be the connection between death and defective drainage, the places formerly most favourable to the spread of disease became quite free from it, when afterwards properly drained.[35]

No one disagreed.

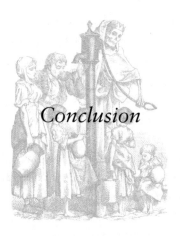

Conclusion

So what had been achieved by all the activity that this volume has examined: all the debates, inquiries, arguments, campaigns, legislation and public works? At the beginning of Victoria's reign most of her subjects lived in the country. By the time of her death most were town- or city-dwellers, earning their living not by tilling the fields but by working in factories, mills, offices, on the railways, canals and roads. And there were far more of them: almost four times as many inhabitants of Great Britain in 1901 as there had been at the time of the first census. Communities like Liverpool, Birmingham, Manchester, Glasgow and Sheffield, which had been small towns at the beginning of Victoria's reign, had become substantial conurbations that had grown rapidly without any attempt to prepare the housing, sanitation or medical facilities that their citizens needed. Yet at the end of Victoria's reign the death rates had fallen and a number of diseases associated with crowded living conditions were in rapid decline. How had this been achieved?

LAISSEZ-FAIRE

Before doctors, scientists, midwives and engineers could make their contributions to improvements in the health of the population, public servants, including politicians, had to be persuaded that the government had some responsibilities in these matters. This was not easily achieved. Victorian politicians of all parties were imbued with the doctrines of laissez-faire: that their task was to defend the kingdom, administer the law and keep taxes as low as possible. This was an especially attractive doctrine for the affluent classes, who would have to pay taxes that were levied and who were, on the whole, better protected against misfortune and ill health than the poorer classes. Social reformers and campaigners like Jeremy Bentham and Edwin Chadwick had to perform some strange philosophical gymnastics to support their reformist agenda. The expenditure of public money was justified with the utilitarian argument that it would reduce the cost of administering the Poor Law, not on humanitarian grounds. Nor were the reformers helped by the temperaments of some of their most prominent campaigners. Edwin Chadwick's energy in promoting causes that would have beneficial, humanitarian outcomes was vitiated by his extraordinary ability to antagonise people who could have been useful and willing allies.

Yet ultimately Chadwick and his fellow campaigners did make their points. The creation of effective municipal government with powers to levy rates and impose certain basic standards of housing and sanitation, best exemplified in the creation of London's Metropolitan Board of Works and, later, the London County Council, would have had to wait longer if it were not for the efforts of Chadwick and people like him. Prominent among these allies was William Farr, whose relentless arguments in favour of better living conditions, backed by hard statistics and persuasive prose, helped to convince his political masters that humanitarian concerns, as well as enlightened economic self-interest, obliged them to assume responsibility for the welfare of their fellow-citizens.

But perhaps, ultimately, it was a force of nature that prompted the ruling classes to find the will and the money to take the steps required, long overdue, to protect city-dwellers from epidemic disease. For two years, from 1856 to 1858, politicians wrangled over Joseph Bazalgette's plans to build a system of intercepting sewers that would shield London's water supply from its disease-ridden waste. The arguments were familiar: whose job was it to complete this task and, above all, who would pay for it? The issue was finally resolved by the Great Stink, whose unpleasant odour, combined with a mistaken belief that cholera was borne by its foul smell and that they were themselves under threat, finally persuaded parliamentarians to give Bazalgette the resources and the authority he needed to carry out his great works. It is tempting to speculate that, if the Palace of Westminster, after the fire of 1834, had been rebuilt on Hampstead Heath instead of the banks of the Thames, we might still be wrangling. Where utilitarian and humanitarian arguments had failed, the Great Stink prevailed.

LIVING CONDITIONS

Parliament's willingness to raise a few million pounds to rid itself of the Great Stink was not extended to comparable concern about the living and working conditions of the great mass of working people living in Britain's cities. As late as 1889 Charles Booth's 'poverty map' of London revealed the degrading conditions in which many of its citizens lived, though in other cities, notably Birmingham, slum clearance measures were more actively pursued. A new century and a new reign had to arrive before the 'wild and Utopian' notion of public housing so apologetically put forward by Dr Buchanan, of St Giles, in 1895 came to be widely accepted as public policy. Likewise, the Cheap Trains Act of 1883 was not effective in encouraging city slum-dwellers to move from densely populated areas until the new century saw the emergence of the Garden City movement, from 1902, and the development of suburban dwellings in Metroland and its sisters. In the meantime, many Victorian city-dwellers continued to live in squalor mitigated only by the philanthropy of enlightened and compassionate individuals such as George Peabody, Angela Burdett-Coutts, Octavia Hill and Lord Rowton, whose memories are preserved into the twenty-first century by the institutions they helped to found. Even such determined philanthropists as these could do nothing about the noxious fumes that issued from factories, potteries, alkali works and other industrial premises and that, when mixed with the smoke from houses, gave names to huge regions with their own 'Great Stinks' like the Black Country of Staffordshire or 'The Smoke' – London itself.

In one respect, the laissez-faire doctrines to which politicians and economists clung so firmly did benefit the poorer classes. The decision to adopt policies of free trade and, in particular, to admit agricultural produce from the Empire and the New World had damaging effects upon British agriculture for which a heavy price was paid in both world wars. Yet the reduction in the prices of some common foods, accompanied by some modest attempts to safeguard their quality, together with that of milk, made a contribution to the nutritional standards of working people, though again another fifty years had to pass before the physical condition of working-class people approached that of the more prosperous classes.

DOCTORS, SCIENTISTS AND DISEASE

While politicians, public servants and philanthropists were feeling their way towards an understanding of their responsibilities for the welfare of their fellow-citizens, professional men and, towards the end of the century, professional women were struggling to understand the causes of disease and their cures. It is easy now to scorn those who held so firmly for so long to the 'miasmatic' theories of disease propagation and denied the role that polluted water played in spreading unpleasant and deadly diseases like cholera, typhoid and dysentery. Yet in the 1850s, when epidemic cholera was accompanied by a smell so foul that, in hot weather, citizens avoided walking near sewage-ridden rivers, and when drinking water looked clean except when examined under a microscope, it would have been perfectly reasonable to assume that disease entered the body via the nose rather than via the throat. It is not, therefore, surprising that William Budd and John Snow were widely disbelieved when they proposed that some deadly agent was passed in water, especially when they were not able to identify or name the agent. It took the work of one of history's most celebrated scientists, Louis Pasteur, and a Nobel Prize winner, Robert Koch, to identify the true causes of disease. Even when they had done this, another half century had to pass before the development of antibiotics by another generation of doctors and scientists offered effective treatments for diseases such as pneumonia and tuberculosis, though smallpox, cholera, typhus, typhoid and scarlet fever no longer posed such a threat as they had in the past.

In the meantime, in the absence of cures, the emphasis had to be on preventing disease from becoming established in the first place. Even here, there was usually a struggle against habit and orthodoxy. Ignaz Semmelweis and Zepherina Veitch, in their different ways, both knew how to prevent the steady death toll of women from puerperal fever, but they both had long, hard and frustrating struggles against ignorance and folly – against the 'gentlemen's hands are clean' school of medicine. Sadly, like John Snow, both died before their ideas were widely accepted and enshrined in legislation or common practice.

THE ENGINEERS

In the meantime, the principal role in preventive medicine was taken, half knowingly, by civil engineers. These were busy men of the heroic age of Victorian engineering, not too concerned with theories of disease propagation or the antiseptic properties of carbolic acid. They did, however, know how to build reservoirs, filtration systems, water supply pipes, pumps and sewers, and many of them became very rich doing it. In the process the clean water they supplied for drinking, cooking and cleaning transformed the lives of those who received it, while the sewers they built ensured that the water remained free of pollution. One writer has claimed of Joseph Bazalgette that 'this superb and far sighted engineer probably did more good, and saved more lives, than any single Victorian public official'.[1] This was certainly a view shared by some of his contemporaries. Less than a year before his death Bazalgette was interviewed for Cassell's *Saturday Journal*, the article beginning with a reference to Bazalgette's home: 'If the malignant spirits whom we moderns call cholera, typhus and smallpox were one day to set out in quest of the man who had been, within the past thirty or forty years, their deadliest foe in all London, they would probably make their way to St Mary's Wimbledon.'[2]

The writer's understanding of medicine (particularly smallpox) was mistaken, but the message was clear. Bazalgette and his colleagues, like Thomas Hawksley, Joseph Simpson and Robert Rawlinson, were better placed to safeguard the health of their fellow-citizens than doctors or scientists who would have to wait for a new century before they were well equipped to treat diseases. When Victoria came to the throne, the average age at death of her subjects fell in the late thirties. When she died in 1901, the average age of death was in the early fifties. All the people whose lives have been examined in this volume contributed to that improvement: politicians, social reformers, doctors, scientists, midwives; but especially the engineers.

Notes

Chapter One

1. W. Bonser, 'Epidemics during the Anglo-Saxon Period', *Journal of the British Archaeological Association*, 3rd series, 9 (1944), 48–71.
2. Bede, *de Natura Rerum*, ch. 37, 'de pestilentia'.
3. Isidore of Seville, *Etymologiae*, bk 14, ch. 6.
4. Voltaire, *On Inoculation: Letters concerning the English Nation*, trans. J. Lockman (London, 1804), letter 11, gives a rather acerbic account of his views on inoculation, which was then becoming commonplace.
5. S. Halliday, *Newgate: A Prototype of Hell* (Sutton, Stroud, 2006), pp. 40–1, describes the incident.
6. L. Picard, *Dr Johnson's London* (Phoenix, London, 2001), p. 79.
7. Voltaire, *On Inoculation*, letter 11.
8. *Edinburgh Review*, 9 (1806), 322–51, contains an account of the early opposition to vaccination.
9. *Journal of Medical Biography*, vol. 8/2 (May 2000), p. 84.
10. *The Times*, 14 November 1871.
11. John Simon, *Papers on the History and Practice of Vaccination* (Parliamentary Papers, 1857), vol. 25, p. 225.
12. A. Hardy, 'Smallpox in London: Factors in the Decline of the Disease in the Nineteenth Century', *Medical History*, 27 (1983), 111–38.

Chapter Two

1. C.M. Law, 'The Growth of the Urban Population of England and Wales, 1801–1911', *Transactions of the Institute of British Geographers*, 41 (1967), 142.

2. B.R. Mitchell and P. Deane, *Abstract of British Historical Statistics* (Cambridge University Press, Cambridge, 1971), pp. 24 ff.
3. A.N. Wilson, *After the Victorians* (Hutchinson, London, 2005), p. 42.
4. G.M. Trevelyan, *English Social History* (Longman, London, 1942), p. 463.
5. W. Cobbett, *Rural Ride* (Dent, London, 1973), pp. 17, 18.
6. G. Rosen, 'Disease, Debility and Death', in H.J. Dyos and M. Wolff (eds), *The Victorian City: Image and Realities* (Routledge & Kegan Paul, London, 1973), vol. 2, p. 626.
7. See Chapter 5.
8. *Registrar-General's Second Annual Report* (1839), app., p. xi.
9. N. Humphreys (ed.), *Vital Statistics: A Memorial Volume to William Farr* (Sanitary Institute, London, 1885), p. 150.
10. B.R. Mitchell and P. Deane, *Abstract of British Historical Statistics* (Cambridge University Press, Cambridge, 1971), pp. 36–7.
11. Humphreys (ed.), *Vital Statistics*, p. 203.
12. See Chapter 6 for an account of the struggle to gain professional status for midwives.
13. *Lancet*, 5 August 1843, p. 661.
14. N. Williams and G. Mooney, 'Infant Mortality in an Age of Great Cities, c. 1840–1910', in *Continuity and Change*, 9/2 (1994), 191 ff.; also *Registrar-General's Fifth Annual Report* (1841). The figures refer to women; men live on average two years less than women in each parish.
15. Florence Nightingale, *Notes on Hospitals* (Longman, London, 1863), p. iii.
16. L. McDonald (ed.), *Florence Nightingale on Public Health Care* (Wilfred Laurier University Press, Ontario, 2004), p. 608.
17. *Selected Writings of Florence Nightingale*, ed. L.S. Seymer (Macmillan, London, 1954), pp. 377 ff.
18. Ibid., p. 392.
19. A.S. Wohl, *Endangered Lives: Public Health in Victorian Britain* (Methuen, London, 1983), p. 12.
20. *Lancet*, 14 September 1861, p. 256.
21. This is discussed in more detail in Chapter 5.
22. Wohl, *Endangered Lives*, p. 147.
23. See Chapters 4 and 5 for an account of these two very different personalities, John Simon and Edwin Chadwick
24. *Royal Commission on Housing of the Working Classes* (Parliamentary Papers, vol. 30, 1884–5), Minutes of Evidence, p. 63.
25. Wohl, *Endangered Lives*, p. 160.

26. See Chapter 4 for a discussion of their careers.

27. *Lancet*, 23 December 1899, p. 1760.

28. Wohl, *Endangered Lives*, p. 62.

29. Briggs, *Victorian Cities*, p. 376.

30. Ibid.

31. S.E. Finer, *The Life and Times of Sir Edwin Chadwick* (Methuen, London, 1952), pp. 92, 218.

32. J. Toulmin Smith, *Government by Commissions Illegal and Pernicious* (H. Sweet, London, 1849), p. 340.

33. Institution of Civil Engineers, *Minutes of Proceedings*, vol. 12 (1852–3), pp. 70–1.

34. The National Archives: Public Record Office, General Board of Health and Home Office, Local Government Act Office Correspondence, MH 13, 1846–71, vol. 261, 15 November 1848.

35. *The Times*, 20 March 1855.

36. *Lancet*, 29 December 1855, pp. 632–3.

37. Parl. Debs. (series 3), vol. 151, cols 27–8 (1857–8).

38. See Chapter 7.

39. F. Engels, *The Condition of the Working Class in England* (Basil Blackwell, Oxford, 1958), p. 63.

40. See Chapter 5.

41. X. Baron (ed.), *London, 1066–1914, Literary Sources and Documents* (Helm Information, Robertsbridge, 1997), vol. 2, p. 399.

42. *Northern Star*, 4 May 1844, p. 6. See Chapter 5 for an account of Blomfield's initiative.

43. Baron (ed.), *London, 1066–1914*, vol. 2, p. 649.

44. *The Times*, 12 October 1843, p. 4.

45. See Chapter 4.

46. See Chapter 4 for the activities of the Medical Officers of Health.

47. J. Simon, 'First Annual Report', in 'Reports Relating to the Sanitary Condition of the City of London', Metropolitan Archives, p. 9.

48. A. Mearns, *The Bitter Cry of Outcast London* (Leicester University Press, Leicester, 1970), p. 59.

49. *The Economist* (May 1848).

50. *Public Health* (June 1895), p. 324.

51. Parl. Debs (series 3), vol. 178, cols 1700 ff. (1884).

52. *Pall Mall Gazette*, 23 October 1883, p. 1.

53. Wohl, *Endangered Lives*, p. 315.

54. M.J. Daunton, 'Health and Housing in Victorian London', *Medical History Supplement*, 11 (1991), 130.

55. See Chapter 7.
56. Parliamentary Papers, 1884–5, vol. 30, p. 19
57. Ibid., p. 78; the dissenter was Jesse Collings, MP.
58. Wohl, *Endangered Lives*, p. 327.
59. See Chapter 1 for an account of the controversies over vaccination.
60. See Chapter 4.
61. J. London, 'People of the Abyss', in *Novels and Social Writings* (Library of America, New York, 1982), p. 140.
62. G. Orwell, *Down and Out in Paris and London* (Penguin, London, 1986), p. 211.
63. See p. 36 for the relevant indices.
64. Rosen, 'Disease, Debility and Death', vol. 2, ch. 7.
65. Wohl, *Endangered Lives*, p. 21.
66. Baron (ed.), *London 1066–1914*, vol. 3, p. 409.
67. See p. 32 for reference to Charles Booth's survey.
68. Wohl, *Endangered Lives*, p. 51.
69. See Chapter 7 for the work of Sir Joseph Bazalgette in this connection.
70. Baron (ed.), *London 1066–1914*, vol. 3, p. 373, n. 1.
71. *Punch*, 20 (January–June 1851), p. 83.
72. Parliamentary Papers, 1878, vol. 44, p. 524.
73. Wohl, *Endangered Lives*, p. 210.
74. Parliamentary Papers, 1878, vol. 44, p. 452.
75. *The Times*, 14 June 1879, p. 8.
76. Parliamentary Papers, 1898, vol. 45, questions 429–30.
77. See Chapter 4.
78. F. Engels, 'The Great Towns', in *Condition of the Working Class in England* (1845; Allen & Unwin, London, 1891).
79. Wohl, *Endangered Lives*, 72–4.
80. Ibid., p. 70.
81. A. Faulkner, *The Grand Junction Canal* (David & Charles, Newton Abbot, 1993), p. 195.
82. *Public Health*, vol. 9, 10 January 1897, p. 286, Journal of the Incorporated Society of Medical Officers of Health.

Chapter Three

1. See Chapter 1 for an account of the conquest of smallpox.
2. Philip Ball, *The Devil's Doctor: Paracelsus and the World of Renaissance Magic and Science* (Heinemann, London, 2006), is a modern and definitive account of the work of Paracelsus.

3. A.E. Waite, *Lives of Alchemistical Philosophers* (George Redway, London, 1888), p. 137.

4. *Dictionary of National Biography* (Oxford University Press, Oxford, 2004), vol. 53, p. 541.

5. R. Porter, *Quacks, Fakers and Charlatans in English Medicine* (Tempus, Stroud, 2001), p. 16.

6. W.F. Bynum, *Science and the Practice of Medicine in the Nineteenth Century* (Cambridge University Press, Cambridge, 1994), p. 60.

7. See Chapter 5.

8. Taken from the Annual Reports of the Registrar-General for the relevant year, available at the Library of the Office for National Statistics, Pimlico, London.

9. The training of midwives is discussed in Chapter 6.

10. *Lancet*, 12 November 1831, p. 216.

11. *The Times*, 12–14 September 1849.

12. M. Pelling, *Cholera, Fever and English Medicine, 1825–65* (Oxford University Press, Oxford, 1978), p. 141.

13. *The Times*, 7 November 1859, p. 6.

14. C. Hamlin, 'Providence and Putrefation: Victorian Sanitarians and the Natural Theology of Health and Disease', *Victorian Studies*, vol. 28, no. 3 (1984–5), p. 383.

15. M. Pelling, *Cholera, Fever and English Medicine, 1825–65* (Oxford University Press, Oxford, 1978), p. 140.

16. W.H. Brock, *Justus von Liebig* (Cambridge University Press, Cambridge, 1997), p. 207.

17. See Chapter 7.

18. Justus von Liebig, *Familiar Letters on Chemistry* (Taylor & Walton, London, 1843), letter 11.

19. *Builder*, 8 November 1862, p. 800.

20. See Chapter 7.

21. *The Times*, 12–14 September 1849. See p. 59.

22. *Dictionary of Scientific Biography* (American Council of Learned Societies, New York, 1975), p. 558.

23. *Health of Towns Commission, Second Report* (Parliamentary Papers, 1845), vol. 18, pt 2, p. 67.

24. *Quarterly Review*, 71 (1842), p. 422.

25. This episode is described in *Dictionary of Scientific Biography*, p. 559.

26. Semmelweis's discoveries are discussed in Chapter 6.

27. *Dictionary of National Biography*, vol. 8, pp. 551–2.

28. W. Budd, *Typhoid Fever, its Nature, Mode of Spreading and Prevention* (Longmans, London, 1873), p. 63.
29. Ibid., pp. 71–5.
30. Ibid., pp. 171–5.
31. *Lancet*, 2 (1856), p. 618.
32. See p. 59.
33. London figures from C. Creighton, *A History of Epidemics in Britain* (Cambridge University Press, Cambridge, 1894), p. 858; Great Britain figures from C. Roberts and M. Cox., *Health and Disease in Britain from Prehistory to the Present Day* (Sutton Publishing, Stroud, 2003), p. 337.
34. See Chapters 5 and 7 for an account of this final epidemic.
35. Just east of the present site of Tottenham Court Road underground station, St Giles was one of London's most notorious slums.
36. A.S. Wohl, *Endangered Lives: Public Health in Victorian Britain* (Methuen, London, 1983), pp. 120–3.
37. S. Hempel, *The Medical Detective: John Snow and the Mystery of Cholera* (Granta, Cambridge, 2006), pp. 52–6.
38. W. Budd, *Malignant Cholera, its Cause, Mode of Propagation and Prevention* (Churchill, London, 1849), pp. 21–2.
39. *The Times*, 26 September 1849, p. 4.
40. *The Times*, 5 October 1849, p. 3.
41. See Chapter 7.
42. Budd, *Typhoid Fever*, pp. 141–3, 153.
43. W. Budd, *Memorandum on Asiatic Cholera, its Mode of Spreading and its Prevention* (Churchill, Bristol, 1866), pp. 5, 3.
44. *Report of the General Board of Health on the Epidemic Cholera of 1848 and 1849* (Parliamentary Papers, 1850), vol. 21, p. 543.
45. S. Roberts, 'John Snow and Benjamin Richardson', *Journal of Medical Biography* (February 1999), and Stephanie Snow, 'John Snow', ibid. (February and May 2000).
46. Hempel, *The Medical Detective*, p. 93.
47. Parliamentary Papers, 1850, vol. 21, p. 543.
48. J. Snow, 'On the Communication of Cholera by Impure Thames Water', *Medical Times and Gazette* (1858), p. 191.
49. J. Snow, *On Cholera* (Wade Hampton Frost, New York, 1936), p. 124.
50. *Report on the Work of the Metropolitan Water Companies* (Parliamentary Papers, 1856), vol. 52, p. 345.
51. See Chapter 5.
52. Parliamentary Papers, 1867–8, vol. 37, pp. 79–80.

53. *Report of the Medical Council* (Parliamentary Papers, 1854–5), vol. 45, p. 7.
54. See Chapter 7 for an account of the work of engineers in this connection.
55. *Dictionary of Scientific Biography*, vol. 10, pp. 266 ff.
56. See Chapter 7.
57. See p. 68.
58. *Dictionary of Scientific Biography*, vol. 10, pp. 351 ff.
59. See Chapter 4 for a description of Lister's work.
60. *Lancet* (1895), pp. 889, 1140.
61. *Comtes rendus de l'Académie des Sciences* (Paris, 1878), vol. 86, p. 1043.
62. *Dictionary of Scientific Biography*, vol. 10, p. 351.
63. F. Adams, *Hippocrates, the Genuine Works* (Sydenham Society, London, 1849).
64. J. Hirsh, 'Pneumonia: Early History of Diagnosis and Treatment', *Annals of Medical History*, ser. 3, vol. 2 (1940), pp. 144–50.
65. R. Woods and J. Woodward (eds), *Urban Disease and Mortality in Nineteenth Century England* (Batsford, London, 1974), ch. 4, J. Cronjé, p. 81.
66. C. Roberts and M. Cox, *Health and Disease in Britain from Prehistory to the Present Day* (Sutton, Stroud, 2003), pp. 335–6

Chapter Four

1. F.B. Smith, *The People's Health* (Croom Helm, London, 1979), p. 140.
2. R. Porter, *Quacks, Fakers and Charlatans in English Medicine* (Tempus, Stroud, 2001), gives a full and amusing account of this phenomenon in English medical practice.
3. William Wallace Currie (son) (ed.), *Memoir of the Life, Writings and Correspondence of James Currie, M.D., F.R.S.* (Longmans, London, 1831), vol. 1, p. 17.
4. A.W. Newton, 'A Liverpool Physician and a Man of Letters', in *Proceedings of the Literary and Philosophical Society of Liverpool*, 65 (1916–17), p. 41.
5. Currie (ed.), *Memoir*, vol. 1, pp. 17–42.
6. Ibid., p. 112.
7. J. Currie, *Medical Reports on the Effects of Water, Cold and Warm, as a Remedy in Fever and Febrile Diseases, whether Applied to the*

Surface of the Body or Used as a Drink (Cadell, Davies & Creech, Liverpool, 1797), p. 201; British Library catalogue BL1509 1286.

8. W. Moss, *The Liverpool Guide, Including a Sketch of the Environs* (Harris & Co., Liverpool, 1796), p. 154.

9. J. Newlands (Liverpool Borough Engineer), *Liverpool Past and Present in Relation to Sanitary Operations* (Harris & Co., Liverpool, 1858), p. 4; Liverpool City Archives ref. H.628.n.

10. Currie, *Medical Reports*, p. 202.

11. B.R. Mitchell and P. Deane, *Abstract of British Historical Statistics* (Cambridge University Press, Cambridge, 1962), p. 24.

12. Quoted in Newlands, *Liverpool Past and Present*, p. 6.

13. W.M. Frazer, *Duncan of Liverpool* (Hamish Hamilton, London, 1947), p. 5. Frazer was a professor at the University of Liverpool and, as the city's Medical Officer, a successor to Duncan.

14. Currie, *Medical Reports*, pp. 210–11.

15. Currie (ed.), *Memoir*, vol. 1, letters dated 29 August and 15 October 1789, app. iv, p. 457.

16. Currie, *Medical Reports*, p. 201.

17. Newlands, *Liverpool Past and Present*, p. 4.

18. A. de Curzon (ed.), *Dr James Currie and the French Prisoners of War in Liverpool* (Howell, Liverpool, 1926), 26.

19. E. Darwin, *Zoonomia, or the Laws of Organic Life* (Erasmus Darwin, Dublin, 1794–6), vol. 2, p. 293.

20. Wallace was the maiden name of Currie's wife, whom he married in 1783. Her family claimed descent from the Scottish hero William Wallace; Currie's son was mayor of Liverpool, 1835–6.

21. Currie (ed.), *Memoir*, vol. 1, p. 15.

22. W. Wright, *London Medical Journal* (1786), contains an early account by William Wright of his experiments with cold douches, reported by Currie in *Medical Reports*, pp. 1–5.

23. *Philosophical Transactions of the Royal Society* (1792), vol. 1, p. 199.

24. Currie, *Medical Reports*, pp. 8, 37–8.

25. Ibid., pp. 16–17.

26. Currie (ed.), *Memoir*, vol. 1, p. 220.

27. R. Burns, *Works, with an Account of his Life and a Criticism of his Writings*, ed. J. Currie (Bell, London, 1816), p. vii.

28. Ibid., pp. 27–284.

29. Currie (ed.), *Memoir*, vol. 2, pp. 307–15.

30. Newlands, *Liverpool Past and Present*, p. 4.

31. See Chapter 3.
32. S. Halliday, 'Duncan of Liverpool: Britain's First Medical Officer', *Journal of Medical Biography*, 11 (2003), pp. 142–9.
33. Liverpool City Archives, ref. Hq.050 KAL.
34. See Chapter 5 for an account of Chadwick's work and his celebrated *Report*.
35. W.H. Duncan, *On the Physical Causes of the High Rate of Mortality in Liverpool* (Liverpool, 1843); Liverpool City Archives, ref. H.614.DUN.
36. See Chapter 5 for an account of Farr's work in combating epidemic disease.
37. Duncan used his lectures as the basis for information he gave to the Royal Commission on the State of Large Towns and Populous Districts; see Parliamentary Papers, 1844, vol. 17, for his testimony.
38. Parliamentary Papers, 1844, vol. 17, p. 50.
39. Ibid., pp. 185 ff., contains Holme's evidence.
40. B.D. White, *A History of the Corporation of Liverpool 1835–1914* (Liverpool University Press, Liverpool, 1951), pp. 40 ff.
41. *Punch*, 12 (1847), p. 44.
42. White, *A History of the Corporation of Liverpool*, pp. 40 ff, describes Newlands's appointment and role.
43. Liverpool City Archives, ref. 352 HEA 1/1.
44. Duncan, *On the Physical Causes*; extracts from pp. 5–21.
45. *Report to the Health Committee of the Borough of Liverpool on the Health of the Town, 1847–50* (Liverpool, 1851); the quoted extracts are from pp. 5–61; Liverpool City Archives.
46. Duncan, *On the Physical Causes*, pp. 56–7.
47. See Chapter 5 for Chadwick's harsh views of the Irish.
48. Liverpool City Archives, ref. Min/Hea II 1/1, minutes of 13 March 1847, p. 100.
49. Ibid., minutes of 17 June 1847, p. 228.
50. The figures of mortality are taken from the *Seventeenth Annual Report of the Registrar General for the Year 1854* (London, 1856), app., table 14, p. 84; available at the Library of the Office for National Statistics, Pimlico, London.
51. London in 1851 recorded a population of 2,362,000 and in the 1848–9 epidemic suffered 14,137 deaths. The figures for Liverpool were 222,954 population and 5,245 deaths.
52. W.M. Frazer, *Duncan of Liverpool* (Hamish Hamilton, London, 1947).

53. Liverpool City Archives, ref. 352 HEA 1/1, letter books, p. 481, contains the letter to Chadwick.

54. *Report to the Health Committee of the Borough of Liverpool on the Health of the Town* (Liverpool, 1851, p. 100; Liverpool City Archives.

55. E. Midwinter, *Old Liverpool* (David & Charles, Newton Abbot, 1971), pp. 80 ff., recounts the process of cellar clearance and house cleansing that Duncan pursued.

56. See pp. 102–3 for this earlier sewer building programme.

57. Liverpool City Archives, ref. 352 HEA 1/1, letter to Dr Head dated 23 November 1853.

58. See pp. 61 ff.

59. The report for 1854 is missing from the Liverpool City Archives, but the *Registrar-General's Annual Report for the Year 1854* (London, 1856), available at the Library of the Office for National Statistics, Pimlico, London, records cholera deaths in Liverpool during the 1849 epidemic as 4,173 compared with 1,084 for 1854; see app., p. 84, table 14; the population in the intervening five years had, of course, increased.

60. *Annual Report of the Medical Officer of Health* (1866), pp. 139–43; Liverpool City archives; Dr W.S. Trench (1810–77) was Duncan's successor as Medical Officer from 1863 to 1877.

61. Frazer, *Duncan of Liverpool*, pp. 101–2.

62. Ibid., p. 98.

63. *Liverpool Echo*, 10 September 2001, p. 9.

64. Duncan Society Literature, August 2001. The Society's website is at www.duncansociety.org.uk.

65. F. Burkhardt (ed.), *Charles Darwin's Letters, a Selection, 1825–59* (Cambridge University Press, Cambridge, 1998), 105 ff.

66. A. Desmond and J. Moore, *Darwin* (Michael Joseph, London, 1991), p. 366. This work also discusses the possible causes of Darwin's mysterious illness.

67. A Medical Guide to the Principal British Spas and Climatic Health Resorts, British Library catalogue, shelfmark P.P.2487.fck.

68. See Chapter 2.

69. S.E. Finer, *The Life and Times of Sir Edwin Chadwick* (Methuen, London, 1952), bk 7, ch. 2.

70. T. Southwood Smith. *Westminster Review*, 3 (1825), pp. 134–67, contains the article.

71. T. Watson, *Lectures on the Principles and Practice of Physic* (Longmans, London, 1844), p. 50.

72. J. Copland (ed.), *A Dictionary of Practical Medicine* (Longmans, London, 1858), p. 564.

73. C. Creighton, *A History of Epidemics in Britain* (Cambridge University Press, Cambridge, 1894), p. 858.

74. John Snow, *On the Mode of Communication of Cholera* (Churchill, London, 1849).

75. *Report of the General Board of Health on the Epidemic Cholera of 1848 and 1849* (1850), p. 10.

76. Report from Dr Sutherland on Epidemic Cholera in the Metropolis in 1854; Wellcome Institute Library ref. WC262 1855 G784.

77. *Report on the Sanitary Condition of Malta and Gozo with Reference to the Epidemic Cholera in the Year 1865* (HMSO, London, 1867), p. 21.

78. *Report on the Sanitary Condition of Gibraltar with Reference to the Epidemic Cholera in the Year 1865* (HMSO, London, 1867), p. 42.

79. *Lancet*, 25 July 1891, p. 206.

80. See Chapter 6 for an account of Semmelweis's work, and J. Sheldrake, 'John Simon, Surgeon and Scientist', *Journal of Medical Biography*, 6/3 (August 1998), p. 136; a Blue Plaque marks Simon's residence at 40 Kensington Square.

81. See p. 90 for an account of Lister's work.

82. J. Simon, *English Sanitary Institutions* (Cassell, London, 1897), p. 166.

83. See Chapter 5 for an account of Chadwick's troubles.

84. *Public Health Reports*, ed. E. Seaton (London, 1887), report for 1861.

85. See p. 134 for details of this legislation.

86. *The Times*, 10 October 1849, p. 5.

87. J. Simon, 'First Annual Report', in *Reports relating to the Sanitary Condition of the City of London* (Metropolitan Archives, London, 1854).

88. See Chapter 3.

89. Creighton, *A History of Epidemics*, p. 858.

90. Simon, *English Sanitary Institutions*, p. 126.

91. Parliamentary Papers, 1857–8, vol. 23, contains Simon's evidence and reports.

92. Parliamentary Papers, 1867, vol. 37, pp. 30–3.

93. *Report of the Medical Officer of the Privy Council* (Parliamentary Papers, 1874), vol. 31, pp. 9, 11.

94. See Chapter 7.

95. J. Simon, *Filth Diseases and their Prevention* (Boston, 1876), pp. 6, 17, 19, 26, 36, 49.

Chapter Five

1. See S. Halliday, *Newgate: London's Prototype of Hell* (Sutton, Stroud, 2006), for an account of these practices.
2. See Chapter 4 for an account of the work of Southwood Smith.
3. *Report of the State of the Irish Poor in Great Britain* (Parliamentary Papers, 1836), vol. 34, p. 6.
4. M.W. Flinn, Introduction, to Chadwick's *Report* (Edinburgh University Press, Edinburgh, 1965), p. 43.
5. John Simon, *English Sanitary Institutions* (Cassell, London, 1897) p. 187 n.; Metropolitan Archives.
6. *The Times*, 29 August 1842; *Morning Chronicle*, 30 August 1842; *Quarterly Review*, 71 (March 1843); and *Tait's Edinburgh*, 9 (1842).
7. Simon, *English Sanitary Institutions*, p. 196.
8. Chadwick, *Report*, p. 410.
9. Ibid., p. 374.
10. Ibid. p. 387.
11. Metropolitan Commissions of Sewers Records, British Library catalogue 8776.h.29
12. Parliamentary Papers, 1844, vol. 17, pp. 150, 170.
13. Chadwick, *Report*, p. 127.
14. Ibid., p. 117.
15. R. Porter, *London, a Social History* (Hamish Hamilton, London, 1994), p. 257.
16. S.E. Finer, *The Life and Times of Sir Edwin Chadwick* (Methuen, London, 1952), p. 356.
17. See Chapter 3 for an account of the Broad Street pump and the work of Dr John Snow.
18. Florence Nightingale, *Notes on Nursing* (facsimile reprint; Harrison, London, 1859), p. 16.
19. Parliamentary Papers, 1846, vol. 10, p. 651.
20. See Chapter 3 for an account of Koch's work.
21. *Builder*, 1 February 1890, pp. 78–9.
22. Ibid., 18 July 1844, pp. 350–1; the writer was Professor Booth, otherwise unknown to history.
23. N. Humphreys (ed.), *Vital Statistics: A Memorial Volume to William Farr* (Sanitary Institute, London, 1885), p. ix. Humphreys worked with Farr from 1856 and made use of a biographical fragment begun by Farr himself.
24. See Chapter 6 for the career of Elizabeth Garrett Anderson.

25. Humphreys (ed.), *Vital Statistics*, p. viii, quotes Chadwick's letter, dated 13 April 1844.
26. *Registrar-General's Fifth Annual Report* (1942), p. 245.
27. *Registrar-General's First Annual Report* (1838), p. xiv; the Library of the Office for National Statistics, Pimlico, London, contains all the annual reports.
28. M. Weatherall, *Cambridge Contributions* (Cambridge University Press, Cambridge, 1997), pp. 28–9.
29. See *Registrar-General's First Annual Report*, pp. 11–12, for the letter.
30. *Dictionary of National Biography* (Oxford University Press, Oxford, 1964), vol. 6, p. 1090.
31. *Registrar-General's Fifth Annual Report*, p. xv.
32. *Registrar-General, Tenth Annual Report* (1847), pp. xv, xvii.
33. Parliamentary Papers, 1854–5, vol. 21, p. 16.
34. See Chapter 3 for an account of Snow's study.
35. Parliamentary Papers (1854–5), vol. 21, pp. 26–31, 47, 48, 52, 155–61.
36. *The Times*, 2 August 1866, p. 10.
37. Parliamentary Papers (1867–8), vol. 37, p. 95.
38. See Chapter 7 for an account of Sir Joseph Bazalgette's work in London.
39. Parliamentary Papers (1867–8), vol. 37, p. 117.
40. *Report of Captain Tyler to the Board of Trade* (Parliamentary Papers, 1867), vol. 58, pp. 6, 8, 20.
41. *Lancet*, 2 November 1867.
42. *British Medical Journal*, 27 April 1867.
43. Parliamentary Papers (1867–8), vol. 37, p. lvi.
44. Ibid., pp. 79–80.
45. Ibid., p. xiv.
46. *British Medical Journal*, 21 April 1883, pp. 783–4.
47. *Lancet*, 15 August 1868, vol. 2, p. 223.
48. Parliamentary Papers (1893–4), vol. 40, questions 10641–5 ff.
49. See p. 136.
50. C. Creighton, *A History of Epidemics in Britain* (Oxford University Press, Oxford, 1894), p. 854.
51. Gustav Jaeger, *Essays on Health Culture* (English edn., London: Waterlow and Sons, 1887); see p. 118.
52. Their activities are described in Chapter 7.

Chapter Six

1. See table on p. 58.
2. I. Loudon, 'Deaths in Childbed from the Eighteenth Century to 1935', *Medical History*, 30/1 (1986), pp. 1–41.
3. See Chapters 4 and 5 for a discussion of the miasmatic explanation for epidemic disease.
4. *Lancet* (1883), vol. 1, pp. 229–30.
5. I. Loudon, *Death in Childbirth* (Oxford University Press, Oxford, 1992), pp. 36–42.
6. See p. 90 for an account of Lister and his work.
7. O.W. Holmes, 'The Contagiousness of Puerperal Fever', *New England Quarterly Journal of Medicine*, vol. 1, no. 4 (April 1843), pp. 503–30.
8. A. Gordon, *A Treatise on the Epidemic Puerperal Fever of Aberdeen* (London, 1795), pp. 2–3.
9. C.J. Cullingworth, *Oliver Wendell Holmes and the Contagiousness of Puerperal Fever* (London, 1906), gives a brief account of Gordon's life.
10. See p. 114.
11. See Chapter 5.
12. W. Farr, *Fifth Annual Report of the Registrar-General* (1841), pp. 384–95.
13. C. Meigs, *On the Nature, Symptoms and Treatment of Childbed Fever* (Philadelphia, 1854), p. 104. R.M. Wertz and D.C. Wertz, *Lying-in: A History of Childbirth in America* (New York Free Press, New York, 1977).
14. C. Meigs, *Females and their Diseases: A Series of Letters to his Class* (Philadelphia, 1847), p. 47.
15. Ibid., p. 19.
16. See p. 149 for an account of the Rational Dress Society.
17. Wertz and Wertz, *Lying-in*, p. 117.
18. See Chapter 3.
19. 98 per 1,000 births in Semmelweis's clinic; 39.9 in the midwives' clinic; Loudon, *Death in Childbirth*, pp. 67 ff.
20. Semmelweis, *The Aetiology, the Concept and the Prophylaxis of Childbed Fever* (University of Wisconsin Press, Madison, 1983). *Journal of Medical Biography*, vol. 2, no.1 (February 1994), gives an account of Semmelweis's life.
21. See Chapter 3 for an account of Virchow's career.

22. *Dictionary of Scientific Biography* (American Council of Learned Societies, New York, 1975), vol. 12, p. 296.
23. Ibid.
24. Pasteur's obituary, *Lancet*, 5 October 1895, p. 889.
25. J.H. Aveling, *English Midwives: Their History and Prospects* (London, 1872), available in the Wellcome Library, Euston Road, London.
26. For example: *British Medical Journal*, 1 (1874), pp. 252–3; *The Times*, 3 March 1875, p. 11, col. 6; *Lancet*, 1 (1891), pp. 110–11.
27. *Transactions of the Obstetrical Society of London* (1874), p. 16; (1875), p. 75.
28. See p. 153 for the Hotel Dieu in Paris.
29. See Chapter 5.
30. *Registrar-General's Thirty-Third Annual Report* (1870), p. 407.
31. N. Humphreys (ed.), *Vital Statistics: A Memorial Volume to William Farr* (Sanitary Institute, London, 1885), pp. 273–4.
32. F. Nightingale, *Introductory Notes on Lying-in Institutions* (Longmans, London, 1871). C. Woodham-Smith, *Florence Nightingale* (Clay, London, 1952), p. 358.
33. Loudon, *Death in Childbirth*, pp. 198–9.
34. Ibid., pp. 200–1.
35. Aveling, *English Midwives*, pp. 3 ff.
36. *Dictionary of National Biography* (Oxford University Press, Oxford, 2004), vol. 10, pp. 970 ff.
37. For this information I am indebted to Louise Silverton of the Royal College of Midwives.
38. Aveling, *English Midwives*, pp. 181–2.
39. *Dictionary of National Biography*, vol. 53, pp. 236 ff.
40. *Select Committee on Midwives' Registration Bill* (Parliamentary Papers, 1892), vol. 14, p. 94.
41. The place is spelt with one 'l'; Lord Elliock added another to his title.
42. A commentary on Zepherina's obituary notice by her younger sister, Sophie, *Nursing Notes*, 1 April 1894, p. 42.
43. *Nursing Notes* (November and December 1894) include a selection of Zepherina's letters.
44. *Nursing Notes*, 1 November 1894, pp. 143–4.
45. Z. Veitch, *Handbook for Nurses for the Sick* (London, 1870), p. 32.
46. The building still exists and is now a restaurant.
47. B. Cowell and D. Wainwright, *Behind the Blue Door: The History of the Royal College of Midwives 1881–1981* (Baillière Tindall, London, 1981), p. 12.

48. J.E. Grundy, *History's Midwives* (Grundy, Bury, 2003), gives a good account of the early rituals associated with childbirth.
49. L. Picard, *Dr Johnson's London* (Phoenix, London, 2001), p. 166.
50. Grundy, *History's Midwives*, p. 10.
51. *Dictionary of National Biography*, vol. 28, p. 551.
52. *Woman's Gazette*, vol. 1, no. 1 (October 1875), p. 3.
53. Ibid., vol. 1, no. 3 (December 1875), p. 46.
54. Ibid., vol. 2, no. 5 (May 1876), pp. 127 ff.
55. Ibid., vol. 1 no. 1 (October 1875), p. 5.
56. *Dictionary of National Biography*, vol. 18, p. 551.
57. *Year Book of Women's Work* (London, 1875); British Library catalogue P.P.2493.ma.
58. *Woman's Gazette*, vol. 1, no. 5 (October 1875), p. 13.
59. Ibid. (February 1878), p. 27.
60. *Year Book of Women's Work*.
61. See p. 160.
62. C. Woodham-Smith, *Florence Nightingale* (Clay, London, 1952), p. 278.
63. *Lancet*, vol. 1 (1866), p. 721. See Chapter 5 for an account of Farr's career.
64. Emma Brierley, *In the Beginning* (Royal College of Midwives, London, 1924), p. 9.
65. Cowell and Wainwright, *Behind the Blue Door*, p. 16.
66. *Nursing Notes*, 1 February 1888, p. 10.
67. Parl. Debs (series 3), vol. 344, col. 1541 (21 May 1890).
68. Parliamentary Papers, 1892, vol. 14, pp. 9–10, 13 May, and pp. 94–5, 31 May 1892.
69. X. Baron (ed.), *London, 1066–1914, Literary Sources and Documents* (Helm Information, Robertsbridge, 1997), vol. 3, p. 369.
70. Parliamentary Papers, 1892, vol. 14, pp. 14 ff, 13 May 1892.
71. Anon., *The Midwives Institute Past and Present* (London, 1911), describes these final struggles.
72. See p. 178.
73. *Nursing Notes*, 1 April 1894, p. 41.
74. See the table on p. 58 for the figures.

Chapter Seven

1. J. Wright, *The Dolphin* (Butcher, London, 1828), p. 71.
2. G.M. Binnie, *Early Victorian Water Engineers* (Thomas Telford Press, London, 1981), p. 71.

3. Ibid., pp. 72 ff, describes the process in Simpson's own words.

4. Institution of Civil Engineers, *Minutes of Proceedings*, vol. 33 (1872–3), p. 334.

5. Anon., *The World of Watson Hawksley* (Montgomery Watson Hawksley, High Wycombe, 1992), p. 6.

6. Institution of Civil Engineers, *Minutes of Proceedings*, vol. 117 (1893–4), p. 369.

7. R.A. Lewis, *Edwin Chadwick and the Public Health Movement* (Longmans, London, 1952), pp. 91 ff.

8. *The Times*, 14 July 1887, p. 10.

9. *Architect and Contract Reporter*, 29 September 1893.

10. Binnie, *Early Victorian Water Engineers*, p. 14.

11. Lewis, *Edwin Chadwick and the Public Health Movement*, pp. 91 ff.

12. Binnie, *Early Victorian Water Engineers*, pp. 39–40.

13. *Newcomen Society Transactions*, 52 (1980–1), pp. 119–38, contains an account of Bateman's work.

14. A. Hardy, 'Parish Pump to Private Pipes: London's Water Supply in the Nineteenth Century', *Medical History Supplement*, 11 (1991), p. 78.

15. M. Daunton (ed.), *Cambridge Urban History of Britain* (Cambridge University Press, Cambridge, 2000), vol. 3, p. 219.

16. Hardy, 'Parish Pump to Private Pipes', p. 81.

17. Chadwick to Macvey Napier, 11 October 1842, quoted in S.E. Finer, *The Life and Times of Sir Edwin Chadwick* (Methuen, London, 1952), p. 218.

18. Binnie, *Early Victorian Water Engineers*, p. 36.

19. Chadwick, in Binnie, *Early Victorian Water Engineers*, p. 172, quoting letter of 9 October 1844 to Councillor J. Shuttleworth.

20. For this long-running controversy, see Parliamentary Papers, 1844, vol. 17; 1847–8, vol. 32; 1852, vol. 19.

21. *Journal of the Statistical Society* (June 1859), p. 233.

22. See Chapters 2 and 5.

23. J. Hollis and A. Seddon., *The Changing Population of the London Boroughs* (Statistical Series no. 5 (1985), ONS Library, Pimlico, London).

24. Parliamentary Papers, 1840, vol. 11, question 3452.

25. See the table on p. 199.

26. See Chapter 5 for an account of Chadwick's robust approach.

27. The consequences of this epidemic are described in Chapter 5.

28. See Chapter 5.

29. *Cassell's Saturday Journal*, 30 August 1890, p. 1160.

30. *Observer*, 14 April 1861, p. 5.
31. *Marylebone Mercury*, 9 March 1861, p. 2.
32. W. Hope, 'The Use and Abuse of Town Sewage', *Journal of the Society of Arts*, 18 (1869–70), p. 302.
33. *Illustrated London News*, 10, 17 and 24 September 1892.
34. *The Times*, 16 March 1891, p. 4.
35. Institution of Civil Engineers, *Minutes of Proceedings* (1864–5), vol. 24, p. 285.

Conclusion

1. J. Doxat, *The Living Thames, the Restoration of a Great Tidal River* (Hutchinson Benham, London, 1977).
2. *Cassell's Saturday Journal*, 30 August 1890, pp. 1160–1.

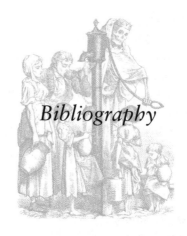

Bibliography

Books and Pamphlets, including Works of Reference

Adams, F., *Hippocrates, the Genuine Works* (Sydenham Society, London, 1849)

Anon., *The World of Watson Hawksley* (Montgomery Watson Hawksley, High Wycombe, 1992)

Aveling, J.H., *English Midwives: Their History and Prospects* (Churchill, London, 1872)

Ball, Philip, *The Devil's Doctor: Paracelsus and the World of Renaissance Magic and Science* (Heinemann, London, 2006)

Baron, X. (ed.), *London, 1066–1914, Literary Sources and Documents* (Helm Information, Robertsbridge, 1997)

Binnie, G.M., *Early Victorian Water Engineers* (Thomas Telford Press, London, 1981)

Brierley, E., *In the Beginning* (Royal College of Midwives, London, 1924)

Briggs, A., *Victorian Cities* (Pelican, London, 1968)

Budd, W., *Malignant Cholera, its Cause, Mode of Propagation and Prevention* (Churchill, London, 1849)

——, *Memorandum on Asiatic Cholera, its Mode of Spreading and its Prevention* (Churchill, Bristol, 1866)

——, *Typhoid Fever, its Nature, Mode of Spreading and Prevention* (Longmans, London, 1873)

Burkhardt, F. (ed.), *Charles Darwin's Letters, a Selection, 1821–59* (Cambridge University Press, Cambridge, 1998)

Burns, R., *Works, with an Account of his Life and a Criticism of his Writings*, ed. J. Currie (Bell, London, 1816)

Bynum, W.F., *Science and the Practice of Medicine in the Nineteenth Century* (Cambridge University Press, Cambridge, 1994)

Chadwick, E., *Report into the Sanitary Conditions of the Labouring Population of Great Britain* (1842; repr. Edinburgh University Press, Edinburgh, 1965)

Copland, J. (ed.), *A Dictionary of Practical Medicine* (Longmans, London, 1858)

Cowell, B., and Wainwright, D., *Behind the Blue Door: The History of the Royal College of Midwives 1881–1981* (Baillière Tindall, London, 1981)

Creighton, C., *A History of Epidemics in Britain* (Cambridge University Press, Cambridge, 1894)

Cullingworth, C.J., *Oliver Wendell Holmes and the Contagiousness of Puerperal Fever* (Glaisher, London, 1906)

Currie, J., *Medical Reports on the Effects of Water, Cold and Warm, as a Remedy in Fever and Febrile Diseases, whether Applied to the Surface of the Body or Used as a Drink* (Cadell, Davies & Creech, Liverpool, 1797)

Currie, William Wallace (ed.), *Memoir of the Life, Writings and Correspondence of James Currie, M.D., F.R.S.* (Longmans, London, 1831)

Curzon, A. de (ed.), *Dr James Currie and the French Prisoners of War in Liverpool* (Howell, Liverpool, 1926)

Darwin, E., *Zoonomia, or the Laws of Organic Life* (Byrne & Jones, Dublin, 1794–6), vol. 2

Daunton, M. (ed.), *Cambridge Urban History of Britain* (Cambridge University Press, Cambridge, 2000), vol. 3

Desmond, A., and Moore, J., *Darwin* (Michael Joseph, London, 1991)

Dictionary of National Biography (Oxford University Press, Oxford, 2004)

Dictionary of Scientific Biography (American Council of Learned Societies, New York, 1975)

Doxat, J., *The Living Thames, the Restoration of a Great Tidal River* (Hutchinson Benham, London, 1977)

Duncan, W.H., *On the Physical Causes of the High Rate of Mortality in Liverpool* (Liverpool, 1843)

Engels, F., 'The Great Towns', in *Condition of the Working Class in England* (1845; Allen & Unwin, London, 1952)

Faulkner, A., *The Grand Junction Canal* (David & Charles, Newton Abbot, 1993)

Finer, S.E., *The Life and Times of Sir Edwin Chadwick* (Methuen, London, 1952)

Frazer, W.M., *Duncan of Liverpool* (Hamish Hamilton, London, 1947)

Gordon, A., *A Treatise on the Epidemic Puerperal Fever of Aberdeen* (Bell & Bradfute, London, 1822)

Grundy, J.E., *History's Midwives* (Grundy, Bury, 2003)

Halliday, S., *Newgate: London's Prototype of Hell* (Sutton, Stroud, 2006)

Hempel, S., *The Medical Detective: John Snow and the Mystery of Cholera* (Granta, Cambridge, 2006)

Hollis, J., and Seddon, A., *The Changing Population of the London Boroughs* (Statistical Series no. 5 (1985), ONS Library, Pimlico, London)

Humphreys, N. (ed.), *Vital Statistics: A Memorial Volume to William Farr* (Sanitary Institute, London, 1885)

Lewis, R.A., *Edwin Chadwick and the Public Health Movement* (Longmans, London, 1952)

Loudon, I., *Death in Childbirth* (Oxford University Press, Oxford, 1992)

Meigs, C., *Females and their Diseases: A Series of Letters to his Class* (Philadelphia, 1847)

——, *On the Nature, Symptons and Treatment of Childbed Fever* (Philadelphia, 1854)

Midwinter, E., *Old Liverpool* (David & Charles, Newton Abbot, 1971)

Mitchell, B.R., and Deane, P., *Abstract of British Historical Statistics* (Cambridge University Press, Cambridge, 1971)

Moss, W., *The Liverpool Guide, Including a Sketch of the Environs* (Liverpool, 1796)

Newlands, J. (Liverpool Borough Engineer), *Liverpool Past and Present in Relation to Sanitary Operations* (Harris & Co., Liverpool, 1858)

Nightingale, Florence, *Notes on Nursing* (Harrison, London, 1859)

Pelling, M., *Cholera, Fever and English Medicine, 1825–65* (Oxford University Press, Oxford, 1978)

Picard, L., *Dr Johnson's London* (Phoenix, London, 2001)

Porter, R., *London, a Social History* (Hamish Hamilton, London, 1994)

Porter, R., *Quacks, Fakers and Charlatans in English Medicine* (Tempus, Stroud, 2001)

Roberts, C., and Cox., M., *Health and Disease in Britain from Prehistory to the Present Day* (Sutton, Stroud, 2003)

Rosen, G., *Disease, Debility and Death*, in H.J. Dyos and M. Wolff (eds), *The Victorian City: Image and Realities* (Routledge & Kegan Paul, London, 1973), vol. 2

Seymer, L.S. (ed.), *Selected Writings of Florence Nightingale* (Macmillan, London, 1954)

Simon, J., *English Sanitary Institutions* (Cassell, London, 1897)

——, *Filth Diseases and their Prevention* (Boston, 1876)

Smith, F.B., *The People's Health* (Croom Helm, London, 1979)

Snow, J., *On the Mode of Communication of Cholera* (Churchill, London, 1849)

Toulmin Smith, J., *Government by Commissions Illegal and Pernicious* (H. Sweet, London, 1849)

Trevelyan, G.M., *English Social History* (Longman, London, 1942)

Veitch, Z., *Handbook for Nurses for the Sick* (London, 1870)

Voltaire, *On Inoculation: Letters concerning the English Nation*, trans. J. Lockman (Davis & Lyon, London, 1804), letter 11

Waite, A.E., *Lives of Alchemistical Philosophers* (George Redway, London, 1888)

Watson, T., *Lectures on the Principles and Practice of Physic* (Longmans, London, 1844)

Weatherall, M., *Cambridge Contributions* (Cambridge University Press, Cambridge, 1997)

Wertz, R.M., and Wertz, D.C., *Lying-in: A History of Childbirth in America* (New York Free Press, New York, 1977)

White, B.D., *A History of the Corporation of Liverpool 1835–1914* (Liverpool University Press, Liverpool, 1951)

Wilson, A.N., *After the Victorians* (Hutchinson, London, 2005)

Wohl, A.S., *Endangered Lives: Public Health in Victorian Britain* (Methuen, London, 1983)

Woodham-Smith, C., *Florence Nightingale* (Clay, London, 1950)

Woods, R., and Woodward, J. (eds), *Urban Disease and Mortality in Nineteenth Century England* (Batsford, London, 1974)

Wright, J., *The Dolphin* (Butcher, London, 1828)

Journals

Annals of Medical History, 3rd series, 2 (1940)

British Medical Journal, 27 April 1867; 21 April 1883

Continuity and Change, vol. 9/2 (1994)

Edinburgh Review, 9 (1806)

Journal of the British Archaeological Association, 3rd series, 9 (1944)

Journal of Medical Biography (February 1994; August 1998; February 1999; February and May 2000; August 2003)

Journal of the Society of Arts, 18 (1869–70)

Journal of the Statistical Society (June 1859)

Lancet, 12 November 1831; 5 August 1843; 29 December 1855; 14 September 1861; 2 November 1867; 15 August 1868; 5 October 1895; 23 December 1899

Medical History, 27 (1983); 30 (1986)
Medical History Supplement, 11 (1991)
Medical Times and Gazette (1858)
New England Quarterly Journal of Medicine, 1/4 (April 1843)
Nursing Notes, 1 February 1888; 1 April 1894
Quarterly Review, 71 (1842)
Public Health, Journal of the Incorporated Society of Medical Officers of
    Health (June 1895; January 1897)
Victorian Studies, 28/3 (1984–5)
Westminster Review, 3 (1825)

Magazines and Newspapers

Architect and Contract Reporter, 29 September 1893
Builder, 18 July 1844; 8 November 1862; February 1890
Cassell's Saturday Journal, 30 August 1890
The Economist (May 1848)
Illustrated London News, 10, 17 and 24 September 1892
Liverpool Echo, 10 September, 2001
Marylebone Mercury, 9 March 1861
Northern Star, 4 May 1844
Observer, 14 April 1861
Pall Mall Gazette, 23 October 1883
Punch, 12 (1847); 20 (1851)
The Times, 12 October 1843; 12–14 September; 26 September; 5 October;
    10 October 1849; 20 March 1855; 7 November 1859; 2 August 1866;
    3 March 1875; 14 June 1879; 14 July 1887; 16 March 1891
Woman's Gazette (October 1875; December 1875; May 1876; February
    1878)
Year Book of Women's Work (1875)

Official Publications

Liverpool City Archives, *Report to the Health Committee of the Borough
    of Liverpool on the Health of the Town, 1847–50* (13 March and
    17 June 1847; published 1851)
——, *Annual Report of the Medical Officer of Health* (1866)
Parl. Debs (series 3) (1857–8; 1884; 1890)
Parliamentary Papers, 1836, volume 34; 1840, volume 11; 1844, volume
    17; 1845, volume 18; 1846, volume 10; 1850, volume 21; 1856, volume

52; 1854–5, volumes 21 and 45; 1856, volume 52; 1857, volume 25; 1857–8, volume 23; 1867, volumes 37 and 58; 1867–8 volume 37; 1874, volume 31; 1884–5, volume 30; 1892, volumes 1 and 14; 1893–4 volume 40; 1898 volume 44

Registrar-General's First Annual Report (1838); *Second Annual Report* (1839); *Fifth Annual Report* (1842); *Tenth Annual Report* (1847); *Seventeenth Annual Report* (1854) (HMSO *et al.*, London)

Report on the Sanitary Condition of Malta and Gozo with Reference to the Epidemic Cholera in the Year 1865 (HMSO, London, 1867)

Report on the Sanitary Condition of Gibraltar with Reference to the Epidemic Cholera in the Year 1865 (HMSO, London, 1867)

Simon, J., 'First Annual Report', in *Reports Relating to the Sanitary Condition of the City of London*, Metropolitan Archives, London, 1854

The National Archives: Public Record Office, General Board of Health and Home Office, Local Government Act Office Correspondence, MH 13, 1846–71, volume 261

Transactions

Duncan Society (August 2001). The Society's website is at www.duncansociety.org.uk

Institution of Civil Engineers, *Minutes of Proceedings*, 12 (1852–3); 24 (1864–5); 33 (1872–3); 117 (1893–4)

Newcomen Society Transactions, 52 (1980–1)

Philosophical Transactions of the Royal Society, 1 (1792)

Proceedings of the Literary and Philosophical Society of Liverpool, 65 (1916–17)

Transactions of the Institute of British Geographers, 41 (1967)

Transactions of the Obstetrical Society of London (1874)

Index